A PATRIOT'S HISTORY
OF GLOBALISM

*To Brandon,
an American Patriot!*

A PATRIOT'S HISTORY
OF GLOBALISM

ITS RISE
AND DECLINE

LARRY SCHWEIKART
NEW YORK TIMES BESTSELLING AUTHOR

Foreword by Stephen K. Bannon

Skyhorse Publishing

War Room Books may be purchased in bulk at special discounts for sales promotion, corporate gifts, fund-raising, or educational purposes. Special editions can also be created to specifications. For details, contact the Special Sales Department, Skyhorse Publishing, 307 West 36th Street, 11th Floor, New York, NY 10018 or info@skyhorsepublishing.com.

Skyhorse® and Skyhorse Publishing® are registered trademarks of Skyhorse Publishing, Inc.®, a Delaware corporation.

Visit our website at www.skyhorsepublishing.com.
Please follow our publisher Tony Lyons on Instagram @tonylyonsisuncertain

10 9 8 7 6 5 4 3 2 1

Library of Congress Cataloging-in-Publication Data is available on file.

Hardcover ISBN: 978-1-64821-005-1
eBook ISBN: 978-1-64821-006-8

Cover design by Brian Peterson

Printed in the United States of America

Contents

To Paul Johnson, who showed us how to write history.

Foreword

By Stephen K. Bannon

The term "Globalism" is a political word freely tossed around by advocates and opponents. Rarely is its history, the meaning of the term itself, or its consequences to America today, explained and described.

Historian Larry Schweikart does far more than explain the term. He describes its origins with the deft pen of a novelist. And he takes the reader on a rollercoaster ride through history.

To begin, Schweikart explains Globalism's origins at the Congress of Vienna in 1814. During a period he calls Monarchical Globalism, a series of meetings followed the fall of Napoleon. They involved major European interests, who were trying to keep peace in the world. It didn't work. Of course, two major European wars erupted in the next sixty-five years.

Next, he takes us to Militaristic Globalism, or the Age of Imperialism, wherein Britain, France, Germany, and to some extent, the United States, seek to extend control over one-third of the world. This, too, failed, as nationalistic movements prevailed instead.

After World War I, Schweikart describes how elites attempted global governance to end wars with a notion of Progressivism. This version of Diplomatic Globalism begat the League of Nations. Unsurprisingly, various dictators arose, and the League of Nations failed.

A variety of Globalisms and their attendant structures and institutions followed, from the creation of the United Nations, the International Monetary Fund, and the World Bank, to non-governmental charities such as the Bill and Melinda Gates Foundation, and the Clinton Foundation. On the health front, the spread of various pandemics, from the SARS virus, AIDS, the Avian Flu, and of course the Covid virus, defied the "Trust the Science" dictates of the World Health Organization.

The bottom line is this: Who should have the right to control the lives and choices of American citizens? Jeff Bezos? Elon Musk? Bill Gates? The Clintons? Or perhaps Klaus Schwab, at his annual meeting in the Alps?

Obviously, no. Americans' sovereignty and destiny must always be in the hands of American citizens. Our Founders knew that, fought for it, and died for it.

The United States of America is a sacred trust. Every patriotic American knows it. Donald J. Trump knows it.

Godspeed.

The Age of Globalism

One can almost envision a scene from *Lord of the Rings*. A sober Gandalf, witnessing the massive orc army arrayed against him and his companions behind their alabaster walls, glumly says, "The age of man is over. The age of the orcs is about to begin." Of course, as anyone who knows the books would counter, "Gandalf wouldn't say that." But not long ago there were those here—now—who believed that the age of nations was over and that the age of globalism was to begin. Indeed, as we will see, there are even those like Yuval Noah Harari who believe that the age of *man* is indeed over and that the age of *transhumans* is about to begin.

It is just as likely that we have seen the apex of this era's attempt at globalism, a quest that dates back to the Tower of Babel (Genesis 11: 1-9) when men sought to become gods. Harari spiked the football at the 10-yard line. It's our ball now.

Common parlance today on both the right and left of the political spectrum refers to a new force in the world called "globalism." Rioters who engaged in "Occupy Wall Street" and supporters of President Donald Trump's Make America Great Again (MAGA) movement both refer to "globalism" as a problem—even an enemy. But its nature, components, and operations, much less its history, are less well known than its main players, or, one might even say, villains. Today those include Klaus Schwab, head of the World Economic Forum, his "prophet," Harari, the Illuminati, and of course whatever members of the Rothschild family are still alive.

Beyond those names, those generally associated with "globalism" are the Rockefellers, Bill Gates, officials of the World Health Organization (the WHO—not to be confused with the great rock band, The Who), the United Nations or anything with a UN-designation, and almost anyone who vacations in Monaco, Corfu, Capri, or owns a yacht over 78 feet long.

Scholars, of course, have their own definitions: Roland Robertson defines globalism as "the compression of the world and the intensification of consciousness of the world as a whole."[1] Sociologist Anthony Giddens described globalism as the "intensification of world-wide social relations which link distinct localities in such a way that local happenings are shaped by events occurring many miles away."[2] Geographer David Harvey also referred to "compression of our spatial and temporal worlds."[3] A somewhat wordier definition was provided by Richard Peet in *Unholy Trinity*: "as the space of a single global experience expands, the institutions that control economies and project cultural themes accumulate into larger entities and condense into fewer and more similar places. . ."[4] Lawyer Robert Barnes defined globalism as "governance over the entire globe by an unelected elite."[5] Finance professor Charles Calomiris took a more nuanced approach:

> Globalism can refer narrowly to a conception of trade that is internationally oriented, or to running a business that provides goods and services in many countries. Politically, it can refer to a public governance orientation that favors decision making by international bodies or multi-lateral institutions rather than domestic governments.[6]

When I posed the question of what globalism was on social media, I received the following responses:

- "an approach to foreign policy in which economic and military planning and execution is carried out on a global scale."
- "a sharing of goods, services, ideas and resources between nations to create an eventual borderless world."
- "a system that exploits the ease and speed of access to communication, currency, goods, and transportation."
- "Old world monarchists marketing themselves as benevolent saviors in their quest to retain unfettered power."
- "The philosophical belief that nation-states represent an immature phase of human development and must give way to a centralized, unified human authority."
- "A new international order that promotes the interests of the world's financial elites at the expense of every nation state's sovereignty."
- "The ability by language and culture to fit in and succeed no matter where you are or travel to in the world."
- "The attempt to apply economy of scale to governance."

Is "globalism" the same thing as "globalization"? Peter Zeihan, who is often described as a "futurist," refers to the process of "globalization" as the "development and industrialization to a wide swath of the planet . . . generation the mass consumption societies" combined with technological progress.[7] He, in other words, sees "globalization" as largely an economic phenomenon.

True globalism, however, is more sinister. From its origins at the Tower of Babel, it has involved a deep spiritual component in which some individuals (today referred to as "elites" because of their wealth, education, and social status) believe they have the moral authority inherent in their status to tell others what to do. And not just other Americans . . . others! As in the entire world.

Attempts at controlling the entire world are nothing new. To the Chinese dynasties, Asia was "the world." To the Romans, Europe, North Africa, and the Middle East was "the world." By the early 1800s, because of the scientific and industrial revolutions, Europe was "the world." Through communications and transport breakthroughs, by the early 1900s, the world was, well, "the world." Our first modern attempt at globalism came with the Congress of Vienna in 1814 through monarchs who saw an industrialized Europe as "the world." Later, Europeans extended their influence and authority through a type of militaristic globalism via imperialism. Neither of those provided the world-wide control the elites desired. It then became possible for elites to envision literally exercising some degree of authority over the entire population of the planet. Diplomats and ministers meeting at Versailles attempted to put in place a type of diplomatic globalism governed by treaties, maps, and agreements. That, too, failed.

After World War II, elites made another attempt at stretching their power over the entire globe, this time in multiple ways. First, the threat of the atomic bomb and scientific concerns about who might use it were subsumed under another new centralized world body, the United Nations. It seemed nationalism, viewed as an evil, would be subdued forever—only to have the Soviet Union flex its muscles and shatter the (phony) global harmony that supporters of the UN thought could exist.

Scientific globalism was abandoned, giving way to an economic globalism that arose de facto out of the reality that coming out of the second World War, the United States stood alone at the top of the productive and consuming world. In the "Golden Accident" of about twenty years that ensued, the United States was both the world's number one producer *and* consumer—something that had never happened in history. This produced a new economic globalist arrangement known as the Bretton Woods system.

Bretton Woods tied the non-communist world's economy to that of the United States, backed by both our military and our dollar. Bretton Woods ensured free trade worldwide, protected largely by the US Navy and buttressed by the American dollar. Yet it contained a contradiction that would need about fifty years to expose: the more foreign aid the US doled out and the more spending that it poured into the military and foreign wars, the higher its deficits. The more deficits the US ran, the less valuable the dollar became. At some point Bretton Woods—even if only limited to economics—would become unsustainable.

However, foreign wars soon produced a culture change as well, one less (or un-) committed to being the world's policeman. At the same time, the rise of China began to eat away at American financial and economic dominance.

On top of that came a new attempt at globalism through medicine in response to Covid-19 (or, as I frequently call it here, the China Virus). For the first time in history, a truly *global* response to a health issue was possible, one in which virtually every nation could be encourage, then strong-armed into accepting the *international* "response" as found in the guidelines of the World Health Organization. Although at one level *nations* still enacted their own practices and procedures, at another level they were subjected to powerful lobbying, shaming, censorship, media "canceling," and restrictive actions by other nations that did agree to the WHO's "guidelines." The entire pandemic stopped just short of falling into a system of global medical tyranny.

Just short.

Reactions to everything from mask-wearing to lockdowns to suppression of "misinformation" differed around the world. Sweden never locked down; Australia and New Zealand adopted policies approaching those of the Third Reich. But the human spirit refused to be crushed, from trucker convoys in Canada to the rebellion by physicians with the Great Barrington Declaration, to the silent resistance by individuals refusing to wear masks or take the vax. It proved sufficient to stifle a once-in-a-generation attempt at total globalist control.

Meanwhile, political resistance to globalism had started with Benjamin Netanyahu in Israel, Vladimir Putin in Russia, then Donald Trump in the USA. They were soon joined by a wave of other international leaders including those of India, Paraguay, Hungary, El Salvador, Slovakia, Italy, and others. The inability of globalist powers, as represented by the governments of most western European nations and the administration of Trump's replacement, Joe Biden in America, to foment a war against Russia in the 2022 invasion of Ukraine constituted a major turning point in the history of globalism. Essentially the "global South" sat out the conflict as did China, even going so far as to use the opportunity to form a regional anti-Bretton Woods alignment, BRICS (Brazil, Russia, India, China, Saudi Arabia). By 2023, BRICS nations had exceeded the growth of the combined West.

And while Trump might have been removed—possibly only temporarily—his "Spartans," consisting of his court appointees, held the judicial pass at Hell's Gate, rapidly deconstructing much of the machinery of the Deep State that had managed to oust Trump.

Over the last two centuries, globalists have tried monarchs, militaries, diplomats, scientists, celebrities, economists, and doctors to install machinery to exert control over the world's populations. Each time, they failed. Occasionally, the people just said "no." This is a record of their efforts.

Chapter One

Monarchical Globalism—
The Congress of Vienna

I n 1822, ostensibly eight years after the Congress of Vienna convened, a Napoleonic diplomat named baron Edouard Bignon assessed the work of the monarchs and diplomats who had assembled there: "The intellectual powers of the peoples are directed toward the improvement of the social order. The cabinets, on the other hand, are deploying all their powers, intellectual as well as physical, to arrest this march of the peoples, and even to make them retrace their steps."[1] This may sound familiar.

To the surprise of many, even though the Emperor Napoleon Bonaparte—the hated and feared vampire of Europe, the monster as many knew him—was now gone, the vision of European civilization led by its policemen was not limited to his depredations. Quite the contrary, the statesmen and kings who had met in Vienna ignored a force ignited by the American Revolution and energized with the French Revolution thirteen years later. That new reality in western politics, the force of public opinion, brought a new awakening the members of the Congress sought to quell.

They failed.

Understanding the current position of modern globalists, it helps to appreciate where they came from and what their nature is. The Congress of Vienna merely constituted the first of a string of failures dating up to the present. Arguments could be made against counting the Congress of Vienna (1814—but really a decade long series of meetings) as the first attempt at globalism. For one thing, it was hardly "global," embracing only the major powers of Europe as defined by the congregants' own definitions. For another, its solutions did not apply anywhere but Europe aside from a few tangential aspects of trade. Virtually all the territory swapped, all the populations moved, all the boundaries changed occurred within the continent of Europe herself. To the monarchs and manipulators who traveled to and fro conducting diplomacy at multiple cities and villas under the title "Congress of Vienna," most of them believed they *were* dealing with the whole world. America, China, Africa, Latin America all existed, but to those gathered to decide the future of post-Napoleonic Europe, well . . . *they* were the only ones who mattered!

Each individual nation, whether represented by a monarch such as Tsar Alexander of Russia personally, or by foreign ministers such as the quintessential manipulator and lovesick diplomat Klemens Metternich or the ultimate survivalist shapeshifter Charles Maurice de Talleyrand-Perigord, at some point employed several actual negotiators, aides, and intermediaries. This alone presented hurdles for modern historians seeking to get at motivations and influences. As author Adam Zamoyski noted, "the decisions taken at a given meeting were not always recorded the same way by all the parties."[2] In addition to different recollections from different people, all with different agendas, scholars had to slog through different languages. But mere interpretation isn't enough, as we are dealing with international diplomacy here, meaning that subtlety and double *entendres* were the rule, not the exception. Precisely determining whether Robert Stewart, Viscount Castlereagh was employing sarcasm, humor, shame, or logic is challenging in its own right.

A second factor requires caution in assessing the Congress of Vienna, in that each player to emerge from the rubble of Napoleon's crumbling empire had his own personal—but not necessarily *national*—motivations. Indeed, the fate of peoples and nations just as often rested on the exuberance of romantic passion or the crushed heart of a spurned lover as they did with concerns about the nation-state or the greater good of the people. If modern-day Baal-like worshippers at the Gotthard Tunnel's opening ceremonies heralded what they hoped was the opening of portals to other worlds with pagan bacchanals and plays celebrating the arrival of a goat-god, the denizens of Vienna that bore the beauty and pain of the world's diplomatic elites lavished themselves in never-ending balls, dinners, and sex. Perhaps such lustful indulgences are just the predictable sordid step-sister of all diplomacy.

One thing is clear: one man, and one man alone was responsible for bringing about the Congress of Vienna and globalism's arrival: Napoleon Bonaparte. For the first time in human history—but not the last—the major powers aligned to defeat one man. Not France. Napoleon the man. The outlaw. The monster. The vampire.

By the end of his "100 Days" return that culminated in his defeat at Waterloo, the diplomats at Vienna were making clear that France was not their enemy. Only Napoleon was. In this, Napoleon was very much like Donald Trump, for not even Hitler was viewed as the singular evil to be removed, as rejected peace overtures from the Germans made clear. Nor were Tojo, Stalin, Mao, or even Saddam Hussein so demonized as a person whose jailing, assassination, or death would change the course of events. Both Napoleon and Trump, however, were. Both men saw the weight of massive national and international organizations mobilize against them. With France, the alignment of the man against the world was so complete that the French diplomat Talleyrand was taking part in the Congress of Vienna even as Napoleon fought his last battles against the other Europeans. Very Mike Pence-ish of him, was it not? Later we will see that Great Britain was entirely amenable to bringing back France so long as Napoleon wasn't involved.

Europe after the Renaissance had seen nothing like Napoleon, the closest European leader to Alexander the Great to ever live. Anyone attempting to claim that social forces, economics, "class struggle," or any other deterministic mechanisms direct human events has only to look at the Corsican. What crystallized the Age of Napoleon was Bonaparte's ability to be in that revolutionary time but not of it; to become one of history's grandest opportunists who believe in little except expediency. Like a surfer who couldn't care less about water, he rode the popular explosion with its corollary necessity of engaging the opinion of commoners. He simultaneously shucked off the new ideologies of human liberty emerging from America, then France, while preempting the dregs of deterministic Luciferians such as Hegel, Marx, and Darwin. Napoleon, for good or evil, stood alone. At all times he harbored a Patton-esque belief that fortune had positioned him for that place in time.

Bonaparte's rise from his birth in Corsica to his training in the military academy where he specialized in artillery to his meteoric ascent through the ranks to sit on the Consulate of France after the chaos of the Revolution has been the subject of a vast number of books. British historian Paul Johnson claims there were more books written about Napoleon than any other person except Jesus.[3] Napoleon's military victories were such that they are studied today. David Chandler's classic *The Campaigns of Napoleon* covers over a thousand text pages alone.[4] At its peak, Napoleon's empire stretched from Spain to the Balkans to Moscow. His forces invaded Egypt and smashed the Mameluk forces there before the French navy was soundly defeated at the Battle of the Nile. He had purportedly planned an invasion of England, even training for it. His best marshals and close relatives, placed on the thrones of various conquered provinces, ultimately disappointed him or betrayed him outright.

Of course, none of that was unique to Napoleon: Alexander's empire likewise stretched from Greece to India, south into Egypt, north into Turkey. He, as well, was subject to plots and conspiracies by his lieutenants. It is entirely likely that the only reason history affixed the name "the Great" to Alexander and not Napoleon was merely tim-ing: Napoleon came along after notions of "rights" and "liberties" had found their way into the language of the common people.

Most Europeans believed in personal freedom at some level by 1800, some more than others. English nobles since 1215 had insisted on certain rights by law. But where Napoleon at first tried to ride the tiger, he soon forgot about it in the high of military campaigning. Before long, the rights obtained by the blood of the French Revolution meant no more to him than the blizzard of treaties and agreements that he discarded. Thus Bonaparte's trampling of so many liberties, his callous-ness toward human life (including that of his own French troops), as well as his whimsical rearrangement of national or provincial boundar-ies, made him enough enemies to deny him such a beneficent label as "the Great." In other words, for all his other good fortune, Napoleon had the bad luck to be born too late to receive good press enjoyed by Alexander and far too soon to completely control the media like a Mao or Francisco Franco.[5]

Unlike Alexander, however, Napoleon recognized that long-term success abroad depended on a content populace at home—that "democracy" or public opinion thing again. While in no way did his reforms have the best interests of the public in mind, he sought to spread the perception that he was a man of the people (as his multiple plebiscites reinforced).

He revised the French education system, ostensibly making it more egalitarian (in reality, he sought only better officers and more accurate gunners). One can almost see a Napoleonic math textbook: "If Jean wants to kill 100 Prussians at a range of 300 yards with a five-pounder cannon, at what angle must he elevate the barrel?" He equalized taxes—a long-festering sore in French history leading, in part, to the Revolution itself. Understanding the significance of religion in people's lives, he at least superficially reversed the church-hatred of the Revolution with his Concordat in 1801 that restored the Catholic Church to its pre-1789 civil status. He emancipated Jews and Protestants in Catholic coun-tries from their ghettos. Indeed, he was so favorable to Jews that the

Russian Orthodox Church called him the "Antichrist and the Enemy of God."[6] Personally agnostic or deistic, Napoleon understood the religious nature of the France that the Revolution unsuccessfully sought to expunge.

Above all, Napoleon recognized what Americans were only beginning to appreciate in the second decade of the twenty-first century, namely that laws must at least appear fair and just for all, elites and commoners. Napoleon went some distance toward that goal by making France's legal system clear and visible to all, even as he routinely arrested political enemies and newspapermen and as his armies looted defeated foreign states routinely. Nor did it hurt that the gold flowed back to Paris, lessening the burden on citizens to pay for his wars. His understanding of propaganda in a mass-population age was cutting edge, including the use of large placards and pro-administration newspapers, while his semaphore system always got his version of events back to Paris before his critics could mobilize. (This is how he presented his Egyptian disaster as a great cultural success.)[7]

David Chandler, referring to a phrase applied to Oliver Cromwell, labeled Napoleon a "great, bad man."[8] To British poet Samuel Coleridge Bonaparte was "the evil genius of the planet," the "enemy of the human race," who waged "war against mankind."[9] Military historian Martin Van Creveld called him "the most competent man who ever lived."[10] Chandler maintains that all biographers fell into the category of worshipers or detractors, and that few works produced balanced portraits of Bonaparte. This is to some degree true: at most times his closest contemporaries were "frenemies" in popular lingo, namely they eagerly worked with him when he was on top and, to appease the allies, denounced him as the Empire fell apart. It also is reflective of the fact that even today, many Englishmen (such as historian Paul Johnson) bear a loathing of Bonaparte that colors their assessment of the man.[11] Napoleon, above all, was a towering military genius, a master manipulator of men, a shrewd diplomat who nevertheless consistently underestimated the strength of the British. Like most men of the time, he jumped into sexual affairs without hesitation or consideration.

A fatalist who believed strongly in the role of chance, Napoleon personally gave God no place in his life. The Almighty was merely another division to be employed at the appropriate moment.

Yet there was an odd religious taint to Bonaparte's success. He had benefitted from an anti-clerical revolution in 1789, which priests were dis-empowered and Catholicism dis-established. Certainly he didn't understand the appeal of the faith, which completely animated his chief rival Tsar Alexander, who genuinely believed he had been called by God to reclaim Europe for Him.

Napoleon's historical appraisal in large part also derives from the fact that, unlike so many other quasi-dictators, his end was not swift. Imprisoned on St. Helena for six years, he drafted an unremitting stream of personal image-enhancing propaganda. That was a blessing not bestowed on Alexander, Leonidas, Cromwell, George III, Saddam Hussein, or Hitler, all of whom died in battle, committed suicide, were murdered, fell from disease, or went mad. His recollections found support in those of his Imperial soldiers, servants, or diplomats whose diaries and memoirs tended to enhance the "good Napoleon" construct. Nor did it hurt that after Bonaparte, France's military defeats stung, causing the nation, like a football team looking back to the glory days of a legendary coach, to point backward to the Emperor's feats.

Indeed, it was in the realm of killing itself that Napoleon's reputation began its swing back to that of an ogre filled with blood lust. Whereas in his younger years Bonaparte routinely faced aging generals stuck in earlier strategies, by the time he invaded Russia he had not modified his tactics or strategies in a decade. Needless to say, the geography and climate of Spain and Russia—not to mention the near-total absence of roads—constituted a towering obstacle to his use of such ingenious military concepts as his *battallion carre*, a giant moving square of corps that allowed any particular army to be in supporting position to another on a day's march. Not just in his military tactics, but in his overall governance, what worked in 1804 had become obsolete and dysfunctional by 1813.

His biography is fairly well known. Napoleon Bonaparte, born in 1769 on the recently annexed island of Corsica, perhaps was born at exactly the right time. Coming of age twenty when the French Revolution swept France, he benefitted from a minor Tuscan noble whose lineage had actually fought the French in the resistance. By then, his father Carlo was an attorney, a member of the Third Estate that had instigated the Revolution with the battle cry of Abbe Sieyes, "What is the Third Estate?" These were hardly laborers or peasants, who by 1769 made up the overwhelming majority of the French population. Nor were they nobility. They were lawyers, merchants, all a step below the aristocrats and could thus claim the revolutionary mantle. It all meant that Napoleon had the connections and money to attend the military academy at Brienne-le-Chateau, and from there, *Ecole Militarie*. (His original ambition was to join the Royal Navy!)[12] While others rushed to join the flamboyant cavalry, Napoleon saw artillery as the wave of the future. He later remarked that only thunderbolts "should be preferred to cannons." This affection for artillery did more than just inform his battles; rather it presented a central tactic upon which he relied, namely massing artillery at a key point against the enemy's line and blasting a hole in it for his cavalry to pour through.

After a successful assault on Toulon, where his cannons drove the British out, he was put in charge of all artillery in France's Army of Italy. The Republic then reassigned him to the Army of the West and its war in the Vendee against royalists—but as an infantry commander. Reassigned to the Bureau of Topography—a position he held briefly—he intuitively came to a second major advantage he would have over his opponents, namely a love and deep understanding of maps. He consumed them, internalized them even as he visualized the topography and landscape on the paper. This repeatedly enhanced a singularly unique talent he had over his enemies in that he could instantly and with astonishing accuracy calculate the rate of march for an entire army over terrain.

Reassigned again to the Republic's defense forces in Paris when a rebellion occurred against the National Convention (the legislature), anxious lawmakers handed Napoleon control of the Republic's military forces. Immediately Napoleon thought artillery would make the difference and ordered a cavalry officer named Joachim Murat to haul in several cannons that, as historian Thomas Carlyle put it, cleared the besiegers with a "whiff of grapeshot." [13] A relieved and grateful assembly rewarded him with the command of the Interior and the Army of Italy. From that point, he leaped in position and legend as he defeated the Austrian forces in Italy, where he won eighteen major engagements and captured 150,000 prisoners. Returning to Paris, he was once again greeted as a hero, whereupon he sold the government of the French Directory on a scheme he could quickly conquer Egypt and move toward India where he could threaten Britain's crown jewel.

France's navy at the time was no match for the Royal Navy, even though it had won a critical battle at Sandy Hook in the American Revolution that sealed Lord Cornwallis's fate at Yorktown. (It remained an irony that the only major battle in which the French defeated the British at sea came when it was critical to American independence.) It transported his army to Egypt, where the French defeated the Egyptian Mamluk cavalry with a shocking disparity in casualties: Twenty-nine French dead to over two thousand Egyptians, thanks largely to the use of a new tactic, the "battle square." But England's Sir Horatio Nelson destroyed the French fleet at the Battle of the Nile, making it nearly impossible for him to return home with his army. He learned that there was a temporary withdrawal of British ships, whereupon he escaped back to France, leaving his men in the desert under another commander. He arrived to find the Directory in chaos, with bankruptcy looming and the government increasingly unpopular despite some military victories. Hastily forming a tight cabal involving the foreign minister Charles-Maurice de Talleyrand-Perigord (known to history as Talleyrand), Napoleon overthrew the Directory and installed himself as the "First Consul."

Critics emphasize the plebiscites Napoleon held that reaffirmed his power were fraudulent, glossing over the fact that *no one else in all of Europe* held such popular elections, save for selected Italian city-states.

Rigged or not, "democratic" or not, Napoleon, alone among the rulers of Europe, actually risked the chance of an unfavorable electoral outcome. Unlike sovereigns "who were born upon the throne," Napoleon observed, who "can allow themselves to be beaten twenty times, and will always return to their capitals; I cannot do that; I am a self-made soldier."[14]

At first the coalitions attacking France had nothing to do with "Boney" as they would soon call him. After the assassination of Louis XVI, monarchies across Europe were terrified that the "French disease" of popular revolutions would spread. Committed to crushing republican sentiments, the First Coalition of Austria (then known as the Holy Roman Empire), the Dutch Republic, Spain, Prussia, and Great Britain engaged in a war with France that ended in the Treaty of Campo Formio and the Treaty of Paris. France won, but in 1798 a Second Coalition with Russia, the Ottoman Empire, Portugal, and Naples joining Austria and Great Britain, and, again, this ended with a French victory. Great Britain then declared war on France in 1803 ending the Peace of Amiens and soon Russia and Austria joined the Third Coalition.

Here the legend of Napoleon, the military mastermind, grew. He moved first, and swiftly. Marching on the Austrians, he managed to envelope a 60,000-man Austrian army and forced its surrender, noting: "I have accomplished my object, I have destroyed the Austrian army by simply marching."[15] Considered a strategic masterpiece, the Ulm campaign sent shockwaves through the coalition, tempered only by yet another major French naval defeat at Trafalgar. Having taken one Austrian army off the board, Napoleon then feigned pursuit of the joint Russo-Austrian armies, only to then apparently fall back. When his men abandoned the Pratzen Heights, luring the coalition into a trap, French legions came close to once again surrounding the entire coalition army. "The battle of Austerlitz," Napoleon said, "is the finest of all I have fought."[16]

At that point Napoleon slowly changed from an elected French leader to an Emperor. He had already named himself as much in 1804, but in the midst of continual fighting against enemies trying to invade France, few concerned themselves with the distinction. By that time, he had a finely tuned military machine unmatched by any one country in all of Europe. It is worth noting that by focusing on the unglamourous areas of warfare such as artillery and map reading, Napoleon gained major advantages over those who will advanced through the ranks in cavalry and whom only paid superficial attention to details of maps. But Napoleon did have cavalry—some of the best. For a decade, the French cavalry, with its exceptional commanders such as Joachim Murat, far surpassed any other in Europe. Advance, audacity, aggressiveness characterized Napoleon's campaigns: he was not a defensive fighter by temperament or equipment. Thus, when he was finally forced to retreat, his forces fell apart faster than expected.

Napoleon, a student of warfare, criticized Alexander's victory at Gaugamela as too risky, as "defeat would have stranded Alexander '900 leagues from Macedonia.'"[17] It was a lesson he forgot in Russia. Even there, Napoleon believed he had made sufficient plans.

With near-computer accuracy, Napoleon used his uncanny understanding of maps and overall knowledge of rates of consumption to accurately predict where he would be, and when. As one of his aides recalled in the 1805 Austerlitz campaign, Bonaparte dictated every detail down to the "orders of march, their duration, place of convergence or meeting of the columns, attacks in full force . . . mistakes of the enemy" from miles away. Even "the very days on which we were to enter Munich and Vienna were then announced and written down as it all turned out."[18] Some claimed he could remember the exact placement of certain cannons out of an arsenal of over 6,000 at specific battles.

His talents led him to massive victories at Austerlitz (1805), Jena-Auerstedt (1806), Eylau (1807), and Friedland (1807). A treaty usually ensued, but for all his victories, Napoleon never completely annihilated the enemy, often allowing the Russian army to rebuild. After Friedland, Russia's Tsar Alexander and Napoleon agreed to a peace at Tilsit on a raft in the middle of the Nieman River. Then after Napoleon captured Berlin two days later, Napoleon signed a treaty with Prussia.

It's conceivable that the French Empire could have stopped there. However, Napoleon's obsession with Great Britain, whom he could never defeat at sea nor lure into major land battles in Europe, ate at him. Attempting to starve England out with an embargo, Napoleon had already issued the Berlin Decree in November 1806 in which he proclaimed the British Isles "in a state of blockade" and prohibited all commerce with Great Britain.

Napoleon, however, faced a fundamental problem: his navy had been ravaged and could in no way even enforce a small part of the Berlin Decree. The Decree foolishly placed burdens on potential allies, caused smuggling to skyrocket, and allowed England to gain a foothold in Portugal, where Lisbon had never been shut down to the Royal Navy. It was in the Iberian peninsula that Napoleon's downfall began. Bonaparte demanded Portugal evict the British and declare war on England, both of which the Portuguese refused to do. In 1807, Napoleon therefore ordered in some twenty-five thousand troops through Spain to attack Portugal. Before long, even Spain herself became intertwined in the Portuguese war. When Napoleon put his brother Joseph on the Spanish throne, the entire Iberian Peninsula came unraveled and France was sucked in.

Once the British smelled an opportunity to bleed the Emperor's forces dry, they inserted troops of their own under Sir Arthur Wellesley, better known as the Duke of Wellington (or, to his men, "old Hooky" for his nose). Warfare continued through three Portuguese campaigns under until Wellington finally defeated the French at the Battle of Salamanca.

Napoleon had left Spain himself in 1809, inspiring Russia, which saw that France in a weakened state could be pushed out of the Grand Duchy of Warsaw (Poland). The Emperor had created the Grand Duchy after the then-decisive battle of Friedland in 1807, wherein Napoleon had encircled a Russian force with their backs against the Alle River. Now in 1812, an older, wiser Alexander saw a chance to peacefully force the French out. Napoleon chose invasion, and disaster.

Much has been written about the invasion of Russia. Suffice it to say that contrary to popular belief, Napoleon was *not* unprepared for the assault. His logistics planning surpassed anything ever attempted in human history, as "the preparations for the great undertaking were made with the greatest possible forethought and attention to detail."[19] Again, David Chandler's magisterial *Campaigns of Napoleon* noted that:

> Every available book on Eastern Europe was carefully read and digested; every published map pored over and memorized. Histories of Charles XII's ill-fated campaign in 1709 received particular attention.[20]

As early as 1810 Bonaparte began preparations, provisioning key German and Polish fortresses. Already Napoleon planned on the largest European army ever seen for the campaign—over 600,000 men. (Many of these were forced conscripts from "allies," including Westphalia, Poland, Italy, Austria, Prussia, and Germany, and while they could, at times, fight well, the heterogenous nature of the force—of which less than half were French—necessarily produced lack of cohesion, misunderstood orders, and a general lack of enthusiasm.)

Most important of all, Napoleon realized there would be no living off the countryside, no scavenging. And, again, contrary to myth, Napoleon expected a scorched earth policy. His *battalion carre* movement, however, would be impossible. Russia had few roads. The rapid convergence of men he repeatedly conjured in his battles in Austria and Prussia would be impossible in Russia's vast, roadless lands. That meant a return to the pre-1789 style of long supply columns. To that end Napoleon formed twenty-six transport battalions with 600 light carts, 600 heavy wagons, and over 250 four-animal wagons. All of that was to be supplemented by herds of oxen. But the animal consumption needs of 120,000 draft animals and 80,000 cavalry horses (!) could be somewhat offset by the vast plains, so long as they stayed unfrozen.

Of course, war never goes as planned, even for someone as meticulous as Napoleon, and before his offensive even got into Russia proper, men dropped out due to ravages of diphtheria, dysentery, typhus, and other maladies. One of his Bavarian corps lost half its men due to illness before it ever saw a Russian.

The rest of the story is well known. Despite knowing in advance that the Russians would retreat, the French seemed unable to catch up for a major pitched battle. Launching the invasion in June 1812, the *Grande Armee* captured several cities, including Minsk and Smolensk. Napoleon finally got his battle at Borodino in September. Defeated Russians retreated again. The French took Moscow on September 10, found no one to treat with (not to mention a ravaged city, mostly burned, with no food or loot and poor shelter). Napoleon's forces left Moscow on October 19, by which time he was nearly out of cavalry horses, was continually harassed by guerillas, and was attacked by the Russians in open battle. The Emperor's magnificent cavalry now marched on foot; wagons littered the scorched roads; and Russians captured key supply depots. Only 110,000 of the original 612,000 who entered Russia exited.

The Emperor gathered for one more battle. Theoretically, he had a chance. Recovering so many troops scattered across the Empire was nearly impossible though. Worse, even by some miracle if he had managed to pull them together, they had been lounging in garrison detail for over a year and were not in fighting shape. And worse still, the aura and mystique of Napoleon was broken.

The coalition crossed into France in 1814. He sought to trade land for peace, but England in particular demanded the removal of Napoleon as emperor of France. Viscount Castlereagh told other delegates "you scarcely have an idea of how *insane* people in [England] are on the subject of any peace with Bonaparte" and Stratford Canning added "The Methodists and the women are particularly warlike."[21] In April 1814 the French Senate deposed Napoleon, who agreed to abdicate in favor of his son. Instead the Coalition insisted on unconditional abdication. He was sent to the island of Elba with one thousand of his elite guard but under British observation, though not before he attempted suicide unsuccessfully.[22] The monarchy was restored under Louis XVIII—the most legitimate Bourbon. He was old, so incredibly fat he could neither walk effectively or get up if he fell and was notorious for his gluttony. When dining with a group of princesses, a large dish of strawberries was placed on the table. Without offering the women any, he added sugar and cream and consumed it all. This was the man who effectively ended the French Revolution in all its manifestations.

Although a bored Napoleon managed to escape Elba the following year and appeal to the already-disgruntled French who suddenly recalled what a monarchy felt like, his hopes for full restoration had no basis in reality. By then he was personally the object of the Coalition offensives—not France per se. In 1813, the allies drafted a declaration to the French people claiming they were not making war on France but French "preponderance."[23] Surprisingly, the attendees at Vienna were not rattled by any of Napoleon's victories after Leipzig, as they were used to losing on the battlefield. Eventually defeated at Waterloo, this time Napoleon was subjected to much harsher treatment and barely avoided execution. (The British feared his execution would turn him into a martyr, and the British public's love/hate relationship with him prohibited him from being jailed in the Tower of London; thus he was exiled to the remote Atlantic island of St. Helena where he remained until his death in 1821.) By that time, caricatures of him as a "vampire," "ogre," and "thief of Europe" were as much for public consumption in newspapers as they were actual descriptors. (Even Napoleon's wife, Marie-Louise, called him the "Corsican Anti-Christ" in her youth.)[24] The names became a farce. When King George IV, having dealt with an obstinate and unruly wife, was told by a messenger, "Sire! I have to tell you that your greatest enemy is dead!" George replied, "No! By God! Is she?"[25]

Bonaparte's personal exit from the stage hardly stopped the production. Behind the curtains at Vienna, monarchs and other *lieux de diplomati* served as the cauldron for the first age of elite globalism. Of course, at the most basic level each nation had fundamental foreign policy objectives. Austria, which had lost lands to Italy, wanted them back. Poland wanted independence. Russia wanted no such thing, instead viewing a Polish state as a threat. Great Britain actually would not have been unhappy with a Bonaparte-less French state with its pre-war borders intact. Prussia wanted unification. And what did France want? It depended entirely on to whom you spoke: monarchists were thrilled with the return of the Bourbons, Republicans were outraged at the betrayal of the revolution by Napoleon, and Bonapartists still thought they had a legitimate claim to power.

Robert Stewart, Viscount Castlereagh was probably the only diplomat present at the meetings who not only thought France was redeemable but necessary in the new world order. He attempted to get Spain and Portugal into the coalitions for some time and recommended that it be illegal for any nation to withdraw.[26] He had drafted an early working treaty for the nations in 1813. His expansion of the coalitions looked similar to NATO in the twenty-first century, ever-expanding around the designated enemy.

Anyone who thought Napoleon stood alone in his nearly insane ego needed only to look at some of the new overseers of Europe. Count Metternich boasted, "It is I alone who has vanquished everything—hatred, prejudice, petty interest—to unite all Germans under one and the same banner!"[27] On another occasion he called himself the "Best Master of Ceremonies in the World" and condescendingly said "All Europe is in my antechamber."[28] Writing to his girlfriend, whom he was trying to impress, Metternich said "I spent the day carving up Europe like a piece of cheese."[29] (This will sound shockingly similar to the admissions of the diplomats at Versailles a century later.) Again, Metternich told Wilhelmine, his lover, that he had "accomplished a task greater than any achieved by a mortal" in overseeing the Congress's negotiations.[30] Or, as one historian, Albert Sorel wrote, "Metternich was in his own opinion the light of the world."[31] On New Year's Eve, 1815, a lonely Metternich sent the Duchess a night delivery containing a gold bracelet embedded with a diamond, a ruby, an emerald, and an amethyst, each stone representative of their birthstones or a time they spent together.[32]

Metternich's obsession with Wilhelmine occupied him even to the point that, predating President Bill Clinton in the 1990s who was being serviced in the Oval Office while on a phone with commanders in Europe deploying troops, Metternich sat in a corner drafting love letters while the other monarchs sat across the room, struggling with maps and a lasting peace. It is not known if Metternich was aware his wife was cheating on him at the same time!

In other ways, the elites "carving up Europe" in 1814–15 differed little from their counterparts at Versailles in 1919 or at the United Nations twenty-five years later. Czar Alexander of Russia, for example, while eager to force Napoleon out, hated the Bourbons with an equal ferocity. However, he had his own opinion of who should be leading France, and it certainly wasn't anyone the French people chose. Instead, as with modern elites, he favored someone from the upper class, a dashing former marshal of Bonaparte's, Count Charles Bernadotte of Sweden. Nor did Alexander shy away from letting Metternich and others think he would scrap the whole agreement and reinstate Napoleon if he didn't get his way.

Unlike the others who arrived at Vienna, Alexander was consumed by a sense of a divine mission. Lord Grey thought him a "vain, silly fellow," but Alexander believed himself to be God's agent, asking his fellow monarchs to sign a declaration committed themselves to each other "upon the sublime truths which the Holy Religion of Our Savior teaches."[33] (Wellington and Castlereagh called this behavior a "piece of sublime mysticism and nonsense.")[34] If Alexander's religiosity had been smoldering when he left Russia, it burst into flames during a jaunt from Vienna when he re-connected with his estranged wife, Elizabeth, vacationing in Bruchsal, Germany. Elizabeth, however, had nothing to do with it: one of her ladies-in-waiting, Roksandra Sturdza, caught his attention. And she had, in turn, taken up with a pietistic former school teacher Jung Stilling, who had developed new and exotic aspects of Christianity. Stilling met with Czar Alexander. Amidst much drinking, Stilling announced he and Roksandra had prepared a "mystic marriage" for religious strength and Alexander insisted on horning in, with the three of them praying for divine support amidst their frolicking.[35]

Alexander continued back to Russia, where all who saw him noticed his more spiritual nature. After consulting with advisers and church leaders in St. Petersburg, he returned to Vienna, indued, he believed, with the power of God. When he arrived, however, his fervor took a different turn as he attempted to rekindle his earlier association with the apple of Metternich's eye, the Duchess of Sagon, Wilhelmina. They spent much of the night together, where the jealous Czar questioned her about her relationship with Metternich. Such was the grip she had on not one, but two of the major principals at the Congress.

The Vienna into which these luminaries were drawn was a pauper city, with soup kitchens and hunger marches. Money had no value, while rents in the inner part of the city were the highest in Europe. Partly to maintain the peace, the Austrian monarchy had let the poor participate in events at the fringes, allowing them to take down and keep decorations, and giving them free access to any leftover food. Kitchens would set out bowls of fruits, nuts, and desserts. And the "rabble" turned out to provide a great audience for all activities.

Now arriving in the city came huge entourages of ministers, monarchs, ambassadors, aides, ladies-in-waiting, support staff, all making up the largest gathering of aristocrats in history. Talleyrand personally brought along valets, barbers, hairdressers, cooks, and others for his embassy, as well as a piano player to help him relax. Armies of others unattached to any particular delegation arrived to ply their trade, including musicians, card sharps, actresses, ladies of the night, hotel help, and tailors, as well as construction workers and set builders for the never-ending theatricals and plays. Merchants experienced a "golden age" of business: innkeepers, theater managers, hatmakers, wigmakers, glove makers, toymakers, butchers, bakers, florists, hairdressers, and even florists did land-office business. Rents soared, so much so that the Prussian Ambassador, who arrived in August 1814, complained he could find no appropriate quarters. Candles and firewood, needed for the grand balls, as well as soap all skyrocketed in price. An eye-witness, Hilde Spiel, insisted that the Viennese population, though they "mocked and sneered, railed and grumbled [nevertheless] hugely enjoyed the spectacle."[36] Spiel, a German, found the Viennese "full of self-mockery, envy, laziness and cunning . . . ."[37] But she noted that they may have had reason to complain: at all hours carriages and state coaches "blocked the roads, sedan chairs became motionless in the melee, horses pranced and the 'Graben nymphs' traipsed along the sidewalks."[38] Costs for just five months of the Congress, she estimated, were 40 million francs (roughly $800 million in contemporary dollars).

Even as the Congress members dribbled in, a new musical genius, Franz Schubert, premiered his first completed mass. Another great, who had once supported Napoleon but then abandoned him, Ludwig von Beethoven, was present. He had conducted his "Battle Symphony" in Vienna in 1813 to commemorate the Duke of Wellington's victory at Vitoria. Reinstituting the monarchies nevertheless was draped over a bubbling pot of cultural and social revolution. It was a time of Beethoven, Schubert, Chopin, Strauss, and Mozart, and even a time of a revolution in production processes with Eli Whitney's mass production changing the way such things as pianos were made. With all their identical parts, pianos were the peacetime versions of muskets—easy to make, but substantially more expensive. In literature, Lord Byron, Victor Hugo, and the entire Left Bank movement characterize the era.

Those, of course, were the names everyone would later know. A wide variety of other, far lesser talents, however, honed their acts in Vienna as more statesmen and royalty arrived. Street marionette shows dotted the city; gambling halls flourished; and animal acts abounded. For the higher brow crowd, the Schonbrunn Palace Zoo displayed dozens of exotic animals, including bears, camels, kangaroos, and buffalo. Perhaps anticipating today's "food trucks," cafés everywhere sported unique themes designed to catch the eye. There were Indian kiosks, Swiss chalets, Chinese pavilions, and, of course, plenty of native Viennese food. Nightly fireworks, a la modern Disney World, were expected.[39]

It was also assumed that each of the central participants would alternate in hosting parties, some of which had ten thousand or more attendees. Metternich did his part. He had constructed a grand entrance to his residence with a covered staircase leading into a series of chambers decorated as a military encampment of each of the allied armies. One contemporary observed that "Every royal person had a separate equipage, with six or eight horses, and equerries, and a crowd of servants."[40] Richard Bright, who visited Vienna at the time, recorded, "I have heard it asserted, that between two- and three-hundred imperial carriages were in daily use . . . They were all painted green, and adorned with either silver or gold."[41]

As the sovereigns arrived, bands played martial music and troops dragooned in by Metternich waved their bearskin coats and shakos on the ends of their bayonets.[42] An elaborate buffet then greeted them; but not for them—it was for the "lesser" nobles! Next they were led to an amphitheater and a short play, followed by a walk into a Russian village who raucously welcomed the Czar. More dancing, including a ballet followed, until at the end masses of bouquets of flowers were laid at their feet amidst more singing.

That was just the entrance!

The party then ascended a stairway flanked by orange trees, saw more soldiers perform an intricate drill, then entered a ballroom, whereupon they were escorted to a balcony for fireworks. Then and only then did the 150 guests begin eating and dancing. On the ensuing morning, a wild game hunt commenced, resulting in over 100 boar shot.

Not to be outdone, the British held a ball in which men attended in full dress uniform while women were dressed to represent the elements. "Air" consisted of twelve ladies wearing blue gauze and garlands and gossamer wings. "Fire" featured red dresses along with headdresses of red and gold. "Water" had "nymphs" dressed in light green gauze with reeds on their head and rough coral or seashells worked into their hair. Then "Earth" brought silver cloth with diamonds covering their breasts and baskets of diamonds on their heads.

Women in particular had to cope with the never-ending parties because, normally, they would have been expected to show up in different dresses. But the sheer number of events precluded this, and even the richest women in Vienna took to increasingly simple dresses. They likewise only wore jewelry for the most major of events. Men toted a different type of jewelry, with a flurry of honors and medal presentations at each affair.

When dancing began, it started of course with the Minuet—the dance of the upper classes—but eventually incorporated the waltzes gaining in popularity, as well as the quadrille and the *ecossaise*. After guests retired for rest, the next morning began again, this time with visits to the Napoleonic battlefields.

The parties themselves became the focal point for two great activities, procuring sexual partners and spying. King Frederick of Denmark found a young working class woman on the spot at a ball, and stayed with her so regularly that when he finally departed she was referred to as "the Danish widow."[43] Spies (especially in the employ of Metternich) were so ever-present that a visitor said "My children cannot sneeze but that Prince Metternich is sure to hear about it."[44] Chambermaids proved particularly useful in supplying information by rummaging through desks, wastepaper baskets, fireplaces, and even luggage. Scraps they produced, known as *chiffrons*, were dispatched to Metternich's offices. Women, of course, traded sexual favors for political information. But open cafés also provided an endless source of gossip and occasional hard news. Churches offered excellent gossip and information-gathering locations. So were ladies' salons, which were not hairdresser establishments but at the time were sitting rooms where women gathered to talk. (Men occasionally found their way in, with a knock: Metternich himself was known to serve the ladies from fine china.)

Visiting the Duchess of Sagon's salons provided Metternich with an excuse to see her. Czar Alexander had temporarily given up on Wilhelmine and instead turned his attention to another, the wife of

Russian General Pyotr Bagration, Catherine. With Wilhelmine, how-ever, it was only a matter of time before she flitted back to the Czar.

The apex of all festivals came in October 1814 just as the Congress commenced, with the Grand Ball. A catering budget for a similar number of guests required 300 hams, 200 partridges, 200 pigeons, 150 pheasants, 60 hares, 40 rabbits, 20 large turkeys, and 12 boars, plus roasted and cold meats and 600 pickled tongues. Side-dishes included 3,000 liters of soups, 2,500 biscuits, 1,000 oval shaped pastries, 60 sponge cakes, finished off by pies, pastries, almonds, and French puff pastries. All was washed down with thousands of gallons of almond milk, lemonade, tea, and of course, wine.

Next came the spectacular Peace Festival. Again preceded by a ball in which the entrance was lit up by rows of Bengal torches and hand-railings consisting of muskets captured from Napoleon's armies, guests arrived with footmen "whose liveries were so heavily embroidered with gold that it was impossible to tell their colour."[45] Some twenty thousand soldiers stood at attention with flourishes from trumpets as the festiv-ities began with a hot air balloon raising an artificial sun embroidered with the coats-of-arms of the three sovereigns. Guests then moved to a lawn adorned with "temples" erected to Mars, Apollo, and Minerva, then to another lawn with an amphitheater containing three temples— one for "peace," one for the "arts," and one for "industry."

Following a short play and requisite fireworks, a figure called "Discord" accompanied by demonic creatures arrived in a chariot pulled by black stallions. He drove around brandishing a torch as actors pretended to be the denizens of Europe fled before him. His "armies" defeated their opponents, "burned" villages, and chased peo-ple to the temple of peace. A giant parade ensued in which each of the allied nations, represented by a general riding in a chariot sporting the flags of the nations, gathered around the peace temple to sing hymns, dispatching "Discord."

When not partying, the ministers and monarchs trudged through the business of setting up the post-Napoleonic world. The assembly in Vienna had been endowed with uniquely unprecedented powers and a remarkable air of legitimacy. Even the Pope said he might attend. However, these elites rode a wave of public opinion for something they had no intention of addressing: causes such as the slave trade, the oppressed masses, the establishment of a more democratic order. One English writer said "Never has a speechless Europe been seized by such violent and such just anxiety; never has the heart of the world itself been troubled by such expectation . . ."[46] For the first time in history, the rights of peoples and the rights of nations were discussed as distinct from those of the rulers. And for the first time, discussions about the "good of the Continent" surfaced. Even Metternich wrote "Public opinion . . . is one of the most powerful weapons, which like religion penetrates the most hidden corners where administrative measures lose their influence; to despise public opinion is like despising moral principles . . ."[47]

Tallyrand, of all people, insisted that the "rule of law," the natural order of things was a key component of the new system, necessary to the "peace and happiness of peoples, the most solid, or rather the only guarantee of their strength and continuance." Legitimacy, the "safeguard of nations," had to be the guiding principle of the new Europe.[48] Always quick to invoke higher ideals, Talleyrand insisted justice must be the "chief virtue" of international affairs. Any international act by any leader had to first consider justice, he noted, because only justice could produce international peace and harmony.[49]

Alexander's right hand man, Prince Adam Czartoryski, led a foreign policy aimed at a "grand project" for a future international system of governance.[50] Czartoryski thought the old system of diplomacy was ineffective, and instead sought to group nations into small federations based on linguistic or cultural similarities. Unfortunately for the Prince, he never fully took into account Alexander's view that the only possible way such a system could work was with an overriding Christian influence—no doubt with a distinctly Russian tone.

A result of the Congress, the Holy Alliance of Austria, Russia, and Prussia—ostensibly formed as an idealistic and even religious instrument of social improvement—was formed in 1815. In theory this formed an early NATO, a standing agreement that would preserve all the arrangements Congress had made. It, supposedly, would prevent another Bonaparte family member from coming to power again. In practice this constituted an arrangement to resist popular pressures for constitutions and democracies. The original purpose of the alliance had been to dispatch Napoleon and the threat of France, but now members were suggesting it have a more permanent role.

As in most cases, common people wanted a simple return to "normalcy" after all the bloodletting. Thus stability triumphed over democratic ideals. Metternich, in opposition to Castlereagh, sought to manipulate the alliance into an anti-populist body. His ideas won out. In 1820, the King of Spain faced a mutiny that forced him to accept the Spanish Constitution of 1812, which spurred Alexander to threaten military intervention. The other allies refused, and in its first test of squashing popular uprisings, the Quadruple Alliance failed. A similar revolt in Naples failed to move the major powers to intervene.

At home, however, various leaders had begun abolishing popular reforms made after 1807 and stifling dissent. Even in England, *habeas corpus* was suspended in 1817, and two years later a political meeting at St. Peter's Fields was charged by British cavalry resulting in the "Peterloo Massacre."

Contemporaries grew cynical about the achievements of the first attempt at globalism. Fredrich Genz, Metternich's assistant throughout the Congress, recalled:

> Never have the expectations of the general public been as excited as they were before the opening of this solemn assembly. . . People were confident of a general reform of the political system of Europe, of a guarantee of eternal peace, even of the return of the golden age. Yet it produced only restitutions decided beforehand by force of arms, arrangements between the great powers unfavourable to the future balance and the maintenance of people in Europe . . . [51]

Genz observed that because "the congress was never defined, and the powers of its members were never determined . . . it drifted to the very last moment on a sea of uncertainties and contradictions," which favored the great powers.[52] (It should be noted that Genz has been called the "most bribed man in history," and as he departed Vienna he took with him snuffboxes, payments, honors, and even a new carriage delivered anonymously).[53] Genz was not alone among the participants in stating that the Congress was a debacle. Describing Castlereagh's role in the Congress, Lord Byron in *Don Juan* used words such as "botching," "patching," and "cobbling."

Champions of the Congress, most notably former Secretary of State Henry Kissinger, romanticized that a new legitimacy was conferred on the meeting. As Harriet Martineu wrote in her history of the assembly, "the peace of 1815 was constructed without the slightest effort to secure its perpetuity by something stronger than conventions and protocols—by uniting mankind in a bond of common interests."[54]

President Woodrow Wilson at the end of World War I hoped "no odour of Vienna" would be brought to the Versailles Peace Conference a century later.[55] It actually was worse, as we will see. Kissinger expectedly praised the Congress for keeping the peace—a tough sell given that the Crimean War (1856) pitted two of the participants (Britain and France) against a third (Russia), or that the Franco-Prussian War of 1871 saw France and Germany go to war. To virtually skip over two major European wars in less than a century after Vienna and claim it a success requires significant academic gymnastics—and minor revolts and border conflicts are not even mentioned here. Kissinger's "out" was in claiming that the real settlement at Vienna was undone by the Congress of Verona in 1822, when revolts of the kind Genz anticipated broke out in Paris.

Other aspects of the Congress unraveled equally quickly. In August 1822, there was a revolution in Belgium against Dutch rule and in November the Poles revolted against Russia. (The former succeeded, the latter were defeated by the Russians.) Contrary to Kissinger's claims, no new "legitimacy" was established in Europe at Vienna. Utopians had hoped that a unification of mankind would occur, while

Christian conservatives hoped for something more Alexander-like, more spiritual.

Instead, Metternich's spy system actually grew—to the point that the Austrian minister's minions could steam open letters at the post office in London![56] His minions in the police arrested dissidents at the first whiff of disaffection. State terror remained a fact of political life until the defeat of Austria in 1855.

Other sordid aspects of the Congress soon spilled out, challenging the great hope that it would be a reformist gathering that would represent the masses. For one thing, word spread of the way the monarchs and ministers had lumped people into groups and bartered or moved them across the negotiating table—a feat Woodrow Wilson and his cronies would replicate and magnify. A French observer, Dominique Pradt, found it was "easier to be awarded souls than to conquer hearts," but the Congress had no intention of trying to do the latter. Once "souls" could be moved with impunity, it soon expanded into bundling and moving entire nations, leaving entirely stateless groups of people. Indeed, if anything Napoleon had brought to Europe a sense of "statehood" not seen before, and now people rose to claim what they viewed as a fundamental right to belong. Poland would remain one of the most vexing problems for globalists well into the 1930s, when Adolf Hitler and Joseph Stalin split it like the wishbone of a chicken.

A new consciousness of "wrongs inflicted" ultimately not only involved Germans, Italians, and Poles but Jews and slavs. While little was actually done to address the issues, "the new consciousness of the wrongs inflicted on individuals and communities . . . only aggravated their sense of exclusion and consequent alienation."[57] German pride was perpetually wounded after that; Jewish obsession over a homeland increased; France fell into a succession of bloody revolutions and ongoing instability; and the newly re-imposed monarchical globalism ignored the very masses upon whose goodwill it had begun. When new European wars ignited in 1857 and 1871, the last pretense of monarchical globalism's legitimacy vanished. Now, the generals brushed aside the monarchs to impose their own brand of globalism by the bayonet.

Chapter Two

Militaristic Globalism and the Age of Imperialism

J ust forty-four years after the Congress of Verona, a meeting that was to perpetuate the peace promised by the Congress of Vienna, a new war broke out in Europe. So much for a "hundred year peace"! This time, the former antagonists Britain and France now were allied with Turkey against their former Coalition partner, Russia, in a dispute over the rights of Christian churches in Palestine. A disagreement between the Roman Catholic church—supported by France—and the Greek Orthodox church—supported by Russia—caused French Emperor Napoleon III and the Russian Czar Nicholas I to escalate a brewing difference over the Danubian Principalities of modern-day Romania but then controlled by the Ottoman Empire. If this isn't confusing enough, for readers who thought they had seen the last of the Bonapartes in chapter one, not only was there a new Napoleon in France, but this one had the support of Great Britain!

When Russia occupied the contested regions in July 1853, the Ottoman Empire with assurances of assistance from France and Britain, declared war on Russia. The Turks fought a defensive campaign in modern-day Bulgaria but lost the Battle of Sinop in November 1853, in which the Russian Navy, operating out of the Black Sea, attacked and defeated a Turkish fleet in the Sinop harbor. That action was cited by Britain and France as the cause of entering the war. Just like that, the Congress of Vienna was a memory, with a new Napoleon and a new war! And as if matters weren't confusing enough, the Italian kingdom of Sardinia also sent forces to Crimea.[1]

Just fourteen years later, in 1871, France and Prussia went to war, largely on the provocation of the Ems Dispatch telegram. In reality, they both wanted war. Prussia—which became united as Germany by 1871—went on to become a perpetual threat on the mainland due to its growing paranoia about enemies (France, Russia) on two fronts and ultimately, as petroleum became the major fuel source of the modernized world, access to oil. The Germans all but ensured a desire for *revanche* (revenge) by the French after the Franco-Prussian War. They also constantly longed for unification with all so-called "Germanic" peoples, especially Austria. But in the period under investigation here, namely the late 1800s, Prussia-Germany became obsessed with acquiring colonies at the same pace the other powers did. Of course there was a Himalayan-sized problem: the Germans didn't have a maritime history as did the British, nor did they have access to ports comparable to the French. Germany's ports were mostly on the Baltic, with a few on the North Sea. Baltic ports were always subject to the disadvantage of needing to navigate the Skagerrak/Kattegat straits, which an enemy fleet could patrol. Fleets could be bottled up. This limitation at sea also meant that Germany, like France, had to judiciously divide its military funding between and army and a navy, whereas the British could starve their army if necessary to feed the Royal Navy.

To put it bluntly, the Congress of Vienna failed. It gave way to a new dynamic of globalism, that of European military and colonial dominance. Some of this came naturally. European death rates fell much more rapidly than birthrates in the early 1800s, leading the population to rise much faster than in Africa or Asia. Europe's population rose from about 150 million in 1750 to over 400 million in 1900.[2] American growth dwarfed that of Europe (of course many Americans had come over as immigrants), from 5.3 million to 76.2 million. By

1900 Europe had 20 percent of the world's population, and when combined with America and Canada, close to one-third. Great Britain's population alone had nearly tripled from 1800 to 1870, and England had become the most urbanized country in the world. Over one-third of England's population lived in cities, compared to only about 16 percent of America's—but that made sense, given the astonishing availability of land in America. In contrast, even after adjusting for the population decline of slavery, Africa, for example, was already in a state of stagnation if not decline. Places such as Algeria suffered five plague epidemics and Tunisia had three.[3]

The sheer growth of population meant many things, including the fact that Europe, England, and America were industrializing at rates much faster than anywhere else in the world. Most important of all the new inventions was the steam engine, brought to life in the early 1700s by Thomas Newcomen then perfected by James Watt and Matthew Boulton, then commercialized by the Carron Company Ironworks. It didn't hurt that England basically was an island of coal or that America was a continent with endless forests. But another key ingredient graced England and America as opposed to the rest of Europe or much of Asia, Latin America, or Africa. As discussed earlier, England's status as an island nation demanded a powerful and advance maritime presence, while America after the Louisiana Purchase had more navigable rivers than anywhere else in the world. Or, to put it another way, the steam engine appeared in those nations most able to make the best use of it on rivers and oceans.

This would prove a critical factor in the globalization efforts of each nation. Consider the Mississippi River, the world's longest navigable river (i.e., capable of handling drafts of nine feet for three-fourths of the year). Its 2,100 miles make it 30 percent longer than the Danube and triple the length of the Rhine—and it's only one of *twelve* major navigable rivers in America. Those rivers total over 14,600 miles, whereas Mexico doesn't have a *single* navigable river. Add to the American river network an intracoastal waterway provided by chains of barrier islands that stretch for almost 3,000 miles. All of this, as futurist Peter Zeihan wrote, constitutes a 17,600-mile network that makes it unique in the world.[4] In contrast, the Nile, about 4,100 miles long, includes parts of modern-day Tanzania, Burundi, Rwanda, the Democratic Republic of the Congo, Kenya, Uganda, and parts of the Sudan. While it provided a good source of water for agriculture, its variations made cultivation risky. Its rapids made transit difficult, and its papyrus "sudds" (barriers) often blocked navigable channels. In short, the Mississippi it ain't. Similarly, the Amazon—similarly sized at 4,000 miles—is lined with thick vegetation. Even where the river is useful for shipping, building anything on the banks was a daunting prospect. Other rivers, including the Yellow (3,300 miles), the Yangtze (3,900 miles), and the Ganges (1,600 miles) all suffered from flooding.

Thus, blessed with either the ocean (England) or the biggest waterway network in the world (the United States), the appearance of steam immediately opened the two largest western economies to the world—or, more appropriately opened the world to them. For starters, this meant European settlement of many of these temperate regions. By the late 1800s Europe had taken over many of these zones. In Argentina, more than 90 percent of the new settlers were of European descent, in Uruguay about 90 percent, and in Brazil 85 to 95 percent. Even without using (for the most part) their militaries, the Europeans and Americans settled vast swaths of wilderness around the world by the mid-1800s.

Steam power made upriver travel not only possible but decisive. Daniel Headrick in his classic article "The Tools of Imperialism" noted that the combination of steam and iron hulls made remote regions accessible and made defensive positions vulnerable.[5] The clearest object lesson in the application of a steam-powered vessel came in 1825, when the steam warship *Diana* ran down a Burmese imperial prau in a four-hour chase when the Burmese, who had a 100 double-banked oars, simply collapsed or even died of exhaustion.[6] Then, fifteen years later, the British vessel ironclad/steamship *Nemesis* left England for China, becoming the first steamer to sail past the Cape of Good Hope. After arriving in Ceylon, the captain announced the next destination was

Macao, which the vessel reached in November 1840. Two years later the *Nemesis* participated in an attack on Canton through narrow inland channels no wooden warship could enter, decimating forts, destroying Chinese junks, and demonstrating the potential of such ships. In this case, the Chinese were slow learners, requiring a major flotilla up the Yangtze a year later by ten steamers, whereupon China agreed to open itself up to the opium trade.

America joined iron vessel diplomacy when Commodore Matthew Perry steamed into Tokyo Bay in 1853, just as Russian steamers appeared off Japanese coasts.

Access to the interior of Africa, Asia, Southeast Asia, and Latin America by itself wasn't sufficient for the western powers to exert control, for an equally formidable enemy than geography had to be defeated: malaria. A particularly virulent form caused by *Plasmodium falciparum* was found only in Africa and was deadly. Beginning in the 1790s, between 46 percent and 72 percent of European first-year military personnel stationed in West Africa died of the disease. In Sierra Leone, the rate was 48 percent as measured by a British study of the years 1817–36; in the Gold Coast, 66 percent.[7] Some expeditions lost their entire number. Although the transmitter of the disease, the anopheles mosquito, was not isolated until 1898 (and against great resistance of the medical community at the time, which insisted that malaria was transmitted by dirt), a practical treatment was found in quinine prophylaxis. French chemists in 1820 isolated the quinine alkaloid, cinchona, then British experimenters found that quinine worked well against malaria, and by the 1830s, it was being produced cheaply.[8]

At that point, impervious to the ravages of disease and able to overcome the obstacles of nature, the third of Headrick's "tools" emerged as dominant, namely modern weaponry. Armed with new breech-loading rifles, continuously refining cannon technology, and early machine guns (such as the Maxim gun), the firepower available to a company of western troops expanded exponentially. Safely barricaded troops, even without cannon or machine guns, well-armed troops with plenty of ammunition could hold a defensive perimeter—such as they did at the Wagon Box Fight (1867) in Wyoming Territory, where twenty-six soldiers and six civilians armed with breech-loaders were attacked by hundreds of Lakota Sioux and drove them off, or Roarke's Drift (1879) where 150 British barricaded behind mealie bags and wagons fought off up to 4,000 Zulus—were the early warning signs for native armies.[9]

Victor Hanson has explained the sociological/cultural elements of western armies, that had a long heritage of being superior to non-western armies.[10] After the introduction of modern weaponry, that advantage increased. One would have thought that if natives could get Enfield rifles they would have been more of a match to the Europeans; in fact, it was just the opposite because of the factors Hanson illuminates. Prior to World War I, volley fire was particularly morale breaking. A thousand attacking natives who saw hundreds go down in an instant suddenly reconsidered the wisdom of a frontal assault. Firing in unison; keeping up a constant cycle of fire while other troops are reloading; and moving in echelon to cover breaks in the ranks are cultural aspects of military training that were distinctly Western and which were learned over countless hours of drill.

This is not to say that native armies did not drill. Zulus practiced combat relentlessly and were highly organized. So were many Islamic armies. But practicing with spears or out of date weapons is far different than drilling with modern weaponry. Moreover, as Hanson shows, the "Western Way of War" was far more about a style of combat—staying in rank, fighting toward unconditional surrender, and so on—than about particular battlefield tactics. And many African and Asian rulers did not trust their troops with more advanced weapons lest they revolt.[11] Artillery was an entirely different matter, and even large civilizations in the Islamic world, such as the Ottomans, had to get their advanced technology from the West, often through traitors. Even then, however, they were not only a step behind, but faced difficulty getting spare parts and repairing broken guns. Smuggling or obtaining European weapons through trade also saddled the rest of the world with armaments of various calibers and makes, preventing uniform training and dispensing of weapons. Every once in a while, such as at the Battle of the Little Big Horn, native armies managed to acquire weapons more advanced than their enemies (in this case, repeating rifles vs. the 7th Cavalry's carbines). These were in such small numbers as to have made no difference in the long run.[12]

Literacy added to the Western advantage: a squad assigned to fire a machine gun could read an instruction manual and minimize (though certainly never eliminate) actual practice time. As weapons grew more complex and expensive, training manuals both for operation and repair became even more imperative. Any society that lacked mass publications and the ability to distribute them to ordinary troops was doomed. Historian David Hackett Fischer noted that as early as 1776 "Yankee regiments may have been the most literate army in the world. Nearly all New England privates could read and write."[13]

And yet another factor endowed Western militaries—and especially Americans—with a major advantage. The West cherished individuality and autonomy as essential to their very political character. In America's militaries, it was common for ordinary soldiers to assume command if senior officers were killed on the battlefield. Indeed, Americans even adopted the "brevet" promotion for battlefields until ranks could formally be affirmed by the War Department. As of 1892, virtually any soldier could apply for officer training. Ordinary American sailors and soldiers contributed important mechanical improvements, which their superiors—far from obstructing—embraced in the spirit of overcoming challenges. For example, the US Navy, at sea, adopted the innovation of a chief petty officer to use CO_2 in the piping to put out fires on carriers; and the invention of the "Rhino" hedge cutting Sherman tank was credited to Sgt. Curtis Culin of the 2nd Armored Division and a "Tennessee hillbilly named Roberts"; no one knows who first welded two long steel "forks" to the front of a Sherman tank to defeat the hedgerows in France.[14]

Certainly European-style combat met certain geographic realities in Africa, the Middle East, and Asia. Topography, mountains and especially jungles, made hash out of file-and-line formations and prevented heavy artillery from being of much use. Likewise, such natural obstacles greatly minimized any use of European cavalry. Nevertheless—especially after the advent of the Maxim gun and repeating rifles—a company of 100 men in any setting could quadruple the firepower of native armies, even if those were armed with semi-modern weapons.

One final aspect of industrialism involved the improvement in the standard of living of the average European. For example, the purchasing power of a French or German wage earner rose by about 30 percent in the mid- to late-1800s; British wage earners saw an even stronger growth at 45 percent, largely because of free trade. The Cobden-Chevalier Treaty opened trade between Britain and France and was opposed by the majority of the population and the parliament, and was pushed through by Napoleon III. Except for Germany, which established protectionist tariffs in 1879, and France which responded four years later, most of the world remained engaged in free trade. Worldwide trade exploded by 600 percent from 1815 to 1900.

In short, by the late 1800s western militaries could dominate native armies, even well-armed ones, that were several times their size. At its imperial peak, Great Britain administered 440 million people dispersed over 11 million square miles, often with an army of less than 500,000 (and even sometimes as small as under 150,000). Add to the advantages they possessed the diplomatic control westerners exerted (as did all nations and empires) of pitting one ethnic group or tribe against another, and dominance came quickly. Consider India, where the British Army featured Hindu regiments, Muslim regiments, and Sikh regiments, each under the command of a British officer, and each usually separated by a British regiment of regulars. Only in 1857, with the Great Mutiny, did this system break down. It did so due to a masterful campaign of propaganda coinciding with the introduction of a new cartridge into British munitions that had to be bitten to expose the powder. Sepoys who were Hindu were told the cartridges were coated in cow fat; Muslims were told the cartridges were coated in pig fat; in fact it was a vegetable grease. But this united the warring Hindus and Muslims against a common enemy, the British.[15] Of course, there were much deeper reasons and ongoing resentments.[16]

Such transportation, scientific, medical, and firepower dominance led the Europeans (less so the Americans) to not only settle other continents but to colonize them. Obviously—to Europeans—the natives had never undergone a Renaissance. Equally obviously, they were backward. Next came the illogical leap: because they were backward scientifically and in military power, they must likewise be less developed intellectually and morally. That logic indirectly supported, at the very least, a type of peon-like servitude to the European powers. It was not important that a few centuries earlier, the Europeans were the "backward" societies.

Although missionaries would prove the most common and practical explorers, a strong geographical movement arose in the period 1820–1900. For example, the *Societe de Geographie de France* (1821), the Royal Geographical Society of London (1830), the American Geographical Society (1851), and another hundred societies worldwide produced thousands of members. France alone in 1896 had 20,000 members.[17]

European globalist ideas were enhanced and buttressed by Christian charity and a strain of do-gooder-ism that well into the twenty-first century would continue to taint evangelizing efforts. It was understandable that the Great Commission given by Jesus to "make disciples of all nations, teaching them to observe all I have commanded you" (Matthew 28:19) directed missionary efforts toward saving souls. Once in the field, however, missionaries found themselves co-mingling that charge with others not direct included in the Great Commission, such as feeding and clothing the poor and making natives literate so they could read the Bible. Indeed, the "so-called 'bush school' served as a school during the week and a church on Sunday."[18]

Rather quickly the arrival of missionaries forced a foreign policy decision when it came to development of colonialized countries and whether—or when—to intervene. Sooner or later, a clash between political and military settlers of a region (such as Mexico or Tasmania) and missionaries would become inevitable. With the Spanish in the New World—as priests often accompanied every expedition—this came sooner, although in Australia and Tasmania the government frequently appointed churchmen to mitigate the damage.[19] Usually, it worked to some degree. Priests frequently—but not always—took the part of natives, working for humane treatment. Protestant missions more so, though they too were connected to the larger objective of European dominance.

One of the most powerful and influential of the religious bodies involved in imperialism was the Baptist Missionary Society (BMS World Mission). Founded in 1792 by the classic Christian Missionary William Carey as the "Particular Baptist Society for the Propagation of the Gospel Amongst the Heathen" in Kettering, England, the group first sent missionaries to India in 1793. His essay "An Enquiry into the Obligations of Christians to Use Means for the Conversion of the Heathens" was a seminal missionary statement. Carey was fluent in multiple languages, which allowed him to translate the Bible into Bengali, Oriya, Marthi, Hindi, and Sanskrit.[20] The following year, 1794, the Society opened a mission in China.

Voluntary lay ministers who went forth from the BMS and other societies have been described as "innovators, creating institutions as they went" driven by "God-intoxicated opportunism," the missionaries saw a "glorious door opened by God" and left the details of bureaucratic support back in England.[21] England at the time had an active churchgoing population of about 40 percent, about half of which was not associated with the Church of England, though few were congregational in structure.[22]

Carey himself started as a street preacher in the bazaars, then eventually got a paying job in the indigo trade, where he conceived of a community of missionaries modeled on the Moravians. He specialized in Bengali, the language of the people, not other languages spoken by the ruling classes in India. At Serampore he joined a group of Baptist missionaries and immediately began to start schools, teaching poor children to read, write, and do accounting. Carey campaigned against *sutee*, wherein a Hindu widow had to sit on top of her husband's funeral pyre. Conversions came slow, and his wife and closest associate both went insane.[23]

The General Baptists formed their own missionary society in 1817; the Church of Scotland followed in 1824. Although the Great Britain passed the National Service Act in 1819 allowing the Bishop of London and the Archbishop of Canterbury to ordain missionary ministers, the evangelical horse had long left the barn. Anglicans were playing catch-up to the volunteers as were Wesleyan Methodists, who organized a missionary society in 1811. Non-Anglican societies tended toward anti-elitism and anti-establishment positions. Regardless of all other traits, the missionary societies were of a single mind when it came to spreading the gospel.

Voluntarism, street preachers, and lay missionaries were inevitable after the Act of Toleration in 1689. Anglicans whined that there was no way, legally, to suppress those who "assembled in barns, in rooms of private houses, or in other buildings of the most improper kind, to hear the wild effusions of a mechanic or a ploughboy. . . "[24] Former Prime Minister Henry Addington, then Lord Sidmouth, sought to constrain lay preachers—"cobblers, tailors, pig-drovers and chimney sweepers" from dispensing the gospel.[25] Training missionaries, however, lagged: not until 1846 with the founding of St. Augustine's College in Canterbury did a school exist exclusively to prepare them. Most theological education came through Sunday Schools, which also provided nearly one-fourth of missions giving.

Whether church-endorsed or lay-originated, the missions needed money. By then, it was common for individual households to have a "missionary box" for special tithes. Virtually all the missionary societies raised funds for foreign fields. Some, such as Carey, established businesses to pay for the mission.

Individuals such as Henry Stanley (1841–1904) and David Livingstone (1813–1879) became the popular model of missionaries in the Age of Imperialism, though in fact women made up a large majority of all Protestant missionaries. Livingston was a doctor and seasoned explorer who followed the Lualaba River to the headwaters of the Congo River, thinking it was the Nile. Stanley had made himself unpopular in British society: the Queen called him a "determined, ugly, little man—with a strong American twang," and the British Geographical Society "considered him a charlatan."[26] Preachers such as Sidney Smith saw them as unfit to represent either England or the cloth. Such itinerant lay ministers were "the lowest of people" he complained, and likely were insane.[27] Nevertheless, until recently when missionaries were painted as evil fellow travelers of the greedy Europeans, they were generally ignored altogether. For example, Owen Chadwick's two-volume history of the Victorian Church did not mention missionaries at all, and a more recent *Religion and Society in Twentieth-Century Britain* scarcely mentioned missions.[28]

As British missionaries replaced the wave of Spanish priests who had accompanied the early explorations of the 1500s and 1600s, coercion was abandoned. After the Indian Mutiny of 1857, the concept became formal policy. Queen Victoria stated, "Firmly relying on the truth of Christianity and acknowledging the solace of religion, we disclaim alike the right and the desire to impose our convictions on any of our subjects," including those overseas.[29] (This, of course, exempted Irish Catholics!) William Wilberforce, Britain's antislavery champion, thought the conversion of India was more important than even the abolition of slavery. In particular, the British were obsessed with ending Indian law, which they considered an abomination for its toleration of *sutee*.

British churches emphasized ordination of non-whites as fast as possible to shed the taint of imperialism. If Britain ruled without the consent of the governed, the missionary movement was "committed in principle, if not in practice to the voluntary consent of those non-western peoples who became Christians."[30] However, despite the multiracial and multinational character of British missions, for the most part Anglicans still operated from a top-down structure, meaning the spread of Christianity by the British—even the lay volunteers—did little for the natives when it came to cultivating that crucial element found in America of bottom-up congregationalism.

Not only did the British lack a method to require men and women to go into missions, the established church elites saw the volunteer missionaries as a nuisance or even a threat. Clergyman Sydney Smith, in the *Edinburgh Review*, dismissed them as "little detachments of maniacs."[31] Committed to not only preaching the gospel but in teaching natives to read, missionaries constituted a means by which the locals could acquire written anti-colonial propaganda. This was nothing new to the British, who sought to keep the American colonists from becoming literate with the infamous Stamp Act. American newspapers had reacted with vitriol.

By 1860, BMS had missions in Asia, the Caribbean, Africa, and South America. African chieftains in particular welcomed the missions, which often brought clinics. However, missions often brought delegates who could argue cases in front of white magistrates if there were disputes. And the presence of Europeans provided some small buffer against other African invaders who risked the wrath of the British or French if they harmed any whites from those nations.

Regardless of whether such organizations were politicized or utilized by the colonial governments, there is no doubt most of the missionaries themselves were sincere, faithful believers who often paid with their lives merely for being Christians. In the 1900 so-called "Boxer Rebellion" in China, all the missionaries in the Shanxi province were killed by the Boxers, as well as all 120 coverts.[32]

Whether Christianizing the natives constituted a stated major objective of imperialism, there is little doubt that the quest for empire itself proved sufficient for European expansion without advancing men's spiritual condition. Depredations such as piracy also fueled imperialistic growth. For example, the Mediterranean had long been a locus of piracy and hostage-taking. Attempts by governments and Christian groups to redeem the hostages only fed the fire. Each new hostage became even more valuable.

The United States, despite its remote distance from the Mediterranean compared to the Europeans, was the first nation to stand up to the brigands. President Thomas Jefferson launched the first "war on terror" against the pirates of Algiers, Morocco, and Tunis.[33] America's Puritan/Yankee character infused with its Scots-Irish rebellious streak was in no mood to tolerate Muslim bullies stealing and threatening US citizens. Operating with a joint resolution (and not a declaration of war, which would become problematic in the future), Jefferson sent a flotilla to the Mediterranean in 1804. As Lt. Stephen Decatur set fire to the captured US frigate, the *Philadelphia*, which had run aground, a "rogues gallery" of Turks, Greeks, French, English, and Egyptians led by the American Consul William Eaton and eight Marines crossed the desert from Cairo and took Tripoli from the landward side.[34]

Stamping out the pestilence of the Barbary thugs required another mission, this time in 1815 with the Second Barbary War against Tripoli, Tunis, and Algiers. Commodore Stephen Decatur arrived with another flotilla and imposed a new treaty in the summer of 1816 that was not ratified until 1822 due to an oversight. Thus ended the payment of tribute. The Second Barbary War, however, may have impressed the British enough that they redoubled their efforts to modernize and increase their own naval presence in the world. Most notably this included building and maintaining effective ports in far-flung regions.

Efforts of the young American Republic notwithstanding, it was Great Britain's Royal Navy that constituted the first mechanism of expanding its empire. It alone could enforce a global order and act as "world policeman." For example, early in the 1800s, Thomas Raffles, who was put in charge of Java from 1811 to 1816, then supervised all the port facilities that became the base at Singapore. Raffles himself designed Singapore as a *world* trade port (which he intended to "eventually destroy the spell of the Dutch monopoly").[35] Almost immediately Raffles's vision paid off: in just under three years over 2,800 ships entered and departed the harbor (383 European) and the number leaped to 10,000 quickly. Both Penang and Malacca saw the British exceed their trade. But Singapore was just one of the numerous British trade bases that spread its influence around the globe.

And not just influence, but a search for knowledge. Accompanying the Royal Navy were contingents of explorers, cartographers, and all sorts of scientific investigators, made famous in the film *Master and*

Commander by Dr. Stephen Maturin, the ship's surgeon who collects insects, flora, and fauna. If possible, though, England offloaded the costs of exploration onto its businesses and missionaries (though many questioned the accuracy of missionary maps).

One element of imperialism reinforced the next. As western nations could extend their reach deep into the interior of Africa, Asia, and Latin America, they came into growing contact with natives. Lacking any form of industrialism, and having not gone through an intellectual Renaissance, indigenous peoples seemed backward and lacking "civilized" behaviors. Take Raffles, for example: he wanted to "spread the rule of law, with all races subject equally to it, and trade flourishing freely in its consequence."[36] He wrote to William Wilberforce that "the foundation has at least been laid on which a better state of society can be founded." Not only would "our commerce . . . extend to every part [of Southeast Asia], and British principle will be known and felt throughout."[37] Trade and "not territory is our object," he claimed, and it was in Great Britain's interests to promote "improving the energies and resources of [native] states, upholding their independence and strengthening their power and importance."[38] Raffles's arguments were amplified and amended in 1830 by Rear Admiral Edward Own, who insisted that naval forces alone could not change societies, only direct colonization—something Raffles hoped to avoid.

Unlike many Europeans (but quite like Charles "Chinese" Gordon), Raffles looked favorably upon native peoples, founding a college in Singapore that introduced them to science, European laws, and constitutional government. What he did not grasp was that without the "Four Pillars of American Exceptionalism," constitutional systems were less robust and more vulnerable to systemic breakdowns. At the time, however, most missionaries confirmed Raffles's perception, but with the attendant requirement that the natives also be Christianized. Any resistance on the part of locals merely confirmed in Europeans' minds that the heathen didn't know what was good for them. Europeans therefore advanced into a form of militaristic globalism that wove together scientific superiority, medical improvement, and spiritual salvation. Encounters with peoples whose own religious habits were less than civilized—to the European eye—only further confirmed the westerners' own superiority.

Slavery provided just such an example. By the mid-1800s the Europeans had concluded slavery was an evil that must be stamped out. England's role in the slave trade was abolished largely through the efforts of William Wilberforce, a wealthy Member of Parliament. He saw the suppression of the slave trade as the singular purpose of his life. In 1807, he attained his goal with the abolition of the slave trade. From that point on, England, sometimes by official policy, sometimes (as in the case of General Charles "Chinese" Gordon) by individual initiative, led the way in abolishing slavery in Africa and Asia.

Gordon characterized this "second wave" of reformers who were out to change policies, not just save individual souls. In doing so he personally established a form of imperial globalism. After serving in Crimea, Gordon went to China and was handed command of the "Ever Victorious Army" of Chinese officered by Europeans. Gordon's forces smashed the Taiping rebels, whereupon Gordon, after an interlude in England, was appointed Governor-General of the Sudan where he suppressed the slave trade.[39] The French abolished slavery in Madagascar in 1896, freeing nearly half a million slaves, then in 1905 abolished slavery in most of French West Africa.

By the mid-1800s, the fusion of commerce, religion, and politics was nearly complete in the British Empire. Livingston described the British presence in Africa in three words: "Christianity, Commerce, Civilization."[40] No one personified this trinity more than Samuel Crowther, who sailed up the Niger River for a meeting with the emir of Bida. Crowther wore three different hats. One was a bishop's miter, which signified his position as an Anglican Bishop and head of the CMS in West Africa. Then he had his Victorian top hat, which identified him as a representative of Queen Victoria's government, a position that allowed him to dispense gifts to the Emir to end the slave trade. A third was his straw hat, which he wore as the agent assisting commercial traders in the region. Crowther was an African, from the Yoruba tribe, and a former slave himself.[41]

Ending slavery, of course, did not end race-based discrimination in most of the empires: the British maintained a three-tiered racial society in South Africa with blacks at the bottom, "coloreds" (Indians, mostly, imported for laborers) above them, and whites at the top. Even there, the battles between the white British and the Dutch Boers for the southern tip of Africa continued until Britain's final victory in the Second Boer War in 1902, with England controlling all of modern day South Africa and Zimbabwe.

France, as did England, justified its control over native peoples in Africa and Asia on the pretense of a *Mission civilisatrice*, or "Civilizing Mission." This included spreading the French language, Catholicism, and education. In theory, the end-goal of the mission was assimilation. In practice, the policy was *sujet francais* (natives) and *citoyens francais* (Europeans). Fewer than seven thousand native Algerians, for example, were granted French citizenship between 1830 and 1946. Like the British, Belgians, Dutch, and Germans, most French subscribed to the notion that "higher races" have a right of dominion over lower races. French liberals (known in the twentieth century as progressives or socialists) strongly favored a genuine assimilation, especially in Algeria—but that is a story for another chapter. Europeans thought more highly of Asians, holding the culture of the Orient in high esteem. This was somewhat ironic, given that the Chinese viewed themselves as the only true "people"; that other races were inferior or devils; and that only its civilization was the repository of art and knowledge.[42] China's Emperor (*Teen-tze*, or "Son of Heaven") held much the same position as Japan's emperor held.

Nevertheless, China remained outside the West's ability to control it, partly due to its size, partly due to the strong anti-European bias among all Chinese people, and partly due to the highly advanced levels of corruption operating inside the country. Rebellions and secret societies had racked China—particularly the White Lotus cult of the 1790s—and it proved difficult to use China's own administrative machinery against her because of the galactic levels of corruption at every level. Intelligentsia governed the country, such as it was, through a bureaucracy top-downward, with merchants at the bottom. Important jobs were for sale. In what seemed a template for much modern education, all students were taught was "how to write examination essays."[43]

Virtually all taxes came in the form of grain tribute, which sailed up the Yellow River in boats: each boat was manned by a hereditary official (who got his cut), but whose actual sailing was handled by deputies (about fifty thousand of them) who also got a cut. All trade had to go through Canton; all involved imperial licenses (and bribes); and the Imperial Superintendent of Maritime Customs took a slice of all that. A big slice. Any foreign trader could plan to pay double or triple bribes to an ever-changing landscape of bureaucratic grifters. And because all this caused westerners to view China with scorn, few had any qualms about supplying Chinese with opium, which began to flow into China in the 1820s in increased quantities. A ship would harbor in Canton, a Chinese official would come aboard, get his bribe; perhaps enforce any number of obtuse and otherwise ridiculous regulations; and punished any westerner brutally for the slightest violation if they chose. Thus, the missionary-merchant base from which most other colonial empires grew never took root in China, which, in the long run, probably proved far worse for the Chinese when westerners, plus the Japanese and Russians, carved out their spheres of influence later in the century.

Outside of China, the Europeans settled down to the actual governance of the empires, coopting or consolidating the informal influence exerted by missionaries. While different in each imperial nation, the construction of an administrative apparatus followed a somewhat similar course. In English possessions, colonial responsibilities had first resided with the Ministry of War. Then, early in the 1800s, duties fell to the Secretary of State until 1854, when a separate Colonial Secretary was appointed.[44] But there was a separate Secretary for India after 1858 and the Foreign Office also had a say in overseas.

In Britain's case the colonies were divided into "colonies," "protec-torates," and "protected states," with the Crown Colonies administered by a governor and an appointed executive council that was assisted—but not responsible to—a legislature. Over time, those legislatures became more active, often splitting into two houses as in the United States. Whitehall governed most of these Crown Colonies. Files were stored at the colonial office in London in a building so damp that paperwork had to be stored in the walls and perpetual fires burned to keep the files from dissolving.[45] A Secretary of State, an undersecre-tary, then a variety of thirty-one other officers and staff supported the Office. Surprisingly, it was a small operation worldwide, administered by only 1,000 in the 1860s and only 2,400 by century's end. When sol-diers on the ground were included, the total grew to 120,000. Needless to say, except for native regiments, no colonial people served in any of those offices.

Financially, England's Colonial Office watched costs to the shil-ling, no doubt due to the constant criticism by Treasury on the waste-ful nature of colonial administration. British administrative expendi-tures were extremely low, amounting in India to one-tenth of a pound sterling per person per year. Capital investments constituted an entirely different matter, and England accounted for 75 percent of the interna-tional movement of all capital in 1900.[46] Contrary to traditional claims, such investments did not "starve" British domestic industry: the so-called "dependent empire" only received about 10 percent of all the empire's capital as a share of total overseas capital. In short, "Britain was indeed a major supplier of the world's finance, but, apart from the last decade [of the 1800s], the Empire was not a major recipient of those funds."[47] Most of the attraction to economic gains in the Empire came from India, and there, from transportation. By 1902, India had a rail-road network of over 26,000 miles. Nevertheless, the dependent empire played little role in shaping the Mother Country's home economy.

By 1900, England exported about 5 percent of its gross national product, which accounted for three-fourths of British private savings. And it was there that the Leninist-imperialist interpretations completely unraveled. Instead of money flowing into the Empire, it went to the United States (as it mostly still does, with the exception of China). Despite the lure of exotic markets and the necessity of railroad construction in India, Africa, and Asia, British investors saw the United States as a better return. "The dusky bosoms" of the undeveloped lands proved far less lucrative than the American dynamo.

In their study of British capital markets, Robert Huttenback and Lance Davis asked if it was rational for the British to invest in the legal and political structure required for an empire, and if determined rational, who benefitted? Profits in the early period (prior to 1880) were high, but quickly reversed after that decade, and domestic investment or betting on America remained the better choice—as the authors observed, for the general investor, the Empire constituted "a flame not worth the candle."[48] Equally important, expenditures to maintain the Empire were hardly inconsequential. Defense costs probably ate up about 12 percent of British savings per year.

Without question, individual entrepreneurs and businesses prospered, yet on the whole, the notion that England conquered large swaths of land and vast numbers of people for the almighty pound sterling falls flat. Certainly other motivations not only enabled, but perpetuated empires. The public found overseas conquest "politically desirable [and] hypnotically alluring."[49] And the dangling carrot of many empires drove further expansion, namely that "the next one" will bring profitability and success. In the end, though, the average Briton did not benefit economically from acquiring large areas of the globe. Economics could not suffice to successfully perpetuate militaristic globalism.

As often as not, as with the case of the South African Dutch Huguenots and Germans (known as "Boers"), a nation emerged from small individual settlements and trading posts that at the time were all but devoid of any native peoples.[50] For about sixty years the Boers remained relatively isolated. Eventually, however, they came into contact with the Bantu, skirmishing, then establishing a dividing line at the Fish River. For the most powerful African tribe in the region at the time, the Xhosa, Boer farms served as an attractive lure. Conflict with Boers, but more important within various native tribes, weakened native resistance, leading to even further Boer incursions. When the British briefly took over some of the territories, the Boers made the Great Trek north to set up their own independent states, Transvaal and the Orange Free State. Britain recognized the two Boer Republics in treaties in the 1850s. After pacifying the new native threat, the Zulus, the British maneuvered to take control of Transvaal. When it formally declared its independence, the First Boer War began in December 1880.

The British were stunned at how quickly the Boers, who had no regular army, only civilian militia, besieged and took British garrisons across the region. A humiliating defeat for the British at Bronkhostspruit was followed by an equally embarrassing assault on Laing's Nek, where the Boers' sharpshooting killed one-third of the British redcoats. But the supreme shame came at Majuba Hill— where, for a change, the British had actually attained the high ground through a night march. Even while firing down from the summit, the British were unable to stop the Boers from storming the hill and routing them, in the process killing, wounding, or taking prisoner more than half. Some historians argue that Majuba Hill was a bigger blow to the British psyche than the Zulu massacre of 1,400 British troops and native allies at Isandlwana in 1879; some suggest that moment was the high point of British imperial power.

Gold was discovered in Boer lands in 1884 making Johannesberg a magnet for British entrepreneurs and miners from Britain's Cape Colony. President Paul Kruger was horrified at the thought of Uitlanders (British) having a major voice in Boer Government. From May 31 to June 5, 1899, Kruger, Orange Free State President Martinus Steyn, and British High Commissioner Alfred Milner met at Bloemfontein, with Milner demanding the two Boer Republics essentially subject themselves to British rule. Milner had no intention of negotiating, only concocting grounds for a war, which started in October.

After the Boers besieged Ladysmith, Mafeking, and Kimberly, and won tactical victories at Stormberg, Magersfonetin, and Spion Kop, the British changed tactics. It took two years, but the British brutally herded Boer families into concentration camps and destroyed Boer farms, fencing off territory in the process to make guerilla warfare more difficult. When the Boers surrendered in 1902, they were promised self-government with the creation of the Union of South Africa eight years later.

A different situation arose with the French in northern Africa, where Algeria constituted something quite apart than anything in the British dominion. France viewed Algeria as a colony that was considered a part of the mother country, and which (in theory) would be groomed for admission into the French political system as a province. Most other possessions were protectorates, which featured local governance through a ruler who voluntarily placed himself under foreign control to retain his position. In return, he wielded considerable domestic power, but was limited in foreign relations. The British ditched protectorates fairly early, only to be saddled with them again after World War I. (It goes without saying that under any colonial rule, divisions within any colony were purely arbitrary. In the so-called Maratha states of Gwalior, Indore, and Baroda, there was a total population of over six million, of whom only the rulers were Marathas.)[51]

In France, protectorates were administered by the Minister of Foreign Affairs, and, after 1871, a Ministry of Colonies. Again, Algeria was an exception: technically not a colony, it was administered by the Department of Interior. Other nations had similar colonial structures. Britain had a "Viceroy" in India for local government, while France used a "governor-general" in Africa. Both were top down, with little true local democratic input.

Colonial administration followed one of two general ideologies when it came to native peoples. One was assimilation. France used this in Algeria through *departments* that aimed to spread French ideas and culture. More common, however, was "association," wherein the empires respected native traditions, customs, and religions as far as possible. For example, the British followed the association system with regard to the Zulu for some time. British authorities searched for a chief who had pre-colonial authority and influence. The French were less generous: to them the *chef* was a "mere functionary," whose principal task was tax collection.[52]

Colonial powers discovered they not only needed natives as translators, whom they divided into several classes of master interpreters, honorary interpreters, and so on. But unless they planned to dump millions of dollars worth of personnel into each colony, they required natives who would support them and adopt their culture and views. To that end, they created colonial civil service structures. These positions involved education and training of natives, who were then selected by an exam. Fluency in the European tongues, of course, constituted a necessity. France developed the Corps d'Administrateurs Colonaiux at home to prepare French youth for the foreign service while England recruited candidates for the Indian civil service from Oxford, Cambridge, Trinity College, and Sandhurst. One politician referred to this as "a gigantic system of out-relief for the aristocracy of Great Britain."[53] Indeed, after Napoleon, fewer wars meant fewer paths to success for the English aristocrats. A poem at the Colonial Office expressed these sentiments:

> The greatest glory of our land
> Whose crimson covers half the maps
> Is in the field where the wicket stands
> And the game is played by DECENT CHAPS[54]

India's administration contained a hierarchical structure of native offices, with the British District Officer on top of each district. He began a daily tour on horseback, usually meeting with the *tabsildar* (magistrate with second-class powers in charge of revenue). Below him came the *patel* (the village chief who collected taxes), then the *patwari* who was the village accountant and record-keeper, then finally the *chowkidar*. Officers rode or walked through towns, inspecting roads and canals, talking with farmers, visiting schools, then setting a place at the edge of camp, hearing petitions and legal cases, dispensing licenses, and otherwise adjudicating legal conflicts.[55]

While education was emphasized, and whereas early Europeanized natives gravitated toward commerce and trade, by the twentieth century they eschewed agriculture, industry, and engineering for the "liberal arts" and politics, enabling elite Africans to advance through the French bureaucracy and control their fellow Africans. Ultimately, France still operated all of its possessions on the structure of the old Code Napoleon—a top down, government-oriented structure that told people what to do.

In 1858, a French diplomat Ferdinand de Lesseps obtained permission from Said Pasha to build a canal connecting the Mediterranean and the Red Sea. At first the British objected, thinking such a canal would give France a major commercial advantage. De Lesseps built the canal regardless, commencing construction the following year. The canal opened in 1869, reducing the distance to travel from the Arabian Sea to England by about 5,500 miles and 10 days at then-common shipping speeds. While Egypt formally owned the Canal, European shareholders, most notably British and French, owned the company that actually operated it. Quietly, Benjamin Disrali had acquired shares to the company from the Khedive. That, along with the fact that British directors dominated the board by 1884, and that the Royal Navy would be the only effective policeman in the neighborhood, meant that England now had a link from Gibraltar to Cairo to India, thereby allowing the British rapid (for the day) access to India, the African interior, and the Middle East. The Canal highlighted a political struggle within England over a "comfortable England" (also known as William Gladstone's "Little England") or a vast worldwide empire that would, as Benjamin Disraeli claimed, "command the respect of the world."[56]

From the outset, the motivations for settlement and conquest embodied a sincerely-held view that an act of self-sacrifice on the part of the colonizers was taking place. Too often historians have glossed over this as camouflage for the imperialist's "real" objectives, territory and power. It was far more, however. A genuine culture had developed (in some ways attendant to masculinity) that expected loss and burden to accompany the colonizers' work. The most famous example, of course, is Rudyard Kipling's poem "The White Man's Burden":

> Take up the White Man's burden—
> Send forth the best ye breed—
> Go bind your sons to exile
> To serve your captives' need;
> To wait in heavy harness
> On fluttered folk and wild—
> Your new-caught, sullen peoples,
> Half devil and half child.[57]

Or consider the poem from the beginning of the *History of the Baptist Missionary Society* originally written in 1842:

> These went not forth, as man too oft hath done,
> Braving the ocean billows' wild uproar
> In hopes to gather, ere life's sands were run
> Yet added heaps of mammon's sordid ore—
> . . . . They left not home to cross the briny sea
> With the proud conqueror's ambitious aim
> . . . . For they went forth as followers of the Lam,
> to spread his gospel-message far and wide
> In the dread power of Him, the great I AM,—
> in the meek spirit of the Crucified—[58]

Lest anyone think this was mere cover for "deeper" motivations, one need only consider the number of missionaries and administrators who were killed by natives. Or ponder the comments of Lord Rosebery, a former prime minister, who said "an empire such as ours requires as its first condition an Imperial Race—a race vigorous and industrious and intrepid. Health of mind and body exalt a nation in the competition of the universe."[59]

Such sentiments were likewise tied to concerns that urban British society had become weak and feminized. Thus "the determination to endure burdens and make sacrifices, the self-abnegation which will face loss, and suffering, and even death, for the commonweal[th], are bracing tonics to national health, and they counteract the enervating effects of 'too much love of living,' too much ease, and luxury, and material prosperity . . . Strength is not maintained without exercise."[60] Certainly such sentiments are common in twenty-first century society, in which American sloth, indulgence, and weakness is viewed as stemming from a dearth of physical and mental challenges.

With the Berlin Conference of 1884–1885, the imperialist powers drew up agreements to primarily settle conflicts over the Congo and Niger regions, permitting freedom of navigation on the two rivers but giving the Congo over to Belgium's control. Also, in what would become Tanganyika, German acquired control over that East Africa. England consolidated its grip on the south thanks to Cecil Rhodes and his British South Africa Company (1889), which created the De Beers Company and the diamond monopoly. Queen Victoria recognized the Company in October of that year, which kicked off construction of a flurry of railroad, roads, telegraph systems, and banking systems.

This investment stood entirely contrary to the Marxist thesis that the colonies existed solely to grow the imperial powers' capital machines.[61] A popular variant of this was that in England, for example, free trade constituted an "informal empire" that was a much easier approach to conquest than formal acquisition of territory. Economic historians Joseph Schumpeter, David Landes, and others saw the "informal empire" as neither racist nor cloaked in any particular morality, but as inevitable when a disparity arose among regions.[62] Most interpretations, however, drift toward either outright racism or greed, the latter being the most popular. "Finance," wrote John Hobson, "manipulates the patriotic forces, which politicians, soldiers, philanthropists, and traders generate" and concentrates them in a foreign direction.[63] When missionaries sought to fulfill the Gospel not only by preaching, but by supplying people's needs, including food and clothing, modern scholars saw only a "happy marriage of the spiritual and material."[64] Such cynicism ignored real Christian motivations that as a by-product included material improvement.

While no doubt it was true in the strictest economic sense that Britain poured more into the empire than she took out, the major purpose of overseas possessions was not economic, but political and geostrategic. The Empire existed to expand British power and control world trade routes, not to exploit backward areas for their resources. Of course, obtaining tin, bananas, coffee, lumber, palm oil, diamonds, gold, and other food and raw materials constituted a powerful bonus. If imperialism is solely viewed in a Marxist light, the glow of understanding will be dim indeed. In fact, the Soviet Union, not the West, would later exemplify the essence of Lenin's thesis that "imperialism is the highest stage of capitalism," for the Soviets had to acquire constantly more territory to divert their own populations' attention from the shocking failures of communism.

However, there was one more burst of militaristic globalism left in the West, this time involving America, and that was directed at China. There, England, France, and other European nations—as well as Japan and Russia—had established trade sectors. With the possibility of multi-lateral conflicts erupting, US Secretary of State John Hay dispatched a circular of notes to all the powers in the region calling for protection of equal privileges and administrative integrity of each zone. All countries would have equal access to all ports. History has known this as the "Open Door" policy, to which all the participants readily agreed.

England had already forced the "door" open in the Opium Wars and had dominance in China until the Sino-Japanese War of 1894–95. China was handed a sop in that only the Chinese could collect taxes on trade—a small concession to gain access to a large market and to extensive natural resources. Of course, not all Chinese were enamored of the agreement, leading to the Boxer Rebellion of 1900 which was put down by an early version of the United Nations in which the Americans, British, French, Germans, Italians, Japanese, and Russians assembled a force of 19,000 men to march on Beijing and relieve the embassies there.

By that time, the United States had its first taste of empire with its victory in the Spanish-American War, seizing the Philippines, Guam, Puerto Rico, and Cuba. Unlike the Europeans, though, the US Congress demanded that Cuba be liberated quickly, passing the Teller Amendment to ensure that America did not retain the island. This was one of the rarest times in history when a victorious power willingly handed control of a conquered land back to the natives. With the Philippines, however, the situation was different, as both a German and British fleet stood ready to move into the islands if the US evacuated. Thus the Philippines became an American protectorate with a plan set for independence under a governor.[65] Two consecutive Philippine Commissions explored the status of the new territory, with the second (under future territorial governor William Howard Taft) establishing a transition from US military to civilian rule.

Taft differed from his political contemporary, Theodore Roosevelt—known as a "Large Policy" advocate (meaning he favored US acquisition of strategic possessions)—in opposing expansion, but admitted that the Philippines came into American hands without any other viable alternative present. Moreover, in 1904, Taft said the US should just declare the ultimate aim of Philippine policy was independence for the islands.[66] As the reality of instability sank in, however, Taft's opinion changed.

Neither he, nor most Americans, had given serious thought to the fact that possessions acquired from other countries, particularly Spain (which had Catholicism and civil law, not a common law tradition), could not be instantly infused with the "Four Pillars of American Exceptionalism." For that reason, Taft thought the Philippines might require a century of trusteeship in which they were taught, in essence, the four pillars. Without ever elaborating the four pillars, or specifically addressing the problems of top-down Catholicism, Taft implicitly understood that America had something different than the

Philippines that would not be rectified by simply governing them in the traditional manner.

In 1898, the United States' victory over Spain in the Spanish-American War not only left the Philippines in American hands, but it produced something quite remarkable in the entire history of militaristic globalism. Not only did the US announce a plan for self-government of the islands—which did not come immediately—the US nevertheless did what virtually no other western nation did: it voluntarily and quickly handed over another seized possession, Cuba, to the natives.

With China effectively off the table and with Africa, the Middle East, India, and some of Asia colonized, militaristic globalism reached its zenith. The Second Boer War essentially ended the "age of imperialism."

Europeans had modest success at inculcating native peoples with European culture and ideals—confined almost entirely to the upper classes. But they also quickly discovered that the cost of maintaining the empires exceeded the benefits, and at any rate, only England, France, and the United States on a practical level after 1900 possessed navies that were powerful enough to ensure free overseas trading lanes. None of the militaristic globalists that had gained overseas territories had the slightest idea as to how to either "make them European" or teach them western political structures in a way that they would remain loyal.

Quite the contrary, by establishing top-down governance with no application of common law, the imperial powers ensured the failure of their globalist colonial schemes. They hung on to many colonies into the 1950s when their administrative structures had exploded. It was as if the Europeans concluded that all that was needed to turn natives into good French or British or Belgian subjects was . . . more administrators! They would indulge in an "orgy of constitution making," saddling newly-independent countries with paper constitutions from a nation that never had one.[67] Frenzied bureaucracy-building, which had commenced in the 1800s, reached near comedic heights in the mid-twentieth century, where the British West Indies likely had more legislators per person than any nation in human history. No one was exempt. In Ruanda-Urundi, the Belgians

> constructed one of the most rococo constitutions ever devised by man, with multi-roll elections to the Councils of Sub-Chiefs, Councils of Chiefs, Territorial Councils, African Council, and, on top, a General Council to advise the [Belgian] Vice-Governor-General: a five-tier system [located in] one of the most primitive countries with a political structure more elaborate than that of the United States.[68]

Equally ludicrous and other-worldly were the western attempts to hammer African nations into western-style democracies: in the two Rhodesias and Nyasaland, a string of commissions, conferences, and constitutions resulted in a government structure deemed too complex for most voters to understand.

Perhaps the Europeans knew where this all was headed, for by the end of the nineteenth century they had soberly concluded that militaristic globalism was no more effective than monarchical globalism. Consequently, in 1889, a forerunner of the League of Nations, called the Inter-Parliamentary Union (IPU) was formed.[69] The IPU actually survived to the present day as a group promoting democracy (as understood by Europeans) and world governance. It lacked the most critical power, namely the authority of righteousness that came from being victorious in a major war. It also accomplished nothing because, in allowing different opposing states with opposing agendas—in contrast to the League, which allowed in no dissenters—it could not impose its will on minorities. Thus, with the failure of militaristic globalism, it was now the diplomats' turn.

Chapter Three

Diplomatic Globalism—Versailles and Remaking the World

F or anyone attuned to the ebbs and flows of human history, to its constant conflicts, wars, realignments, and rise and fall of empires, World War I should have come as no surprise. Of the failures at the Congress of Vienna, perhaps the greatest was to fail to foresee—perhaps even to accelerate—the formation of a new, oversized German state in the 1870s. This new Germany, whether in war or peace, would in the subsequent 170 years become a perpetual source of mischief.

While England, France, and others extended their imperial canopies across the globe, Prussia found herself isolated, smack-dab in the middle of Europe. Massive and populous Russia was on one side; equally densely populated (and traditional enemy) France hovered on the other; and the Austro-Hungarian Empire blockaded the south. Whatever seaports the Prussians had were either contained inside the Baltic Sea—with their access contingent on good relations with Norway and Sweden, which possessed numerous islands gatekeeping the entrance—or on the North Sea, where the Royal Navy stood guard.

In other words, Prussia, even after unifying with the numerous states into the German Confederation (later simply Germany), constantly faced the prospect of isolation or a multi-front war. Naturally, seeing themselves as behind in the imperial push for overseas lands, Germany scrambled for colonies, which they obtained over the next twenty years in German East Africa (present day Burundi, Rwanda, and Tanzania) and German West Africa (Cameroon and Togo). These had started as trading posts; then, after the Anglo-French Convention of 1882, which seemed to threaten German overseas possessions, more formal status was announced. With its own version of gunboat diplomacy and a belated militaristic globalism, Germany assigned military vessels to guard its ports. Subsequent agreements with France solidified Germany's grip on the African colonies.[1]

Germany's problems in seeking an overseas empire were twofold. First, the Germans got a late start. Few prize possessions remained by the time they got to Africa. Second, overseas empires are, well, over seas and the German navy, even with the pre-Great War buildup, was no match for either the British or French navies (and by 1898, the American navy could be added to that list). Germany had to place considerable resources into maintaining and administering possessions that in time of conflict it might not even be able to communicate with, let alone supply and hold. Again, though, even had the Germans possessed a top-quality navy, the geographic limitations of ports and access to open water proved a persistent problem.

After the Boer War (in which the Germans supported the Boers) and the Moroccan Crisis (1905–06) where the former enemies, Britain and France, reached an accord, Kaiser Wilhelm came to believe there was an attempt to prevent Germany from obtaining any overseas acquisitions: "Against France and England an overseas policy is impossible."[2] Even when Germany gained some territory in modern-day Cameroon, it did nothing to assuage concerns and the agreement received sharp criticism in the German press.

In this respect both the previous efforts at globalism—by monarchs in Vienna and by militarists since—now came together in a giant act of failure by creating a new, different, powerful state with a chip on its shoulder. As we will see, Germany represented a concoction to the new reality of a mass citizenry still bottled up under a quasi-monarch.

Otto von Bismarck had seemingly pulled this off with the introduction of social security and other reforms that sought to align the masses with the state and achieve international legitimacy through overseas possessions. Elites in Vienna thought they had tamped down the popular urges, now only to see them rise in a powerful new form under the control of a centralized state that had to appeal to popular sentiment.

Thus, the Congress of Vienna had not only failed to prevent a new major European war, which came with the Franco-Prussian War of 1870, but had laid the groundwork for the consolidation of a Prusso-German power that probably exceeded that of France alone and threatened both France and Russia. When combined with other peoples seen as "Germanic," such as the Austrians with their own large (if highly fractured) empire, a German alliance already covered much of Europe by 1900. Conflict that would split the world was almost inevitable.

Perhaps surprisingly, then, it seemed almost unthinkable between 1900 and 1910. Norman Angell, the best-known proponent of the "war is obsolete" view, saw his 1910 book *The Great Illusion* attain cult status. "Angell clubs and organizations, more than forty in the major universities, took root" and his book was translated into nearly a dozen languages.[3] Throughout the west, debates and discussions took place, from the halls of Cambridge and the Sorbonne to the inner chambers of kings and ministers. Angell insisted no new war could occur. It would simply cost too much. Wars between nations would result in "commercial disaster, financial ruin," and unparalleled suffering.[4] (In 1915, Angell would publish a book called *America and the New World State* in which he said the US should make itself the governor of the world.)[5]

In those views, Angell—whose nostrums gained far more cache— only embellished what a young Winston Churchill said after he emerged from the Boer War. "A European war," he noted, "can only end in the ruin of the vanquished and the scarcely less fatal commercial dislocation and exhaustion of the conquerors."[6] Churchill had seen England, after a handful of sharp defeats in South Africa, ramp up its commitment to the Boer War by over 300,000 additional men. This was to put down irregular militia forces whose heaviest weapons were a few cannons. "Democracy" he observed, "is more vindictive than Cabinets. The wars of peoples will be more terrible than those of kings."[7]

Quite accurately, Churchill recognized that in previous ages the undeveloped transportation systems and the length of growing seasons tended to limit conflicts. Such factors would not be present in the modern, mechanized age. A somewhat different, but equally optimistic, argument came from Churchill's acquaintance, English economist John Maynard Keynes. He described the interconnected world:

> The inhabitant of London could order by telephone, sipping his morning tea, the various products of the whole earth, and reasonably expect their early delivery upon his doorstep. Militarism and imperialism of racial and cultural rivalries were little more than the amusements of his daily newspaper. [8]

In the early part of the twenty-first century, this would become a common rationale for why wars were no longer possible. Thomas Friedman in his best-selling book *The World is Flat 3.0: A Brief History of the Twenty-First Century* would make similar arguments, such as that any two nations with Dell computers or McDonald's would not go to war with each other.[9] (The later edition came after the US went to war with Iraq and overthrew governments in Egypt and Libya, all with Dell computers.)

Others entering the twentieth century insisted that the elites and bankers would not permit a war. Walter Rathenau said in 1909 that "Three hundred men, all of whom know each other, direct the economic destiny or Europe. . ."[10] In 1914, even the bankers were shocked by the rapid onset of an international war: the Rothschilds lost half their capital in the four years after the guns of August. (After the war, the *Financial Times* would maintain that "half a dozen men at the top of the Big Five Banks could upset the whole fabric of government finance by refraining from renewing any Treasury Bills.")[11] Prosperity in Europe and America had reached new heights: in London there were only 100,000 known paupers.

On top of all those reasons against war, most of the monarchs were related to each other. Surely families would not send the world into conflict, would they? Cataclysm came nonetheless.

In retrospect (as seems always the case) all the warning signs were missed. Of the particular German psyche described earlier, victory in the Franco-Prussian War, far from ushering in an era of confidence and national calm, had the opposite effect. Germans obsessed over the *kultur*, or self-esteem, that derived from war. It was, as General Friedrich von Bernhardi labeled it, a "life-giving principle." The "desire for peace," he wrote, "has rendered most civilized nations anaemic," and was "directly antagonistic to universal laws."[12] Author Ludwig Thoma lamented that Germany had to "purchase with its blood the right to work and create values for mankind."[13] In a modern term, Germans felt "dissed." They believed that "high esteem which is due them" throughout the globe "has hitherto been withheld."[14] Such views soon generated a paranoia, leading the Kaiser, after receiving word of Russian support for Serbia in a war with Austria-Hungary, as an "*excuse* for waging a *war of extermination* against us" (emphasis in original).[15] Images of an entangling web of anti-German states surrounding them filled German minds. Intellectuals, in particular, embraced such notions. Emil Ludwig, who later would pivot to being a war critic, at the outset of hostilities said "even if a catastrophe were to befall us such as no one dares to imagine, the moral victory [of August 1914] could never be eradicated."[16] Novelist Ernst Glaser wrote of the world around him, "the war had made it beautiful."[17] Another described the Great War as a "European Civil War" against the inner invisible enemy of the European state."[18] Although they would feel much differently in five short years, the youth of Europe lusted for war. Indeed, at its outset, it's possible that World War I was the most popular war in history. Henri de Montherlant said he "loved life at the front, the bath in elemental, the annihilation of the intelligence and the heart."[19] Charles Peguy went "eagerly" to the front (where he died).

Germans exhibited no less enthusiasm for combat. Ernst Junger labeled the outbreak of hostilities a "holy moment"; novelist Fritz von Unger found it triggered a "new zest for life." British youth like Rupert Brooke called the war a "fine thrill," and Robert Nichols said of those who would not go, "he is dead who will not fight." Italians likewise agreed. Said one Italian poet, "This is the hour of triumph of the finest values . . . the Hour of Youth," and another wrote, "only the small men and the old men of twenty [sought] to miss it."[20] Hermann Hesse insisted that the war was "good for many Germans" and that "a genuine artist would find greater value in a nation of men who have faced death and who know the immediacy and freshness of camp life."[21]

Only a few saw a much different cloud on the horizon, even if it resulted in an ultimate sweeping away of all in sight. Kurt Reizler, Bethmann Hollweg's secretary, wrote in July 1914 that the Chancellor "expects that a war, whatever its outcome, will result in the uprooting of everything that exists."[22] Or, as Betthman Hollweg put it, "Doom greater than human power [is] hanging over Europe and our own people."[23] Doubtful, however, that he envisioned the Kaiser abdicating once the demands of the allies hit Germany, or that the Habsburg emperor, Charles, would follow him three days later. When the murder of the Romanovs in Russia was included—courtesy of Lenin's terrorist-communists—the monarchical pillars that had supported the world of 1900s Europe were gone.

As we assess the Versailles Conference, then, it is imperative we take note of all the motivations and causes of war that they missed, for they would make up new ones they would "address," only compounding the problem. To review: 1) everyone wanted war and saw it as a glorious experience; 2) Germany felt disrespected and treated as unequal in the fraternity of free states; and 3) France seethed with revenge for the humiliation of the Franco-Prussian war. And underlying all these, there was an as-yet un-addressed expectation of popular government spreading out from Europe to the colonies.

Almost all notions of heroism and optimism changed within months of the trenches, as shockingly high casualty lists brought instant sobriety to all. Then, for four bloody years, with the exception of the failed Dardanelles campaign, the war on the Western Front turned into an unimaginative charnel house of a slog. Unsurprisingly, before it was over (as with the Congress of Vienna) the victors had a plan in mind to prevent another war through the reorganization of populations, redrawing of borders, and creation of and a new world organization. Globalism had arrived to postwar Europe. As with Vienna, Versailles became the vehicle for the elites to foist upon a shattered, defeated foe a new vision of the world, one far less conciliatory to the vanquished, tainted by the destructive nostrums of Progressivism and virtually all the costs coming at the expense of the defeated.

First it should be noted that the leaders who arrived at Versailles never even addressed the two towering psychological forces that had helped perpetuate the war: Germany's paranoid insecurity and France's lust for *revanche*. Certainly neither was mentioned in Woodrow Wilson's "Fourteen Points." They did not arise at all among those who descended on the Versailles proceedings, particularly by Britain and France, eager to protect their overseas possessions. Germany and Austria-Hungary were not even invited. Their concerns, their "side of the story" could never even be told, let alone considered. Thus had nothing else happened, the self-styled titans who sought to impose a global government and establish world peace ensured that their proceedings would ensure future conflict.

Second, as had occurred in Vienna a century earlier, the forces of popular change and democracy, while cited incessantly by the Versailles glitterati, were nevertheless the *objects* of the elites' actions. Those forces did not *shape* the changes—indeed, most of the truly democratic voices of the Arabs and Asians were carefully contained, sequestered away from the real secret meetings where maps were being redrawn and agreements concluded. Masses of people were moved simply by changing lines on paper, lumping them in with other groups who had centuries-old grievances or, at the very least, a well-founded distrust.

Other myths, misunderstandings, and mistakes underlay the participants in Versailles. One of the more common World War I myths was that of the "lost generation" in Great Britain. This was the notion that the greatest minds of Oxford and Cambridge had fallen in the trenches. British historian Paul Johnson pointed out that a bevy of postwar poets and writers "obsessed with death, futility, and waste," always unheroic and replete with the moral that "national goals were meaningless," helped cultivate this myth of the lost generation.[24] Over the years, the most quoted British figures of World War I were not generals, statesmen, or even men in the trenches, but the "War Poets" such as Rupert Brooke, Wilfred Owen, Ivor Gurney, and Siegfied Sasson.[25] H. G. Wells, in *The War that Will End War*, welcomed a conflict that he thought would produce an international order that would forever end bloodshed.[26]

Of course, as they had at the end of the Congress of Vienna, many elites at Versailles proclaimed victory over all human impulses. This was a new globalism infected with Progressivism, the late-eighteenth century notion that humans were perfectible in this world. (Recall these same dons had just as smugly predicted that progressive ideas would prevent such conflict in the first place.) But whereas the Vienna elites sought a type of globalism—again, as they knew it meaning Europe—many of the new Progressive globalists wanted to say farewell to many aspects of the nineteenth century itself. For example, the outdated philosophy of personal guilt or responsibility had to go, replaced by collective and societal guilt. Present-day readers will recognize in this the origins of "Critical Race Theory" and "systemic racism," as well as "systemic-this-or-that" applied to any group perceived as a victim. Group guilt easily was manipulated by both the terror-states of Nazi Germany and Soviet Russia: the Nazis with race guilt for the Jews, the Soviets for class guilt by the *bourgeoisie* and kulaks. Modernism and Progressivism, thought the Versailles globalists, could usher in a new era of morality when in fact it ensured an unprecedented wave of human horror based on its fundamental principles.

Winston Churchill, in fact, claimed the war killed the promise Progressive ideas. Torture, cannibalism, were the "only two expedients that the civilized, scientific, Christian States [of western Europe] had been able to deny themselves," while they willingly followed the Germans "in the van of terror."[27] But every other horrific practice or technique had been fully utilized by all sides, and, he noted, that the evils were all engaged in by "educated states." Woodrow Wilson himself had warned before entry into war that should the time come that Americans had to fight "they'll forget there ever was such a thing as tolerance . . . The spirit of ruthless brutality will enter into every fibre of our national life."[28]

Those predictions were forgotten once the brutality of the Great War swept over the world. Again, the time had come for the elites to fix things. Some, such as Harold Nicolson, took pride in thinking that theirs was a new approach. Contrasting the impending Versailles conference with what had occurred at the Congress of Vienna, Nicolson became "aware of the differences with the last great conference, the Congress of Vienna in 1814. . . They'd worked in secret, we were committed to 'open covenants openly arrived at.' We were preparing not only Peace, but Eternal Peace."[29] Nicolson's understanding came from the January 8, 1918 address by Woodrow Wilson where he revealed his "Fourteen Points," the first of which promised no secret treaties. Without consulting Britain or France (let alone Germany, Russia, or Austria-Hungary), Wilson added "Four Principles" then "Five Particulars" in an orgy of numbering.

Wilson's vanguard was led by Col. Edward House, who chose as his point man Stephen Bonsal, an army major who had accidentally met House in Berlin in 1915 and worked as a translator. Upon arriving in House's quarters just prior to the Armistice, Bonsal received his instructions from the unctuous House:

> I think I can handle Lloyd George [of Great Britain] and the "Tiger" [Georges Clemenceau of France] without much help. But into your hands I commit the mighty men of the rest of the world. . . The war that has destroyed cities has puffed up some little men until they find their hats and their boots too small, much

too small for them. I shall count on you to present them to me in
their original proportions.[30]

The whole attitude toward Wilson and the Americans had changed
in the few months since Wilson arrived: now crowds in theaters were
silent when his face appeared on screen, whereas upon his arrival they
had greeted him like the resurrected Christ.

Some, such as Harold Nicolson, arrived thinking that Versailles
would be different from Vienna a century earlier. In fact, the elites' opinion of themselves in 1919 differed little from those of Metternich or Czar
Alexander in 1814, which is to say they thought of themselves as superior
beings who needed to control the masses. And it wasn't just Wilson. His
supposed antithesis, political opponent, and briefly Secretary of State,
William Jennings Bryan, held similar globalist notions:

> Behold a republic increasing in wealth, in strength and in influ-
> ence, solving the problems of civilization, and hastening the
> coming of an universal brotherhood . . . a republic gradually but
> surely becoming the *supreme moral factor in the world's progress*
> and the *accepted arbiter of the world's disputes*—a republic whose
> history 'is as the shining light that shineth more and more unto
> the perfect day.' [emphasis added][31]

Wilson did not absorb much from Bryan, whom he considered too
rough around the edges. Others, however, such as Herbert Croly
(considered "the intellectual leader of the American Progressive movement"), recoiled at the thought that the masses might actually govern.
In *The Promise of American Life*, Croly sneered that the common man
could never rise to the level of saints or heroes: "Faith in the people . . .
and confidence in popular government means . . . an utter lack of faith
in those personal instruments . . . "[32] Croly ridiculed "confidence in
the average man," which automatically meant "distrust in the exceptional man."[33] To Croly, elevation of the masses meant the sacrifice of
the individual.

Wilson's own views on the state were clearly presented in his 1889 book *The State*. The origins of the state, Wilson said, lay in the authority of the father in the family and was inherent in the European race. Discarding consent and the social contract, Wilson insisted that a cadre of civil servants "cultured and self-sufficient enough to act with sense and vigor, and yet so intimately connected with the popular thought . . . as to find arbitrariness or class spirit quite out of the question."[34] Put the right "cultured and self-sufficient" elites in power, and they would not be capable of tyranny. Why, it was beneath them! For Wilson, government had to be powerful and free of the influence of rival interests—quite the opposite of the Founders' view to let, as Hamilton wrote, "faction check faction" and interest offset interest. The very concept of division of power and checks and balances refuted Wilson's concepts. As a hard-core Presbyterian, Wilson viewed the congregation with suspicion; he despised congress, which he thought did nothing. But under the Constitution, America had descended into a "scheme of congressional supremacy."[35] It would be immediately recognized that not only had Wilson ignored the radical explosion in the power of the presidency under Theodore Roosevelt, but that the driving impetus for the Founders in creating good government was to hold with Whig views that elevated the legislative over the executive. He embraced the notion that a president could re-form and restructure the office of the presidency as he saw fit, all toward more power. Problems had arisen, Wilson wrote in 1908, from the "too literal application of Whig doctrine, to the infinite multiplication of *elective offices*" (emphasis added).[36]

Internationally that translated into a view of a law or body of rules that "ought" to govern nations. Addressing Congress in 1917, he proclaimed, "We are at the beginning of an age in which it will be insisted that the same standards of conduct and of responsibility for wrong done shall be observed among nations and their governments that are observed among the individual citizens of civilized states."[37] Wilson's view of trade was that "since trade ignores national boundaries and the manufacturer insists on having the world as a market, the flag of his nation must follow him, and the doors of the nations which are closed against him must be battered down."[38] His religion was a social-gospel top-down Presbyterianism that had no room for congregational input.

Meanwhile popular leaders who represented the populist movement of the day arrived from the far-flung empires, including Nguyen Tat Thanh of Vietnam (later known as Ho Chi Minh); Feisal ibn Hussein of the Saudi Bedouin tribes; Edvard Benes of Czechoslovakia; Winston Koo, the Chinese ambassador to Washington; and the Polish chemist Roman Dmowski. They were to find the elites at Versailles had not the slightest interest in them or their worlds.

Two presidents, Wilson and Henri Poincare, were joined by nine premiers and dozens of foreign ministers as the conference started its work. While this seemed markedly contrasted with the kings and nobility who had graced the Congress of Vienna, only the titles of the elites had changed, except in place of a group of rough equals, Wilson stood apart. Another Army officer and Harvard graduate, Ralph Van Deman, had the assignment of insulating the American delegation from outside pressures. Like Metternich, Van Deman had nearly seventy intelligence police working under him, preparing for the next wave of Ivy Leaguers led by House. This patrician horde of researchers, historians, economists, and philosophers included journalist Walter Lippmann, Harvard educated Charles Seymour, Harvard historian Samuel Eliot Morrison, and nearly 130 other acceptable elites who went by the name "The Inquiry" and who were kept in housing at the American Geographical Society Building in New York. They met in secret, drafted a thousand reports—including some written by Allen Dulles—that addressed every problem the peacemakers might encounter.

Nicholson came to relish the American scholars. An elite and his fellow Oxbridge dons found his "liking for the Americans becoming a vice . . . I like the scholarly sort, such as Coolidge, Seymour, Day, and Allan Dulles because they are quiet and scholarly and because they like the truth."[39]

Contrary to their pious pronouncements, the Versailles cabal wanted nothing to do with transparency. Charles Seymour complained about being "hampered by the atmosphere of Paris," and Nicolson agreed, saying "We felt like surgeons operating in the ballroom with the aunts of the patient gathered all around."[40]

But that was the public. In fact, Versailles was riddled with spies and secret agents communicating through a maze of coded messages. Herbert Hoover, in charge of food administration, demanded that the espionage agents "imbedded in his relief organization report only 'in clear' (in plain English), not code, to deflect suspicion they were serving a double function of intelligence agents and relief workers."[41] Yet to thwart the spies, Hoover's organization developed *its own code*. So much for transparency. When Hoover's subordinate reported that the Archduke Joseph would be prevented from returning to power in Austria-Hungary, he transmitted a cable: "ARCHIE ON THE CARPET 7 P.M. WENT THROUGH THE HOOP AT 7:05."[42] The British, particularly Nicolson, followed the more tried-and-true methods of diplomatic spying, making use of their extensive missions abroad to feed information on, say, what the Romanians were thinking.

In a development that would not shock anyone, the diplomats and effete *soireei* attendees in Versailles looked and acted remarkably similar to those in Vienna a century earlier. A young Elsa Maxwell, who accompanied Henrietta Brooks—attending the festivities with an eye toward catching a husband (whom she did, in Douglas MacArthur)—wrote:

> The exhilarating atmosphere of Paris during the peace talks. Every day was like a sparkling holiday. There was an aroma in the air as though a thousand girls wearing a wonderful perfume had just passed. The city echoed to the music of bands welcoming returning soldiers. Shops, theaters & cafes were jammed with people who'd lived under the drab shadows of war for four years. Everywhere, every hour of the day & night, there were parties.[43]

Wilson himself arrived in January 1919 to some two million people at the Champs-Élysées, greeted by weeping and people carrying flowers. Captain Harry Truman, then in Paris, observed "I don't think I ever saw such an ovation."[44]

Then there was Wilson with his numerology of points, principles, and "particulars." Specifically, the Fourteen Points included:

- Open diplomacy without secret treaties (which had already been violated by the time the Germans were presented the Fourteen Points)
- Economic free trade on the seas during war and peace (which in practical terms meant only the US and England could take advantage of this because of the size of their fleets)
- Equal trade conditions
- Decrease armaments among all nations (This was partially achieved with the Washington Treaty of 1922, although it only fostered resentment by the Japanese)
- Adjust colonial claims (by which was meant stripping Germany of her colonies)
- Evacuation of all Central Powers from Russia (which had already occurred with the Treaty of Brest-Litovsk of March 1918)
- Belgium to be evacuated and restored
- Return of Alsace-Lorraine region and all French territories
- Readjust Italian borders
- Austria-Hungary to be provided an opportunity for self-determination
- Redraw the borders of the Balkan region creating states of Romania, Serbia, and Montenegro
- Creation of a Turkish state with guaranteed free trade in the Dardanelles (again, possible only for nations with powerful navies)
- Creation of an independent Polish state
- Creation of the League of Nations

Wilson operated from a theological perspective of his own making, exuding righteousness and rejecting countless practical measures the Europeans knew would be essential to keep peace. (Lloyd George called him "Jesus" in private.) In his opening remarks on January 18, a cold, snowy day, channeling Metternich, Wilson insisted that Versailles represented "the supreme conference in the history of mankind."[45]

In these, he had been heavily influenced by the South African prime Minister Jan Christiann Smuts in his 1918 document, *The League of Nations: A Practical Suggestion*, which Wilson quickly presented as his own. Even Smuts hadn't originated the idea of an international body: that came from Walter Phillimore, of the British Foreign Office, who in 1918 had chaired a committee that produced a report championing an international body; and Under Secretary of State for Foreign Affairs, Robert Cecil, another quasi pacifist who "saw [the League "not as a device for resisting aggression by collective force but as a substitute for such force" using the vague impetus of "moral authority."[46] Ironically, however, it was Vladimir Lenin who spurred Wilson to adopt the League of Nations concept with a call for general self-determination. Wilson was not to be outdone by a communist.

What most wanted, including Clemenceau, was not some do-good international nanny with "moral authority" but a solid treaty backup from the United States. Clemenceau actually favored an alliance akin to modern day NATO with joint planning and military staffs. There was the issue of participation: if the "League" was to be inclusive, why was Germany left out? Would that not create a problem in the future?

Then there were the Soviets, who regarded the League "merely as an instrument of the victorious capitalist Power to maintain their position at the expense of the vanquished and of the proletariat of all countries. . . "[47] Lenin, in typical sneer, referred to it as "a band of robbers, an association of bandits who only squabble among themselves and do not trust each other in the slightest," as apt a description of a gathering of Bolsheviks as anyone could concoct.[48]

The Versailles congregants ignored more than transparency. Addressing items 11 and 13 of the Points (creating new nations and redrawing boundaries), the diplomats waded into a quagmire. They ignored the fact that Europe was home to over 200 different peoples and languages, many of them cobbled together over centuries by compromise, marriage, and power-sharing within the government. Consider Austria-Hungary, which had 12 million Germans, 10 million Magyars, 8.5 million Czechs, 1.3 million Slovaks, 5 million Poles, 3.3 million Romanians, 5.7 million Serbs, and another 5 million of other groups or nationalities.[49] As was later learned again and again by moderns—with the dissolution of communist Yugoslavia in the 1990s, by the American deposition of Saddam Hussein in Iraq in the 2000s—many nations with strongman leaders survived through a Byzantine labyrinth of family connections, shrewd placement of different ethnicities or tribes in government positions, and even marriage. It did not help that two of the principal Versailles players, Great Britain and France, had vast overseas multiracial and multi-ethnic empires. As discussions of carving up the Hapsburg state got under way, Nicolson himself asked if self-determination should be granted to the Cypriot Greeks. Sir Eyre Crowe of the Foreign Office asked if he was also ready to grant self-determination to India, Egypt, Malta, and other possessions. A chastened Nicolson did not bring it up again. But as with the Bedouin in Arabia, deals were cut with promises of independence and territory. The infamous Balfour Declaration of 1917 promised the Jews a national homeland in Palestine to lure them from the Central Powers . . . land also being dangled in front of the Arabs for their support against the Turks.

Most important, however, when the Fourteen Points were transmitted to Germany on November 5, and had been accepted as the basis of an armistice, a week earlier, on October 29, Col. House met with George Clemenceau and David Lloyd George, who only agreed to the Fourteen Points under certain conditions. Among those several reservations, called the "Commentary," was the removal of any of the advantages for the Central Powers. Moreover, the stipulations also set up the dismemberment of Austria-Hungary, stripped Germany of her colonies, separated Prussia with a "Polish Corridor," and included reparations payments. *None of these was conveyed to the Germans or*

Austro-Hungarians who had accepted the unedited "Fourteen Points" as the basis for the armistice.[50] Deceitfully, Wilson continued to deal with the Germans as though no extra conditions existed, and the Germans, for their part, did not press for clarification until it was too late.

So as the peace conference unfolded—very much like the Congress of Vienna—it did so without a specific agenda, without form, and without solid organization. Having arrived with hundreds of specialists, the allied negotiators met "without an agreed programme of procedure and never acquired one."[51] Britain's Prime Minister David Lloyd George arrived fresh off an overwhelming victory in British elections with a campaign based on imposing a harsh peace on the Germans. As the conference unfolded, Wilson increasingly became obsessed with only one of his Fourteen Points: the League.

He soon traded one point after another for specific demands by the French and British. Most notably, the French focused on carving away as much German territory as possible while creating a "big Poland" that would sever Prussia and dispossess Germany of her Silesian industrial belt. Additionally, France wanted an occupation of the Rhineland for fifteen years, denying Germany of the Krupp ammunition factories at Essen. Older diplomats, such as Clemenceau, sensed the situation would generate its own problems, warning "in six months, in a year, five years, ten years, when they like as they like, the Boches will again invade us."[52] Then there was the "war guilt," which both the British and the French demanded, as if they had not belligerently ramped up the rhetoric of destruction themselves.

It must be kept in mind that Germany, with an army of nine million men still mobilized, had lost *none* of its prewar territory as of the Armistice. The newly-named German Chancellor, who replaced Kaiser Wilhelm as the head of state, welcomed back demobilizing troops as "unvanquished from the field."[53] Since the bulk of the most important allied negotiations took place in secret, ordinary Germans felt they had won.

When the Germans actually arrived, expecting a negotiation, they were greeted with a *diktat* and the smug condescension of Bosche-hater

Clemenceau. The former editor of a radical newspaper, *La Justice*, he had earned the nickname *le Tombeur de ministries* ("the destroyer of ministries"), which aptly reflected his hostility toward traditions. As interior minister, Clemenceau had used the army to crush strikes. Offered the position of justice minister during the war, he refused so that when the government collapsed, he was a viable alternative. Like Wilson, he proved an autocrat, harshly censoring the press. And as much as he despised the Germans, he scorned the United States: "America is the only nation in history which miraculously has gone directly from barbarism to degeneration without the usual interval of civilization."[54] The ceremony at Versailles saw Clemenceau bluntly tell the Germans, "You asked for a peace. We are disposed to grant it to you."[55]

Lloyd George was somewhat less enthusiastic about imposing a severe peace on Germany. The son of a Welsh teacher, Lloyd George as a member of Parliament had opposed the second Boer War and charged British generals with failing to adequately care for their sick and wounded. During the war itself, Lloyd George served as the munitions supremo, then secretary of state for war. As would occur with Churchill two decades later, he was admired and by 1918 one of his Conservative opponents admitted, "He can be dictator for life."[56]

He had arrived at Versailles committed to making Germany pay the full brunt of the postwar burdens but changed his mind in France. Concluding that bankrupting Germany would achieve nothing, he tried to convince Wilson to ameliorate his terms, correctly fearing the same kind of "*revanche*" that festered in prewar France would now transfer to Germany. He failed. Outmaneuvered and isolated, the Germans signed. Robert Lansing, who had replaced Bryan after his resignation in June 1915 after America's drift to war, wrote of the Germans that they looked like "men being called upon to sign their own death-warrants . . . With pallid faces and trembling hands, they wrote their names quickly . . ."[57]

Lansing was one of the few to sense that the odious terms inflicted on Germany would come back to bite Europe. He was not, contrasted with Col. House or John Foster Dulles, anti-German. (Dulles referred to the "enormity of the crime committed by Germany.")[58] Some subsequently argued that if Wilson had included more Republicans in the delegation, they would have extracted more concessions from him. Certainly the Republicans of the day were more isolationist—but only when it came to Europe, as under Teddy Roosevelt they had cheered his interventions in the Caribbean and South America. They were also slightly less anti-German and somewhat more suspicious of the British.

One voice loud enough to challenge the Carthaginian Peace being imposed was that of Cambridge economist John Maynard Keynes, a representative of the British Treasury department who thought mostly in terms of supply and demand, and who knew that if Germany was to pay anything, it had to be able to make *something*. Examining Germany's proposed war debts, Keynes actually turned the lens back on England's debts to America, and argued that by reducing the former, the incentive was created to reduce the latter. While Keynes later proved to be wrong about much, he was correct in fearing that too harsh a peace would push Germany toward communism. It was the street-strife between the communist gangs and the fascists that eventually enabled Adolf Hitler to rise.

Despite letters from the Chancellor of the Exchequer espousing Keynes's more lenient view, Wilson plodded on, ignoring economics and concentrating with blinders on the League. Keynes insisted that the resulting terms were a recipe for disaster and ruin, not just for Germany, but for the entire European economy, and labeled Wilson the "greatest fraud on earth."[59] A Reparation Commission, established in 1921, was to decide the final numbers and amounts, but between 1919 and 1921, Germany had to pay 20 billion gold marks (roughly $5 billion US at the time) in gold, commodities, ships, or securities. In theory, that money would not only be used to pay the costs of Allied occupation, but also to buy for food and raw materials for Germany herself.[60] In other words, the allies under the Versailles Treaty in part took from Germany . . . to pay Germany.

Reparations payments were originally to be made in gold, and the prediction by Keynes—later to be accepted as fact—was that when

Germany's gold reserves ran out, she made payments in paper money that became the source of an inflated mark. Historian Sally Marks has questioned this connection. American investment in German industry offset some of the dislocations, and as Marks showed, there was "a net cash flow into Germany and 'the victors paid the bills.'"[61]

Many argue that Germany refused to tax, choosing instead to inflate. A sort of "merry-go-round," as historian Adam Tooze described it, emerged as "Germans borrowed money from the Americans to pay the British and French who then paid the Americans . . ."[62] The French spent francs, not marks, and converted the paper money, which was then sent back to Germany. England followed the same policy. So initially the inflation was mostly in Germany, which turned to hyperinflation, bled everywhere, wiping out the savings Continent-wide in the growing middle class. Here came a result Keynes had not predicted, as resentment turned not against Germany but "against constitutions and parliaments put in place after the war."[63] (America had avoided inflation because the Fed was systematically deflating the economy—one of the causes of the Great Depression later.) France, concerned about getting her money from Germany, sent troops to occupy the industrial Ruhr area, further humiliating Germany and eroding public confidence in the Weimar government. Meanwhile some German industrialists such as Krupp, Thyssen, and Farben welcomed the inflation that made German exports cheaper.

Images of ordinary Germans burning money, pushing wheelbarrows full of it through the street, or children making castles with it are abundant. A Freiburg University student who purchased a cup of coffee for 5,000 marks ordered a refill and the price had gone up to 7,000 marks. By July 1923, "300 paper mills were working nonstop and 150 printing companies had 2,000 presses running constantly" in order to print enough money.[64] In October, on a single day, the Reichsbank printed 120,000 trillion marks, yet even then, the demand was many times more than that.[65]

Hyperinflation wasn't unique to Germany—Hungary (1945–6) and Yugoslavia (1992–94) would come to have worse hyperinflation.

The difference was that this hyperinflation was afflicting a beaten, new republic that started off weakened in the eyes of the public. As usual, the US rode to the rescue with the Dawes Committee, in 1924, which reduced reparations and gave Germany loans to pay them. Later, Owen Young of General Electric, which had a major affiliate in Germany, negotiated a final arrangement to let the Germans reduce their overall debt yet again. The Americans had now saved Europe twice in seven years, but the Germans saw in the new loans an opportunity to tie the United States to the new Weimar Republic economically and thereby put the United States in a position of eventually seeking to advocate for the end of reparations.[66]

As it turned out, fixing the Weimar economy and reparations was child's play compared to reconstructing the map of Europe along Wilsonian lines. In this Wilson was not deceitful. He genuinely expected American-style democracy to work in reconstructed Europe as it had in the United States, properly balanced by the Progressive world view. Yet all the terms of his conversation ("democracy," "representation," "self-determination") "flowed from a heritage in the United States that went back more than 120 years, enmeshed in and enriched by a tapestry that took on an entirely different meaning in Europe."[67] Almost none of the new or reconstructed states had true American-style checks and balances. None of them had the "Four Pillars of American Exceptionalism," or even understood why they might be necessary. For example, the Dutch and some of the Scandinavian countries were Protestant, but few were congregational in their church organization and lines of authority. Britain had some separation of powers, but parliament and the executive (prime minister) were fused and the House of Lords had been stripped of its veto power in the early 1900s. Poland had no history of democratic government; Romania, Greece, and Bulgaria were prewar monarchies; Hungary had a four-year stint as an independent nation; and perhaps only the newly-created Czechoslovakia had the structure of a republic.

Thus, when Wilson spoke of "democracy" he meant one thing; the Europeans meant something quite different, and certainly far less "democratic." Then there were the problems associated with "national self-determination." Could a country choose to return to a monarchy? Wilson thought not, of course—but had no fleshed-out arguments to support his view on this. Not surprisingly, many nations, theoretically banned in sentiment if not in actual law from restoring monarchies, in short order settled for the next best thing, "democratically elected" dictators such as Francisco Franco of Spain, Ionnis Metaxis of Greece, and Benito Mussolini in Italy. Albania's King Zog I was a fascist. Poland yielded its democratic rule for a dictator, Joseph Pilsudski. Hungary was a monarchy with a regent while Bulgaria was an autocratic monarchy. The list continued as the years unfolded, with Antonio Salazar taking over Portugal, and, of course, Hitler. Nor was the Far East spared as Japan, ostensibly democratic, instead was governed by an Emperor, below whom a structure of assassins and gangs and the army directed policy. China maintained a form of democracy but was mired in corruption and chaos.

Another factor foiled Wilson's vision of "democracy" in Europe. True popular government failed repeatedly because of the un-American multiparty systems that encouraged the growth of radical fringe parties, who found themselves the swing vote among larger parties. A popular joke of the day was that it took three Englishmen to start a colony, three Germans to start a war, and three Frenchmen to start five political parties. America's system encouraged moderation, to the point that Alabama governor and presidential candidate George Wallace once said, "there's not a dime's worth of difference between the two parties." He was right. The requirement that candidates get (usually) 51 percent of the vote made it difficult for radical agendas to advance, but also made change slow and painful. Europeans, on the other hand, saw governments disintegrate as fast as sandcastles on a beach. Often cabinets lasted only two years. In post-war Weimar, the average lifespan of a cabinet was eight months, compared to only five in Italy and only four in Spain post-1931. Worse, the system of having prime ministers selected from the legislature prevented further checks and balances. Fittingly, when Joseph Paul-Boncourt formed his new

French government in 1932, he said "Restoring the authority of the State in a democracy . . . will be . . . the first and most essential element of our intended programme," whereupon his cabinet fell apart.[68]

Over the decade following globalism-by-diplomat, the three major objectives of Versailles, namely forcing the Central Powers to economically atone for the war, re-forming the territorial map of Europe to take better account of ethnic groups, and establishing an international body to keep peace, all failed. By 1930, much of the reparations component had been eliminated or restructured (mostly through US loans); newly-created nations such as Czechoslovakia and Poland were already viewed by Germany and Russia as territory to be reclaimed; and the League proved toothless.

No sooner did Wilson come home with the treaty than the US Senate, led by Republican Henry Cabot Lodge, viewed the mutual security aspects of the League as unrealistic and impracticable. Lodge feared the League committed the US to go to war for Britain's empire, among other problems, and instead offered his "Reservations" that would only accept an American membership in the League if Congress (as was its duty under the Constitution) had a right to review and evaluate each use of force abroad.

The "Lodge Reservations" meant the death of the League, and not even Wilson's eight thousand-mile railroad swing backing the treaty could save it. Instead, the pressure likely contributed to a stroke he suffered on September 25, 1919, then another on October 10 wherein he was left paralyzed. (This, in turn, allowed Edith Wilson to forge Wilson's signature on bills.) When Senator Albert Fall tried to console Wilson, saying "Mr. President, we have been praying for you," Wilson shot back, "Which way, Senator?"

In any event, the US did commit to de-militarization over the next decade under Republican presidents Warren Harding and Calvin Coolidge. Seeking a "Return to Normalcy," Harding sold off shipyards and government-owned railways. Then there was Senator William Borah of Idaho, known as "The Great Opposer," who resisted a postwar naval buildup. He managed a six-month freeze on naval construction in 1921 and with House support lowered naval appropriations. Harding was forced to call for a naval conference in November 1921 that included Britain, France, Italy, and Japan. The resulting Washington Naval Treaty attempted to limit construction of what all believed was the most dangerous weapon in the world, the battleship, through the "5:5:3" ratio in which for every fifty thousand tons of capital ships the US and Britain built, Japan could build thirty-five thousand tons and France and Italy fifteen thousand tons each. (Japan's low numbers were ensured by the fact that the Americans had broken the Japanese code outlining their negotiating points.)

Almost immediately nations scrambled to evade the treaty, often by increasing the armaments, which did not affect the displacement numbers much. Japan cheated by evading the restriction that it have only twelve cruisers with eight-inch guns by building a heavily-armored class of cruisers that had triple-six-inch guns that could easily be switched to eight-inch guns. Few limitations were put on the most important ship—though perhaps few knew it at the time—the aircraft carrier.[69] Planned battleship and cruiser hulls quickly were converted into aircraft carriers, and in fact there was a "bonus" whereby a carrier was limited to twenty-seven thousand tons, but a cruiser converted to a carrier could reach thirty-three thousand tons. All of this was beside the fact. The real issue was that by limiting Japan to a lower tonnage than the "white" nations, the Washington Conference grated on the Japanese. Japan left the treaty at the first possible opportunity. And it was still more ironic in that it was the Americans thought they had been "had" in the negotiations and that England was the winner, when in fact Uncle Sam came away the biggest beneficiary.

Perhaps the fitting apex of all these idealistic agreements came in 1928 when the French Foreign Minister, Aristide Briand, hoping still to tie an American guarantee to French borders, suggested a compact between the US and France. American Secretary of State Frank Kellogg, keenly aware of what the French were pulling, adroitly turned this into a blanket prohibition of war as an "instrument of national policy." Consequently the Kellogg-Briande Pact and its sixty-five signatories outlawed war. Nothing could have been more representative of the age and the emotion; nothing could have been more irrelevant at keeping the peace.

There was one final, largely unintended consequence of the diplomats' efforts at globalism. Governments everywhere grew larger and more powerful. As Paul Johnson correctly claimed, "the effect of the Great War [and its ensuing peace] was enormously to increase the size, and therefore the destructive capacity and propensity to oppress, of the state."[70] The next war would demonstrate that "destructive capacity" in the form of a new weapon that, once again, would prove the focus of international concern. Monarchs, armies, now diplomats had tried unsuccessfully to create a world government. Why not let the scientists try?

Chapter Four

Scientists' Globalism, the Bomb, and the UN

With the monarchs, the imperialists, and the diplomats having failed to install an international order, it now fell to the scientists in the wake of the "Physicists' War" and the creation of the atomic bomb. For if any force or weapon could terrorize people into accepting global government, surely it was The Bomb. Yet once again, populations resisted being herded into a one-world government. And what is more remarkable, it only took about two years for the resistance to squelch the latest iteration of the globalist dream even though the organization of the United Nations remains to this day.

Historian Paul Boyer, in his study of American reaction to the atomic bomb, observed that practically "every theme central to American social thought since the turn of the century figured at least implicitly in [speculations about the atomic bomb]: the fear of class conflict and racial unrest; concern over vast concentrations of power—whether corporate or political; forebodings about mass leisure; worry that the individual would be lost in an impersonal technocratic order; uneasiness about the rise of a technological elite; apprehension about the role of the military . . . even a long-standing uneasiness over the rise of great cities."[1] Indeed, these themes would be played out through each of the subsequent globalist efforts we will examine, suggesting that ordinary people had a great deal of concern about power and control from above. This concern, of course, stemmed from the fact that the United States, founded on the "Four Pillars of American Exceptionalism," began with bottom-up religious structures and common law, a layered political structure. Neither of these took well to top-down authoritarianism, whether from monarchs or "the striped-suit boys" as Harry Truman called the bureaucrats in the State Department.[2]

Nevertheless, it is a remarkable feature of the modern world that the victors in the two great cataclysms of the Twentieth Century have, rather than seeking broader power for themselves or their own nations, attempted to construct an international structure in which their national power would no longer be needed. We have witnessed the astounding and often bizarre lengths to which the victorious diplomats of the First World War went to prevent another such conflict from ever occurring. Predictably, those methods ended up putting control of the post-World War I world in their hands. Their efforts unraveled in less than a decade, and in many ways the Second World War could be seen as a logical outcome of the failed globalist structures they created. Also predictably, that reality did not seem to deter them at all when it came to how they intended to remake the world after the next world war with a new world body, the United Nations.

One titanic difference between the two post-war situations was obvious however: in 1945, the United States was the sole owner of the most awesome weapon ever conceived, the atomic bomb. Use of the bomb has been debated endlessly by historians. President Harry Truman said in his memoirs that the project was so secret even he did not have the "slightest idea of what was going on" until after he became president.[3] Truman went on to recount how his advisors had recommended using the bomb as soon as possible on Japan and without specific warning; against a target that would show devastating strength; and against a military target. They saw no way to conduct a demonstration that would have the desired effect of bringing Japan to surrender. Whether it was mentioned that no "gun" type atomic bomb had ever actually been tested, even on a test range, isn't recorded. There were concerns that if the plane carrying the "Little Boy" bomb crashed, there might be an accidental explosion. But there was apparently no discussion of the impact of dropping an untested weapon which, for whatever reason might be a dud, in front of Japanese officials who would only have their resolve to resist strengthened by such a failure.

Of course, the bomb—indeed, both of them—worked with horrific efficiency. But the devastation caused by the bombs has been recounted elsewhere. My concern is with the impact such devices had on the momentum for an international, global body, the planning of which was well under way before the bomb was even tested.

Truman was unreserved in his enthusiasm for the new United Nations, telling the delegates on June 26 that they had "won a victory against war itself."[4] He then credited Almighty God for bringing them "so far in our search for peace *through world organization*." That was an odd comment, given that when men tried that with the Tower of Babel, God destroyed their work.

This produced a strange perception among Americans, that they were the potential victims of the device they themselves had created. As James Reston wrote in the *New York Times*, "In that terrible flash 10,000 miles away, men here have seen not only the fate of Japan, but have glimpsed the future of America."[5]

A mythology has arisen largely through the work of Paul Boyer, the historian of the early atomic age in America, who developed a narrative of the post-Hiroshima period we might call "inventor's regret." Boyer argued that the men who made the bombs were ashamed and repentant for what they had created, an attitude that soon spread to most Americans. One newsman said many would have been happy if the gamble had failed or if the knowledge could be bundled up and discarded. Almost immediately, predictions came about the end of all life on earth. The *Washington Post* couldn't wait to insist that the life expectancy of humans had "dwindled immeasurably in the course of two brief weeks."[6] Of course, the exact opposite happened: people across the globe began living longer and longer, sparking its own set of apocalyptic gloom scenarios by the 1970s. But in the ashes of Hiroshima and Nagasaki, writers couldn't wait to terrorize people with images of firestorms that would "obliterate all the great cities of the belligerents, [and] bring industry and technology to a grinding halt, . . . [leaving only] scattered remnants of humanity living on the periphery of civilization."[7]

As one anthropologist said, America was in the grip of a "fear psychosis," sinking in an ever-deeper abyss of alarm.[8] Yet to the surprise of many, public opinion polls showed little concern by the general public, especially contrasted with that of the intellectuals and chattering classes. Only one-quarter of the public were greatly worried about the atomic bomb, and 65 percent were not too concerned at all. When asked to name the most unsettling world issues, fewer than 20 percent replied the bomb. There did exist a concern that such weapons could be used against the United States herself, but like the weather, people felt there was little individuals could do.[9] In fact, a *Fortune* poll showed 47 percent thought the bomb decreased the likelihood of a world war.[10]

Yet according to the "inventor's regret" thesis, many scientists and political leaders saw the bomb as creating the opportunity (again) for a world government. Predictably, the left-leaning Catholic journal *Commonweal* wrote in November 1945 that the solution to the atomic bomb was "simple." It consisted of creating a "world state; . . . if we do not wish to be morally guilty of suicide, the establishment of such a world power is the only thing left to us."[11] Enter the scientists.

Physicist Harold Urey said in 1945, "A superior world government of some kind . . . is the only way out."[12] Another atomic scientist, Leo Szilard, joined Urey in advocating for a world government: "Permanent peace cannot be established without a world government."[13] He envisioned a blizzard of big-government agencies to supervise disarmament, atomic energy, and a new economic order including a globalist propaganda agency that would be given control over any newspaper in the world. Within two generations, he claimed, those structures could be transformed into a "genuine world government."[14] In retrospect,

Szilard's commentary oozes classism and self-importance: "Many of the men who influence public opinion . . . come from a small class of people—the class of people who have the advantage of higher education . . . Their attitudes and their loyalties will, in the long run, affect the set of values accepted throughout the whole community."[15] Certainly the former members of the Third Reich would have agreed with much of that, arguing that people needed to come from a "small class of proper Nazi people."

Many intellectuals including H. G. Wells and *Leo Szilard himself* had years earlier envisioned a world organization made up of scientists who would control nuclear energy for the purpose of saving mankind![16] Szilard claimed to have thought of the idea in the mid-1920s, whereupon he met Wells to describe his idea. It was, he explained, a new organization called *Der Bund* ("the order" or "the band") which would be "a closely knit group of people whose inner bond is pervaded by a religious and scientific spirit." He went on:

> If we possessed a magical spell with which to recognize the "best" individuals of the rising generation at an early age . . . then we would be able to train them to independent thinking, and through education in close association we could create a *spiritual leadership class* which would renew itself on its own." [Emphasis mine][17]

Szilard saw the members of the Bund as suffering servants who would carry "burdens." His real objectives were more nefarious, seeing the Bund as having a "more direct influence on public affairs as part of the political system next to government and parliament, *or in the place of government and parliament*" (emphasis mine).[18] Actually, Szilard aimed rather high: "The Order . . . was not supposed to be something like a political party . . . but rather it was supposed to represent the state."[19] He envisioned cells of up to forty people to form the backbone of the Bund, which he touted for the rest of his life. As Richard Rhodes noted in *The Making of the Atomic Bomb*, this meant the end of people's democracy, and Szilard eagerly anticipated the fall of parliamentary democracy in Germany in the mid-1920s.[20]

Although fiction and fantasy are not a part of this study, it is worth noting that like Elon Musk, Jeff Bezos, and Bill Gates, H. G. Wells shared a vision of a humankind on a trajectory toward destruction, and that only interplanetary space travel could save it. The source of such space travel for Wells? "The liberation of atomic energy could [provide] the means which would enable man not only to leave the earth but to leave the solar system."[21]

Szilard wasn't alone in his sympathy for a giant international body. Albert Einstein on multiple occasions touted a "supernational organization" with broad powers, and its implementation had to be immediate. Leftist writer Walter Lippmann likewise called for international control of atomic energy, as did Freda Kirchwey in *The Nation*.[22] The Federation of American (Atomic) Scientists also made a documentary film called "One World or None" in 1946. Writing in one of the most "pop" of magazines, *Reader's Digest*, Stephen King-Hall offered the choice "World Government or World Destruction?"[23] A judge, Frank Tyrrell, called for the organized bar to take the lead in "international anarchy" and called for 170,000 American lawyers to mobilize in support of international atomic control. Tyrrell asked, with no small amount of hubris, "Do you for a moment think that anything which the united bar has resolved upon could long be successfully opposed?"[24] Spokesmen for many elite professions, as they had in the past, argued that their particular expertise was uniquely attuned to saving the world.

Americans generally reacted to suggestions for a world government with modest approval. For a time, scientists stood high in public esteem. The public generally assumed that the newly formed United Nations might play a role. Almost immediately, however, the globalists demanded a major overhaul of the UN if it were to play such a role. Raymond Fosdick, as Paul Boyer noted, claimed that those who created the UN would have radically changed its nature if they had known about the atomic bomb.[25] Boyer observed that around one-third of Americans expressed "passive support" for a world government in control of the bombs if it meant that such control would "abolish war," which, of course, it would not.[26] As with all polling, how the question is asked made a world of difference: another poll found just over one-third approved of a situation where the US would have to abide by the decisions of a world body.

The fact that two-thirds of the public disapproved of such a scheme in many ways only made it more attractive to intellectuals—because, after all, they were so much smarter than the Average Joe. Robert Hutchins, the "boy president" of the University of Chicago, thought this meant that he and his fellow educators needed to lead this "moral, intellectual, and spiritual revolution": "we had better set about trying to get war abolished through world government now," he insisted.[27] Another condescending look at the failures to create a world government came from Norman Cousins in *Modern Man Is Obsolete*.[28]

Of course, many intellectuals and some religious leaders did not leap to join the one-world parade, most notably Reinhold Niebuhr, who energetically fought against a world government, viewing it as "secularist" and oriented toward leaving humans with delusions of godlike control.[29] Niebuhr pointed out that the globalist dream rested on the fantasy of a world government that could be created out of thin air somehow changing human nature. Just as twenty-first century Democrats would flee from the word "liberal" and hide behind "progressive," so too did the term "world government" quickly come into disrepute to the point that Robert Hutchins wished it had never been created in the first place.

It is entirely possible that had Stalin possessed a fraction more cleverness, or been a tad less lustful of power, these infant "globalists" might have disarmed the West entirely. In one of the great accidents of history, an utter clod bumbled his way into convincing the United States it'd better hang on to its nukes a while longer! As if to compound this accident of history, Franklin Roosevelt, who had appeased Stalin at every turn, died on April 12, 1945, leaving Harry Truman with the reins of power. It was like night and day: Even before he moved into the White House, on April 23, Truman summoned Vyacheslav Molotov, the Soviet Foreign Minister, to a meeting where he spoke "bluntly." Truman recalled he told his staff he "had no intention of delivering an ultimatum" but "would make clear the US position, which he did in bold, stark words."[30] A shocked Molotov said "I have never been talked to like that in my life," and Truman snapped "Carry out your agreements and you won't get talked to like that."[31] Despite the inability of the three major allies to work to move forward on the Yalta and other agreements, Truman said he had authorized the United States to go ahead with the plans for the organization.

Truman still might have been bamboozled into going along with the globalists, but again Stalin stepped in, or, more appropriately, stepped in it. With his permission, his allies slaughtered up to 20,000 in Bulgaria, set up a communist dictatorship in Hungary, arrested and tried more than a dozen non-communist politicians in Poland, and so on.[32] Stalin singlehandedly removed any appeasement bones Truman may have had: "I am tired of babying the Soviets," Truman told James Byrnes in January 1946.[33] For the time being, the final nail in the coffin arrived the next month with the "Long Telegram" from George Kennan that all but institutionalized the cold war. Then, in March, Winston Churchill gave the tyranny that fell over Europe a name, the "Iron Curtain."

Meanwhile, the effort to contain atomic energy had not faded. For one thing, many of the scientists believed they were inherently better equipped to handle the challenge. James Franck, for example, explained that scientists were of an "international brotherhood," which he compared to a "religious order."[34] These new monks came together in small groups at all the locations where they had developed the bomb—Chicago, Los Alamos, and Oak Ridge. One group even morbidly named itself ALAS (Association of Los Alamos Scientists). Soon they formed the Federation of Atomic Scientists, or FAS, generally known as the "scientists' movement." They worked to defeat the May-Johnson bill that would have put atomic energy under the control of the War Department and won a victory in October 1945 when the Senate created the Committee on Atomic Energy. Then, eight months later, the Atomic Energy Act of 1946 put civilians on the newly-created Atomic Energy Commission in charge of atomic energy, though a Military Liaison Committee still had a powerful influence.

In October 1945, over five hundred scientists issued a statement that insisted that since other nations would soon develop their own bombs, and since no defense was possible, "international cooperation of an unprecedented kind is necessary for our survival."[35] The following January, Undersecretary of State Dean Acheson prepared a plan with David Lilienthal called *Report on the International Control of Atomic Energy*, which reflected the idealism that permeated the activists' views that by the power of reason, and in the spirit of scientific cooperation, the most "dangerous aspects of atomic energy [could be] taken out of national hands."[36] It should strike no one as surprising that these documents and reports were published by the Woodrow Wilson Foundation or the US government itself.

Fear was their tool. They embraced it enthusiastically, obscenely. As the historian of this era, Paul Boyer noted, a June 1946 radio show on "Exploring the Unknown" broadcast an H. G. Wells-like atomic bomb version of *War of the Worlds* with a script about a future atomic war. After producing roaring sounds and a narrator somberly telling listeners that people were "blown to bits . . . to nothing," with sounds of bodies hitting the ground, it culminated with a gavel banging and a voice declaring "I sentence you to a few short years—in which to solve the problems posed by nuclear fission. Penalty for failure—death!"[37] The program ended by urging people to support the Lilienthal report supporting international control.

Harold Urey insisted "nothing less than the total abolition of war will prevent [atomic bombs'] use."[38] As they would with the Covid-19 China Virus pandemic in 2020, the one-world supporters pushed fear in every corner of culture. Even *Reader's Digest*, an otherwise conservative publication, ran an article in 1947 called "Mist of Death Over New York" that depicted an atomic bomb attack on New York City, detailing city dwellers drowning as they leaped into the Hudson or dying of radiation sickness. Robert Oppenheimer was sent an advance copy for his comments, and he urged keeping the most sensationalistic aspects using facts "which are true or *which could be true* [emphasis in original]."[39] Historian Boyer admitted that the public appeals by the scientists was based "almost wholly on fear"; an article in *Collier's* written by the publicist of the Federation of Atomic Scientists began with the words "I want to frighten you."[40]

Boyer contended that the "orchestrations of fear" were undertaken deliberately: "from mass terror would spring a mass demand for the radical transformation of the international order."[41] *Commonweal* magazine admitted that "fear may do what sheer morality could never do."[42] And when fear of nuclear death did not suffice to convince the public of a need for a one-world government, writers delved into the menace of the arms race that would require national police states. In this they were not entirely wrong. Science fiction writer Chandler Davis in 1946 wrote an article in *One World of None* called "Nightmare" that told of a future American society dominated by a police state due to the need to keep atomic secrets.[43] Oxford Professor E. L. Woodward predicted that the new source of atomic energy "must increase enormously the power of the state over the citizen" and saw a "kind of neofeudal system in which an elite of technocrats, strategists, and corporate barons" in control of energy would dominate the rest of society.[44] Strategists and "corporate barons" in control of energy would dominate the rest of society.[45] Influential journalists Joseph and Peter Alsop envisioned a time in which the "great cities will become ghost towns. Population and industry will be dispersed in new urban communities" due to the arms race.[46]

Many of those dark predictions came true to one degree or another, but little of it had to do with atomic bombs as we will see. The future devastation of liberalism and wokeness proved far more deadly than the need to keep military secrets.

Not surprisingly though, just as the monarchs and diplomats had before them, the new elites believed themselves particularly suited to addressing the threat of the atomic bomb. Professor John Perkins of Boston University asked in an essay, "Where is the Social Sciences'

Atomic Bomb?" Only a force equal to that of an atomic weapon could address the problem, and "this is the result the social scientists must produce. This is their atomic bomb."[47] With a typical elitist top-down mentality, Perkins insisted "the top minds of the world must be commandeered to harness the complex and powerful aspirations, actions, and attitudes of men and channel them into the ways of peace." Other academics agreed that they were more brilliant than anyone else: psychologist A. M. Meerloo in the *New York Times Magazine* argued that only a "united social science—embracing economics, sociology, and psychology . . . [led by] free intellectuals with *original thoughts*, who *will not bend to authority*" would be up to the task [emphasis mine].[48] *Science* magazine chimed in, demanding that social scientists devise "an economic, social and political organization" that would promote human values, health, love, and security"[49]

Perhaps not surprisingly, some of the social scientists' great concern for humanity involved money. William Ogburn, in the *American Journal of Sociology*, after chiding Americans for wanting a say in the process ("it is the function of the social scientist to say what the social consequence [of the atomic bomb] should be"), went on to reason that "perhaps hundreds of large projects" that would require a financial commitment similar to the Manhattan Project should be considered. "For every subsided piece of research in natural science there should be corresponding financial aids to research in social science." Since over $2 billion was spent making the bomb, "an intelligent society would aid social research to solve the problems the bomb creates."[50] Many other social scientists joined the conversation, all with the same demands. But one, Louis Wirth, the president of the American Sociological Society, let the cat out of the bag when he complained that in the past, social scientists had not had the power to "persuade *or compel*" others to put their idealistic programs in place.[51] Wirth went on to note that it wasn't enough to investigate the implications of atomic energy, but social scientists had to prepare public opinion as well.

As time passed, however, even the imprimatur of atomic scientists did not sway the public: by October 1945, 71 percent of Americans said the US should "keep the secret" of the bomb, and a second survey a year later by a different pollster yielded the exact same result.[52] Predictably, the pollsters blamed the people for their insufficient "grasp of the world situation."[53] Overall, however, the topic was losing interest: between 1945 and 1948 the percentage of newspaper columns mentioning the atomic bomb fell from 20 percent to about 6 percent.[54] Not long after Hiroshima, the public had already began to turn on the scientists, both the physical and social varieties. One of the Manhattan Project's physicists observed that people were beginning to fear science, seeing scientists as warmongers. One could find headlines such as "Science a Menace" or "Science Moving too Fast."[55] Even Robert Oppenheimer agreed that the atomic bombs had undermined public trust in science. Some called for a moratorium on further bomb development—and the notion of letting scientists control matters disappeared quickly.

All of this took place against a fading backdrop of decreasing public fear about atomic weapons. When the Bikini Atoll public test of an atomic bomb took place in 1946, Americans largely shrugged. One of the scientists who returned from Bikini was "surprised at first to find so little interest."[56] It seemed the fear-mongering had petered out, but then came a book called *No Place to Hide* by a doctor, David Bradley. It sold 250,000 copies and temporarily halted the collapse of the one-world movement.[57] The boost from Bradley's book was short-lived: Just three years later Eugene Rabinowitch wrote in the *Bulletin of Atomic Scientists* that scientists "cannot but admit the fact that their campaigns have failed."[58] Oppenheimer had given up years earlier, writing "I am bankrupt of further ideas," and in 1947, a poll of the members of the Federation of Atomic Scientists itself showed a majority favored America developing more atomic bombs.[59]

As they would decades later, when the public proved less than enthusiastic about their plans, the globalists blamed the public for its ignorance. Lewis Mumford labeled it "moral inertness," while Albert Einstein lamented "The public, having been warned of the horrible nature of atomic warfare, has done nothing about it."[60] Or, as Edward Long, Jr. put it in *The Christian Response to the Atomic Crisis*, the scientist "crusaders became lonely prophets."[61] Christian observer Reinhold Neibuhr had warned that the scientists had ignored basic human nature and the structural elements of national governments. By 1948, polls showed that among the most educated, at least, almost two-thirds believed atomic power would yield more good than harm.[62]

Elites had failed to terrify the population enough with images of atomic destruction. Then a different dynamic gripped the elites: the bomb, as a weapon, demanded secrecy. Even use in peaceful atomic energy projects faced severe limitations due to national security. An article in the *University of Chicago Law Review* complained that the Atomic Energy Commission operated in a "vacuum" and that there was virtually no public discussion.[63] One-time scare-monger David Lilienthal, while urging the public to inform itself on atomic power, provided little specific information. Secrecy was so great about the atomic bombs themselves that even the senator who framed the Atomic Energy Commission law, Brien McMahon, revealed that his Joint Congressional Committee on Atomic Energy did not know how many bombs the US actually had![64] Former speechwriter for Franklin Roosevelt, Robert Sherwood, complained about the strategy of keeping people fearless by keeping them ignorant.[65] Oppenheimer, James Conant, and other birthers of the bomb lamented the secrecy, but it was inevitable. Once the decision was made to abandon international control, there was no way to restore openness.

Others, such as General Leslie Groves, who had actually been in charge of the Manhattan Project, and aviation pioneer Alexander Seversky, attempted to downplay the brutal scenes of a future (such that it was) after a nuclear war. Groves insisted "We will come through all right . . . You don't have to hide under your beds at night."[66] In other words, the indecision about whether to scare the public into support for a global government (which, as we have seen, failed) or bribe them with undefined promises of the benevolence of atomic energy (which likewise failed because of the secrecy needed to maintain atomic weapons when the push for international control failed) largely left the scientists' movement for globalism dead in the water.

Yet at that very moment, a new instrument was being created that seemed to fulfill all their hopes for international control of the terror they had created. And it had come into being without knowledge of the bomb itself. A newer version of the League of Nations, a "United Nations," featured the United States in a central role—something the League clearly lacked—and in theory also included the USSR. All that prevented the UN from taking on the role of a true global government was that the Soviet Union and its allies staunchly resisted almost any measures to operate in genuine coordination with the West. In one of the great ironies of history, the West was saved from a global tyranny by the horror and tyranny of a lesser power pledged to communism.

The United Nations got its formal blessing on January 1, 1942 when Winston Churchill, who had engaged in eight major personal conferences with Franklin D. Roosevelt, returned from a short Canadian trip to Washington to sign a Joint Declaration of the United Nations.[67] The Soviet Ambassador, Maxim Litvinov, and the Chinese Ambassador also signed, committing all the nations to the Atlantic Charter, an agreement between the US and Great Britain that dated to August 1941 and established eight "common principles." Among them were many of the old League points—freedom of the seas, restoration of self-governments for conquered countries—but also both countries agreed not to seek territorial expansion and to pursue the liberalization of international trade.[68] On January 2, another twenty-six nations signed the United Nations agreement, and all pledged not to make a separate peace with the Axis.

Of course, the notion that the Soviet Union would ever give back any territory it took was unlikely. Nor was Stalin planning on allowing free trade with the west. Still, at such an early point in the war, a united front looked encouraging.

Planning continued throughout the conflict. Specifics were discussed at the Dumbarton Oaks meetings from August to October in 1944, which proposed the establishment of a "general international organization." Led by the United States, Great Britain, the Soviet Union, and China, with delegates from other nationals involved, the conference was to expand on the Moscow Declaration of 1943 that called for a postwar international order to replace the useless League of Nations. Held in Washington, DC from August 21 to October 7, attendees included Soviet ambassador to the US Andrei Gromyko, China ambassador Wellington Koo, US Undersecretary of State Edward Stettinius, Jr., and British Under-Secretary for Foreign Affairs, Alexander Cadogan (later replaced by Edward Wood). In reality, Stettinius, Gromyko, and Acheson ran the show. By then, the war's end in Europe was assured: allied forces had held, then expanded their Normandy beachheads under Operation Cobra at Saint-Lô. Conflict in Asia, however, while never in doubt as to the victor, remained murky as to the cost and timing. Moreover, the Soviets refused to meet directly with the Chinese, as they were already supporting a communist revolutionary army under Mao Tse Tung in that country.

Today, fewer names are more associated with the one-world/ globalism movement than that of Rockefeller. Not surprisingly, Nelson Rockefeller played a key unofficial role in the Dumbarton Oaks meetings, officially sanctioned by the FBI to pass its reports on to Stettinius.[69] Rockefeller also immediately embroiled himself in a controversy over the logo of the proposed United Nations by excluding Argentina because of its support of the Nazis. Ironically, however, Rockefeller aligned against globalism and tried to stop a UN-type organization. Instead, he sought to replace it with the Chapultepec Pact (officially the "Inter-American Conference on Problems of War and Peace") that would forge a regional, not international, alliance between the United States and nineteen Latin American countries. Latin American countries feared that a United Nations might interfere with Pan-American goals. Ultimately it was Rockefeller's regional pact idea that, according to historian Stephen Schlesinger, led to Article 51 in the Charter that permitted "individual or collective self-defense" at a regional level. Years later, John Foster Dulles, Secretary of State at the time, credited Rockefeller with the North Atlantic Treaty Organization.[70]

The conferees at Dumbarton Oaks produced a set of "Proposals for the Establishment of a General International Organization" that were reproduced in "Pamphlet Number 4: Pillars for Peace."[71] Among the stated purposes were 1) to maintain international peace and security including "effective collective measures" to suppress acts of aggression and to peacefully settle international disputes," 2) to achieve international economic, social, and humanitarian solutions, and to 3) offer a place to afford a center for international harmony and achieving common ends.

Immediately hurdles appeared. Both involved the relative power of the Soviet Union. Diplomat Charles Bohlen, writing many years later in his memoirs, noted that all issues were settled except for the voting procedure in the Security Council and the attempt by the USSR to get all sixteen of its "republics" counted independently in the General Counsel. The former would entail a veto in the Security Council; the latter, a much larger Soviet-dominated bloc in the General Assembly (as it would be called).[72]

Stettinius accompanied FDR to Yalta in January 1945 where he presented a new American proposal that gave all the five powers the veto on all but procedural issues in the Security Council. While none of the members could prohibit a measure from coming before the Council, any single power could veto any action. This meant that by the time the delegates met to formalize the United Nations in San Francisco, the major stumbling blocks had been overcome. And to ensure he didn't have a repeat of the Versailles delegation named by Woodrow Wilson (all yes-men with virtually no critics), Roosevelt at least included a wider variety of members in the delegation including the Michigan Republican Arthur Vandenberg and the former GOP governor of Minnesota, Harold Stassen. Vandenberg had only recently dropped his isolationist position. (When informed of the Lend-Lease Act that gave the British 50 older destroyers in return for leases to naval bases, Vandenberg wrote in his diary, "I had the feeling I was witnessing the suicide of the Republic.")[73]

Roosevelt died on April 12, 1945, whereupon a different atmosphere descended, though the new president, Harry Truman, was as committed to the UN as FDR. Asked if the San Francisco conference on the UN would still occur, Truman said "it had to take place if we were to keep the peace. And that's the first decision I made as President of the United States."[74]

Two months after the opening ceremonies in San Francisco, by a vote of 20 to 10 (with 15 abstentions and five absent), the charter was approved. (Those into numerology would find it interesting that the date 6/25/45 sums to 76, or "the eye of the Lord," "a sign from the heavens," or "the first and the last" while the date 6/25/1945 sums to 1976 which is "New Jerusalem.") Certainly the delegates and those in attendance felt they were involved in a titanic if not spiritual endeavor: Truman said the UN would keep the world "free from fear," something that has yet to take place some eighty years later. And then in an inauspicious start, the Security Council unanimously elected as the first Secretary General a man named Lie.

Norwegian foreign minister Trygve Lie (pronounced "Lee" but ominously appearing as "lie") was anything but well-regarded. British under-secretary of the United Nations Brian Urquhart, who served under Lie, described him as "out of his depth," and an "unsophisticated man" who relied on peasant shrewdness than on intellectual effort or diplomatic hard work. He had a massive physique of an "athlete who had run to seed," was apt to fly into a rage in which his face would turn beet red, "jowls quivering," and uttering "complex and ominous Norwegian oaths." Lie had a taste for expensive wines and haute cuisine, and once made a reservation at a nightclub under the assumed name of Rodney Witherspoon.[75]

A month after Lie's election, Winston Churchill, now in his seventies but still capable of stellar bursts of genius, delivered one of the most quoted and accurate speeches of the twentieth century at Westminster College under the title "Sinews of Peace."[76] Truman had read it, and found nothing objectionable—until his advisors exploded afterward. Then he denied ever having read it and said the former Prime Minister "put me on the spot." He then described what would later prove one of the clearest strategic assessments of Soviet intentions an "almost catastrophic blunder."[77] Churchill, however, had encapsulated the issues perfectly: an "iron curtain has descended across the continent" of

Europe, Churchill proclaimed, behind which lay "all the capitals of the ancient states of central and eastern Europe. Warsaw, Berlin, Prague, Vienna, Budapest, Belgrade, Bucharest, and Sofia . . ." If anyone was the antithesis of a globalist, it was Churchill. Now out of power and aged, it was beyond his desperate and hopeless quest to save the British Empire, though he would try in his return to the Prime Ministership. For a decade before he came to power in 1940 he had understood the evil of the Nazi regime, and now he more clearly than anyone spelled out the threat of the Soviet Union. Instead of a toothless global body, Churchill favored a "fraternal association of the English-speaking peoples" to stop the godless communists.[78] As to notions that an international body should control the atomic bomb, Churchill said it "would be criminal madness to cast it adrift in the still agitated and un-united world."[79]

If anything, the first few years after the war showed how critical it was for an independent national state called the United States to exist, as America unveiled the Marshall Plan in 1947 which, historians generally agree, saved much of western Europe from communism. It not only prevented teetering democracies such as Italy and Greece from falling to communist governments, but it eliminated the gap between North American and European living standards and "in the process opened an equally cataclysmic one between Western and Eastern Europe."[80] Indeed, this "cataclysmic" gap between the free nations and those enslaved by the communists weighed more heavily on ordinary people than the fear of atomic destruction ever did. This was evidence that could be seen, not believed. A slogan used by the left, "Better Red than Dead," soon turned into a mockery as Americans witnessed people across Europe pushed into a new subjugation equally as horrific as the one they had escaped from. By the early 1960s, with the erection of the Berlin Wall, actual news footage of people fleeing East Berlin reinforced that point.

Occasionally cited as an attempt at globalism, Marshall's economic plan was far more an economic regional relationship in the vein Churchill envisioned than an attempt at one-worldism. It bound

European countries even more tightly to American producers and consumers in a regional compact. Great Britain sucked up over 25 percent
of the total, followed by France (18 percent) and Germany (11 percent).
Marshall Plan money overall accounted for under 5 percent of the
national income of the recipient countries between 1948 and 1951, or an
increase in the GDP of recipient nations of half a percent. What it did
not do in total dollars, however, it accomplished in image, hope, and
instant stabilization. And as if to underscore that it was not globalist
but regional in intent, it was replaced in 1951 by the Mutual Security
Pact of foreign aid to allies.

Public opinion had squashed scientific globalism. The Soviets did
the rest. A shift to regional defense tied to the United States was on
full display in 1949 with the creation of the North Atlantic Treaty
Organization (NATO), which codified the reality that there would be
no "world government" in charge of atomic energy. To a large degree,
NATO broadly represented Churchill's desire for a "fraternal association of the English-speaking peoples" to stop Soviet expansionism.[81]
NATO also cemented the view that the Soviets were simply not trustworthy and that there could be no "world government" that gave them
any kind of serious decision-making power. (The Soviet delegation cast
its first veto in the Security Council just days after it was formed, over
British and French withdrawal from Syria.) Soviet belligerence would
prevent the United Nations from acting in any meaningful way to stop
aggression in all but two cases over the next fifty years.

When North Korea invaded their South Korean neighbors in June
1950, the machinery of the UN whirred to life as planned. And most
members expected the USSR to block any attempt to involve the UN
in the conflict. But here, the Soviets again shot themselves in the foot
with an ongoing boycott of the Security Council over Taiwan being
given "China's" seat on the Council. Thus, there was no Soviet "nyet"
vote when the Security Council authorized United Nations troops to
support South Korea.

A second rare instance in which the UN worked as planned
came in the 1990 invasion of Kuwait by Iraq under Saddam Hussein.

Typically, the Soviets would have blocked UN involvement, seeing the weakening of the OPEC alliance as a means for the Soviets to sell more oil. (In addition, the Soviets never minded seeing western, particularly American, troops tied up in combat around the world.) This time, however, the USSR wheezed in its death rattle, and Mikhail Gorbachev—battling a bubbling democratic revolution at home and a collapsing economy—permitted the UN resolution for troops to evict the Iraqis.

In almost all other cases, the use of UN "peacekeepers" over the decades has proven abysmal, ineffective, and usually counterproductive, as stories of UN "peacekeeper" abuses abound.[82] Research has been split, but the most recent study concluded that peacekeepers only are effective if both sides want them: otherwise they are merely targets.[83]

Meanwhile, the globalist dream for the United Nations and scientists alike—that a non-national body would be in charge of atomic weapons—went up in radioactive smoke when the Rosenbergs enabled the USSR to explode its own atomic bomb. Once the Soviets demonstrated their belligerence, a new reality set in. As one historian of the United Nations put it:

> Americans believed that the UN was strongest and most dynamic . . . when it did America's bidding. . . Oddly, many other countries shared the same attitude: they, too, felt better about the UN when the United States took charge.[84]

In essence, the world had returned to pre-Versailles status where a large nation, or several, determined their own fates. And that meant that scientists had joined the list of monarchs, militaries, and diplomats in forging a one-world body that would ensure perpetual peace. Perhaps the economists and bankers could do better?

Chapter Five

Financial Globalism, Bretton Woods, and the Dollar

F ar more ominous in its implications for globalism than either the Marshall Plan or NATO were the financial machinations going on at Bretton Woods, New Hampshire, on July 1, 1944 even as the structures for the United Nations were being planned. More specifically, the attendees met at the only real hotel in the region capable of handling large numbers of attendees, the Mount Washington Hotel. Its organizers were a homosexual (John Maynard Keynes) and a Soviet agent, Harry Dexter White (whose code name, it was later learned in the Venona papers, was "JURIST"). To Keynes, White came across as rude, lacking "the faintest conception [of] civilized behavior."[1] White responded by calling Keynes "Your Royal Highness."

Bretton Woods began in disarray. The hotel didn't have enough rooms with potable water; there "wasn't enough ice or Coca-Cola to go around; staffing was so thin that some nearby Boy Scouts had to be drafted; and the establishment's manager locked himself in his office with a case of whiskey and refused to come out."[2] With Keynes and White as co-captains, this ship could only head in one direction, that of world monetary control (and that possibly under Soviet influence).

The only questions to be resolved were really who would be at the helm and who would benefit?

Multilateral negotiations resulted in the creation of the World Bank (to provide loans to poorer nations), the International Monetary Fund (to do the same, but also to ensure the solvency of the international banking system), and the International Bank for Reconstruction and Development (to distribute still more money to the Third World). Funding for the International Monetary Fund came from capital subscriptions from member countries in convertible currencies.

Futurist and international economic analyst Peter Zeihan argued that the "banks and the fund . . . were sideshows."[3] Attempting to put a smiley face on the new structures, Keynes described it as follows:

> . . . when one chap wants to leave his resources idle, those resources
> are not therefore withdrawn from circulation but are made available to another chap who is prepared to use them—and to make
> this possible without the former losing his liquidity.[4]

Left unsaid was the reality that the "chaps" would be forced to make their money available whether it was their desire to do so or not, and secondarily that most of that money (and votes on how to use it) came from the United States.[5]

Americans, with Keynes's input, ran the show and everyone else attended just to learn what their role was. By that time, the United States was dominating the entire Allied side of the war except for the Eastern Front. American money had swamped England; US soldiers, Marines, and sailors shouldered the burden of the Pacific War almost alone (Australia having effectively dropped out after the first Guadalcanal campaign and China a persistent tease as Chaing Kai-shek preserved his army to fight the communists rather than using it on the Japanese). Prior to Bretton Woods, European nations and their empires—to the degree any remained—operated their own internal systems with relatively little outside trade. What slapped them as surely as a bucket of ice water to the face was the realization that whatever might unfold politically after the Germans and Japanese were bludgeoned into surrender was that even if they could re-acquire some of their overseas possessions, they had no navies.

France had handed its ships over to the Germans with the Vichy Government, whereupon the British sank the rest in Algeria; the Dutch and Australians had seen much of their naval forces obliterated in the Battle of the Java Sea. Japan, Germany, and what was left of the Italian navy after the Taranto raid would be forced to scrap their seapower. Even the British recognized the awesome cost of maintaining an "empire-sized navy" would not be possible after the war's end. America, on the other hand, not only possessed a giant two-ocean navy, but one fine-tuned to state-of-the-art technological capabilities. Brand new battleships and carriers, armed with an armada of newly-designed aircraft, had come on the scene in 1944. America's merchant fleet, boosted during the war by phenomenal output by shipbuilding heroes such as Henry Kaiser (whose yards set a record building a Liberty Ship in just four and a half days), had supplied England for three years.

Given this breathtaking dominance by the United States, Bretton Woods delegates were dumbstruck when White and Keynes unveiled, not a *Pax Americana* with global tariffs, quotas, or restrictions, but a previously unseen free trade system where anyone could export to the USA. As the delegates pondered this, it dawned on them that the United States was guaranteeing free trade around the world (with the exception of the Soviet Bloc) through its navy and therefore were indirectly subsidizing the economies of almost everyone else.[6] Peter Zeihan called Bretton Woods the "single most important factor" in the economic "miracles" of Japan, Korea, and Germany.[7] Over time, despite the growth of those economies, the United States as of 2023 still produces about 25 percent of the world's GDP . . . right where it was in 1944. But it also accounted for nearly half of the world's defense outlays and controlled half the world's naval tonnage.

It would be another Kaiser-like innovator, Malcom McLean, who at age twenty-four envisioned putting entire cargo boxes on ships that would eventually become "container ships," revolutionizing transport even further. (McLean, a trucker, needed another sixteen years to bring his idea to fruition, ultimately parlaying a small oil tanker business into a $42 million loan from Walter Wriston at Citibank for which his personal contribution was $10,000.)[8] Yet all this started to unwind, or at least reached the "end of the beginning," in 2014.[9]

"Futurists" such as Zeihan and George Freedman agree that the international restructuring that occurred over the last twenty to thirty years constituted an inevitable collapse of Bretton Woods. The system was unsustainable from the get-go. For one thing, this global system rested entirely on American will and a commitment to use it not only to protect American interests, but *all* free trade. Whether this specifically lay behind the Korean and Vietnam wars, or whether it was pure ideological anti-communism, remains an unresolved debate. However, it is entirely likely that, as the great Rush Limbaugh used to say, "the free flow of oil at market prices" energized the mission to boot Iraq out of Kuwait in 1990–91.

In 1946, however, when the Bretton Woods structures went into effect, the world's demand for dollars was insatiable. International trade boomed, moving from a 3 percent per year contraction in the 1930s to a 7 percent per year expansion from 1948–71, even exceeding the growth of the Roaring Twenties. Industrial production likewise grew at a 5.6 percent clip. Indeed, it was a reasonable question as to whether the US Navy ensured the dollar or the dollar backed up the US Navy. What was undeniable was that at the end of World War II, aside from a small Soviet fleet, the American navy was the only one in the world that mattered.

Either way, American money became *the* international currency, all supported by a rapidly growing American economy exploding with new products such as baby foods, televisions, inexpensive housing, fast foods, and undergirded by an astounding revival of the economic engines of the US economy in the 1920s, namely steel, automobiles, and electricity. Historian Paul Johnson wrote that America had "essentially a businessman's economy. Its success lay in great part in the existence of a favourable climate, in which businessmen felt safe and esteemed," and one which had disappeared under Franklin Roosevelt.[10] It is somewhat ironic that even Adolf Hitler used America's economy as the measurement for German performance, writing in his little-noticed *Second Book*:

> The European dreams of a standard of living, which he derives as much from Europe's possibilities as from the real conditions of America. . . [T]he European, even without being fully conscious of it, applies as the yardstick for his life the conditions of American life . . . [11]

America's huge volume of internal sales enabled the US auto industry to adopt "methods of production that in Europe due to the lack of such internal sales would simply be impossible."[12]

Everything was tied together by a vast new advertising universe. Soaps, packaged foods, hula hoops, and Barbie dolls found their way into American homes through *Life*, the *Saturday Evening Post*, and other magazines. They came over the airwaves via radio with the *Lucky Strike Hour* and *General Electric Theater*. Even parents found themselves helpless to keep their children from television advertising when Ruth Handler created a realistic-looking doll named "Barbie" and decided to put commercials on the *Mickey Mouse Show*.[13] Mattel's television ads on Disney's show focused on the little girls, not the cynical adults: the girls, and their mothers "stampeded the stores" when the ads appeared.[14]

What made the Bretton Woods model even more ideal for a time was a single unspoken fact: the United States had emerged from World War II as the only major belligerent whose homeland was not devastated. It simultaneously constituted the *world's* largest consumer *and* producer. Since the navy protected American exports, and since America for many years was the only nation even capable of significant exports, Americans sold everything to everybody. It should be no surprise that the Barbie doll became the *world's* most desirable toy; or that Pan American Airlines (Pan Am), prodded by its CEO Juan Trippe, not only dominated world air travel but by the late 1950s had dictated the very shape of it. While every other airline flew propeller-driven aircraft, Trippe single-handedly pushed the world into the jet age in 1955 by ordering a fleet of forty-five big 707 jets from Boeing at a cost of $265 million.

This shrank the globe in three profound ways. First, Trippe forced every other national airline to scrap its fleet of prop aircraft and substitute jets, making America the leader in the field. Second, Trippe's new jet airliner reduced flight time flew nonstop from New York to Paris to just six hours and thirty-five minutes, only half the time needed by propeller aircraft. And third, only the United States built these planes, creating a massive market for Boeing. In its maiden flight in 1956, the new big Pan Am wowed critics and customers alike. Richard Branson, later to found Virgin Airlines, praised Trippe's exploitation of glamor while maintaining the cost-efficiency of "bums in seats."[15] At the very time that Coca-Cola and Barbie were becoming international sensations, the most identifiable object in the sky was the light blue Pan Am aircraft.

In the new global market that emerged from Bretton Woods, America would have naturally dominated by sheer size and productive capability. Yet another factor energized and accelerated the American global position, namely that many (if not most) of its entrepreneurs at that time held a deep reverence for the American ideal. They were more than proud to tout America's greatness *and goodness*. One could see this not only in the overt expressions of Walt Disney films and theme parks, but in the pragmatic appreciation for the struggles of ordinary people. When John D. Rockefeller said "The common man must have kerosene, and he must have it good, and he must have it cheap" the last thing on his mind was amassing money. Old "Rocky" genuinely possessed a burning desire to provide inexpensive power and light to ordinary people. The same could be said of entrepreneurs such as Ray Kroc or Kemmons Wilson, who brilliantly appreciated the new opportunities and necessitated markets inherent in America's car culture. Wilson, who had stayed at substandard or inexpensive motels in his travels, meticulously measured and annotated everything about the "ideal" hotel room, then founded Holiday Inn to provide low-cost but good quality quarters to families on the road. "Kids stay free" reflected his departure from the practice of charging extra for each child.[16] Kroc, no less a genius, had experienced more than a few "greasy spoon" cafés in his travels. What Wilson did for accommodations, Kroc did for cuisine . . . to use the term loosely! He wanted to ensure that every family could rely on the same quality meal at every location.[17] It is ironic that today, McDonald's is associated with "junk food," whereas to traveling families in the late 1950s and early 1960s—often saddled with subpar roadside diners with food of questionable origin—McDonald's represented a quality oasis!

Kroc had served in World War I, lying about his age to enlist, alongside another of these postwar giants, Walter Elias "Walt" Disney, who would go on to form a film and theme park empire. Like Kroc, Disney held America in the highest regard. Born in Chicago, he treasured a romanticized version of small-town midwestern America. His movies and television shows portrayed only the best in human traits— courage, faithfulness, sacrifice for the greater good, and, of course, love. When he began his theme parks, he started every visitor off with a trip down main street, which reflected his idealized view of the country.[18] His parks were meticulously cleaned, and he banned chewing gum and cigarettes, whose residue could make scenery appear dirty and ordinary. Disney, like Trippe, Handler, Wilson, and Kroc, was not selling a product. He was selling America. These entrepreneurs were the heart of the early Bretton Woods economic system.

In its first two decades, Bretton Woods merely provided the financial and trade highways upon which those entrepreneurs spread American idealism. The United States had just started to taste the contradictions created by Keynes and White's brainchild, contradictions that started to take root in the early 1960s. Most notably, Bretton Woods, with its International Monetary Fund and World Bank, imposed on the United States two mutually incompatible tasks. America's currency needed to remain as "sound as the dollar." Even though America was no longer on the gold standard, virtually everyone inside the financial system understood that money had to maintain its value.

An inevitable problem lurked, however. Known as the "Triffin dilemma," named after a Belgian-American economist Robert Triffin, the requirement of maintaining the dollar's value to gold could only be achieved by keeping inflation low, maintaining low deficits, and keeping the national debt under control.[19] This increasingly became more difficult as the World Bank, International Monetary Fund, and various foreign aid packages drove up American monetary commitments and increased the US deficit. Keynes had in fact anticipated this development and proposed an international reserve currency called the "Bancor," but no one had any faith in such a currency that was untied to real productivity.

When foreign aid combined with irrational and unhinged domestic welfare spending, and the expenses of the Vietnam War were piled on, the Bretton Woods system seemed on the verge of collapse. In 1967, runs on gold seriously damaged the system. Richard Nixon finalized the actual monetary element of Bretton Woods's death in 1971 by closing the gold window (although simultaneously again legalizing individual ownership of gold coins and bullion). Inflation, the nemesis of a sound dollar, began to surge thereafter, reined in only by the election of Ronald Reagan.[20]

Whereas the overall concept of Bretton Woods, in which a powerful American navy would ensure the free trade of goods and services outside the Soviet bloc, remained, by the late twentieth century a number of realities had started to descend on the globalists. Money and finance faced powerful constraints.

The most important of these was geography. It is static, only changed by often Herculean efforts such as building the Trans-Siberian Railroad, the Panama Canal, or the "Chunnel." Other than possessing a mostly moderate climate, the other most important geographical factor over centuries has been access to navigable water, particularly rivers devoid of tides and storms. The United States had not only over 14,000 miles of temperate-zone rivers (vs. a mere 2,000 miles for Germany or China and a near total absence in the Arab world) but also America's oceans have a string of barrier island chains on the southern and southeastern costs that provide an intercoastal waterway of about 3,000 miles. Combined with all the interior waterways, the United States has over 17,600 miles of commercially usable water, maintained at a ridiculously low price of about $2.7 billion for all internal waterways. Excluding the cost of a navy, maintaining the oceans was free.

This meant that the United States had a built-in price-mitigator of ridiculously cheap transportation. Of course, that was only valuable if the land accessed by those waterways was itself useful. Think, for example, of the land on the banks of the Congo or Amazon rivers, where thick and nearly impenetrable jungles make access irrelevant. In those zones, there are virtually no "good weather days." Every day not only features incredible humidity and heat, but drenching and unpredictable rainfalls. Merely building frontage roads alongside the rivers to move freight and people inland would constitute a task equal to building the Panama Canal Railroad for every single mile, or 4,000 miles for the Amazon vs. about 50 for the Panama Canal. And this doesn't even get into the serpentine nature of the Amazon, whereas the Mississippi River for the most part is a straight line.

America's water network constitutes an internal infrastructure that required very little to make profitable. At first, steamboats, then ships powered by oil or diesel, took care of delivering goods; port facilities soon provided loading, unloading, and storage facilities. Thus, major commercial centers such as Pittsburgh, Cincinnati, St. Louis, New Orleans, and others arose, all easily connected by a rail network, then, later, by interstate highways.

Consider, then, what *that* enabled: by 2014, the US consumer base was $11.5 trillion, triple that of anyone else, and larger than the next six countries. And none of those countries were located in the Middle East, Africa, Australia, or Latin America. Indeed, America's consumer base was double that of the BRICS countries combined (Brazil, Russia, India, China, and South Africa).[21]

Further geographic obstacles that afflicted nations' economic development include mountain ranges. Whereas the US Rocky Mountains have six major passes with minimal avalanche risk, the Himalayas, the Alps, and the Andes do not. And mountains usually mean elevation, which makes cultivation of most crops difficult due to snow and an all-around colder climate. A map of global agricultural land shows Africa, Latin America, over two-thirds of China, and Australia are nearly devoid of high-quality land. Argentina's Rio Plata Region and Australia's Murray-Darling Basin are about the only small areas on entire continents where agriculture can thrive.[22] Canada, in addition to being cold, has major geographic barriers with the Canadian Shield and the Canadian Rockies. But Canada has one relatively short useful waterway—the St. Lawrence, and America's southern neighbor Mexico has none.

The implications of these realities are staggering. No—I repeat, no—Middle Eastern country is self-sufficient in foodstuffs. Not even Israel. East Asian nations have managed to be self-sufficient in rice (except for Malaysia), but still import all other food goods. Columbia, Venezuela, Singapore, Jordan, Cuba, Iraq, Saudi Arabia, Japan, and South Korea all import nearly two-thirds of their grain. Except for Israel, not a single Middle Eastern country is even remotely industrialized. On the other hand, of the thirty industrialized European nations, only Norway is self-sufficient in energy. Germany's dependence on the Nord Stream 2 pipeline and Russian energy was exposed as dangerously short-sighted when Russia invaded Ukraine in February 2022. Germany needed 2.2 million barrels of crude oil imports per day. Without Russia, that became a massive anchor around its economy.

Russia itself was trapped in a geographic vise. Only one Russian city was at a lower latitude than Minneapolis! Russia's only navigable river, the Volga, is frozen three months of the year, and doesn't even empty into an ocean but the Caspian Sea. As Peter Zeihan points out, the nation's geography is all wrong: "What barriers Russia does have are in the wrong places: the forests and swamps and mountains of the Arctic and Siberia aren't between the Russians and rivals but between the Russians and even crappier land."[23] With a population half that of the US, Russia has borders of 12,000 miles. Its birth rate, like that of other nations but worse, is falling.

But Russia looks good in comparison to Latin America, where the geography is horrible. There, more capital had to be laid out for infrastructure than almost any other region. To move cargo from Lima, Peru to São Paulo, Brazil might seem like it would involve a (real) distance of only 2,160 miles, or about the same as the distance from New York to Phoenix, but to avoid either the Amazon or the Andes makes the trip a 6,000 mile journey. Caracas, only 10 miles inland, has a steep mountain range separating it from the ports, forcing a typical journey to require four hours. And not a single road connects Venezuela with Brazil. Columbia has a navigable river and coastline, but its cities are above it and leave the population effectively landlocked. Chileans live butted up against the Andes, where winter storms often sever all traffic, including railroads, to the west. Santiago, Chile and Lima, Peru are both on the coast, but are separated by 2,100 miles of desert. Brazil has a commercial capital, São Paulo, but it is located on a mountain where the one single road through can cause twenty-four-hour traffic jams, and almost all the coastal cities are backed by cliffs making transportation of goods into and from the interior extremely difficult and costly. Only Argentina, and, to a lesser extent Paraguay and Uruguay, have access to a decent climate with fertile land.

The point here is that torrents of globalist wealth would be sucked up like a giant mudslide in trying to overcome the simple geographic obstacles. Of course, no amount of globalist money or expertise will solve the *political* problems of Latin America or Mexico. This comes down to a simple dictum: They don't have the "Four Pillars of American Exceptionalism." Those are 1) a Christian, mostly Protestant, religious tradition (that featured congregationalism and bottom-up church governance), 2) common law (featuring bottom-up political governance), 3) private property with written titles and deeds, and 4) a free market economy. What at one time was called the "Third World" did not have the first two at all, and often lacked the others.

Without these pillars, the institutions needed to consistently grow will not emerge; lands and titles are not secure; tyrannies develop easily; governments are unstable; and thus the conditions for long-term private investment are missing. These ideas are addressed at length in *A Patriot's History of the United States* and *A Patriot's History of the Modern World* (two volumes). In a nutshell, after independence, the decolonized nations of the African continent especially (but also India) followed statist policies because that was what they had been taught. But because the colonial masters *themselves* either did not operate from the "four pillars" or, like England, did not apply common law to her Dominions, political instability was inevitable. In Africa, more than seventy coups took place in the first thirty years of independence, and "by the 1990s few states preserved even the vestiges of democracy."[24] The infamous Rwandan genocide produced between 400,000 and 700,000 refugees. After *Inyenzi* rebels invaded Rwanda in 1963, when Tutsi exiles launched cross border attacks, Hutu retaliation resulted in gangs killing over 10,000 Tutsis.[25] It took years to restore peace.

Even when dictators managed to install some stability through the iron fist, African economies continued to suffer under top-down authoritarian economic systems, which stood little to no chance of overcoming geographical barriers. Foreign aid poured in, without ever dealing with the most basic problem of the absence of necessary foundations and geography.

How did the globalists attempt to compensate for these obstacles, to overcome essentially geographical setbacks imposed by God Himself? Indeed, how to control those nations who were no longer under colonial authority?

Whether because of guilt or genuine, misguided compassion, Europeans "re-invaded" their former colonies through massive humanitarian offensives. Those aid missions to the developing world "took on a mystical, quasi-religious quality in the West."[26] Natives who had never seen a telephone, an asphalt road, or advanced machinery were suddenly heralded as the wave of the future if only the globalists could funnel enough money to them. When governments couldn't directly siphon enough money from their taxpayers, a "development assistance industry" arose to share the burden, much of it funded by guilt-ridden leftists who were embarrassed by the success of their businesses.[27]

Thus began the most astonishing and massive wealth transfer in human history. By 2006, $2.3 trillion had been shifted to poorer countries with virtually nothing to show for it. A World Bank economist admitted that despite mind-boggling expenditures by the developed countries, foreign aid had not yet managed to get "Twelve-cent medicines to children to prevent half of malaria deaths . . . [or] to get four-dollar bed nets to poor families" to prevent mosquito-borne diseases.[28] One insider, Thomas Dichter, who had spent years in the Dev Biz with various institutions and organizations, "knew of no organization that really accomplished much in the way of sustained alleviation of poverty."[29] Even when analyzing the role of "good" vs. "bad" government, William Easterly, a research economist for the World Bank, when surveying the period 1970–1993 found "no evidence that aid raised growth among countries with good policies, indicating no support for the conclusion that 'aid works in a good policy environment.'"[30] Nor did it matter if the aid was short- or long-term. It still had no positive effect on growth.[31] Even when aspects of some programs succeeded, other components failed. For example, in Africa, de-worming drugs worked, but educating people on worms and their infections failed.[32]

Certainly failure was not for a want of globalist organizations. Harry Truman kicked it off in 1949 with his inaugural address, turned into actual policy in the Act for International Development. It specifically declared that the United States would provide "technical assistance" so people could develop their own resources.[33] That was soon followed by the International Monetary Fund, the US Agency for International Development, the African Development Bank, the American Development Bank, the World Health Organization, the United Nations Children's Fund, the Asian Development Bank and more. Academia joined in with a new term, "the Big Push" to accelerate Walt Rostow's "takeoff" stage. (These areas never seemed to actually take off). And aid increased when growth fell, rewarding incompetence and malfeasance.

There was the 1960 Freedom from Hunger Campaign, followed by the 1960–70 UN Development Decade (which committed itself to increasing economic growth by 5 percent in the decade), then the Declaration on the Human Environment and a second UN Development Decade (to create a "just world order") and, having failed to meet the goal of 5 percent economic growth in the previous decade, laid out an even more ambitious plan (6 percent) for the next decade. That was followed by the Universal Declaration on the Eradication of Hunger and Malnutrition, then the Lima Declaration that sought to *triple* the undeveloped nations' share of world production in twenty-five years (an utterly idiotic goal, and one that ignored the fact that thirty years after independence almost none of them had moved above their 7 percent of world production). But wait! There was more: the International Decade for Women (1976) was joined by the Decade of International Drinking Water and Sanitation (1980). Not one of these declarations, commitments, resolutions, or grand statements achieved their objective.

Official government aid and international organizations' efforts were joined by armies of new paternalistic non-governmental organizations (NGOs) that colloquially referred to themselves as the Dev Biz. Often the size of medieval armies and as thick as ants, more than 430 NGOs swarmed over the undeveloped world, from World Vision to CARE and Save the Children; from Amnesty International to Oxfam and Action Aid; from Samaritan's Purse to Catholic Relief Services. All of these were interlaced with Doctors Without Borders, Zero Population Growth, and even traditional outfits such as the International Red Cross. They were applauded and encouraged by the International Center for Maize and Wheat Improvement, the Ford Foundation, the Rockefeller Foundation, Columbia University's School of International and Public Affairs, the Woodrow Wilson School at Princeton, and the Kennedy School at Harvard. And as if that weren't enough busybodies, in rolled the entertainers, singers, and entrepreneurs such as Bono, Bob Geldof, and Tom's Shoes founder Blake Mycoskie.

By 1997, the World Bank alone had a staff of 5,500 eating up annual expenditures of $810 billion, or more than half the budget of Chad. And that did not include four thousand part-time consultants. Many NGOs had three thousand or more staff in twenty or more countries. As Thomas Dichter, who worked in these NGOs noted, as of 2003 "a conservative global estimate would be [there were] roughly half a million people whose livelihood depend[ed] on the [Dev Biz] industry."[34]

Without realizing they were confirming the claims of the imperialists and colonialists a century earlier, many in the Dev Biz concluded that some African countries would need foreign assistance in perpetuity. The 2016 documentary *Poverty, INC.* dove into the malignant effects of aid in Haiti, for example. After the Haitian earthquake there was indeed a need for emergency food, clothes, and machinery. But years later, the US still delivered massive shipments of rice to Haiti—long after the emergency—which changed Haitians' very diets from eating rice two times a week to eating rice three times a day. Moreover, Haitian rice farmers were driven out of business, unable to compete with cheaper subsidized rice shipments. To westerners, it seemed logical to get Haitians out of rice growing and into city industrial work, but this led to massive slums and shanty towns constructed on the very mountains that collapsed during the earthquake. Even former President Bill Clinton, asked about the aid to Haiti, willingly admitted he had made a mistake, that their entire policy was wrong, and that it did more harm than good.[35] Likewise, Tom's Shoes, far from ensuring local residents had a regular supply of shoes, drove native shoemakers out of business and guaranteed that Tom's would have to come back again . . . and again.

As Dave Dougherty and I wrote in *A Patriot's History of the Modern World*, vol. 2, "When the verdict on foreign aid finally started to become obvious, namely that it was failing to show any meaningful improvement in development, the advocates of the Dev Biz started to act like adherents of a religion being debunked."[36] The reasons for perpetual poverty not only now included geography—which was unchangeable outside of titanic effort and capital—but now aid itself.

There were other fundamental reasons for Third World poverty that the globalists ignored. And they ignored them precisely because the roots of these weaknesses went directly to the absence of western concepts, even to specifically the absence of the "Four Pillars of American Exceptionalism."

Peruvian economist Hernando de Soto had studied why poorer nations seemed unable to climb out of poverty. Again, for the moment completely ignoring the realities of geography, de Soto found that the culprit was an absence of titles and deeds with private property. For example, in Egypt it took between 6–14 years and 150 administrative steps to secure title deed to desert land.[37] (By contrast, in 2016 when I retired from my university in Ohio, we purchased a home in Arizona and sold our home in Ohio. It took two steps—one for the purchase, one for the sale—and about two to three total hours.) In Mozambique it took 153 days to comply with regulations to start a new business, contrasted to only two days in Canada, and it cost 126 percent of the value of a debt to collect on a contract in Indonesia vs. a mere 5.4 percent in South Korea. Japan's bankruptcy laws yielded nearly 90 percent of the debt under collection, while India's came to only 13 percent.[38] Thus, lacking a Protestant religious tradition, common law, and (for the most part) private property with written titles and deeds, poorer societies were doomed no matter how much aid poured in.

Merely establishing a title deed system is a problem, as William Easterly pointed out: "Would the government give the titles to the *weg Iowo* [patron] or to the *jodak* [client]?"[39] Here was the point: even if under the best of circumstances various specific regulatory changes improved business, the underlying conceptual frameworks were still deeply flawed. It was akin to building state-of-the-art electronics facilities on top of a 1950s television station. A consistent, constitutional, freedom-based, bottom up foundation was entirely missing.

But modern globalist aid did not operate under "the best of circumstances." Quite the contrary, while occasionally genuine Christian charity might be involved (i.e., Samaritan's Purse), just as often foreign development occurred under a radioactive cloud of self-loathing, guilt, and Marxist-redefined history. Most of those involved in the Dev Biz believed that the Third World was poor solely because of the colonial exchange, and without whites, the deepest parts of the Congo would resemble Wakanda and the Peruvian Andes would look like Xanadu. The guilt went deep, to the point of "imputing guilt merely for *being* European or American."[40]

Activists began heaving the new guilt baggage on the US foreign policy train in earnest after JFK's assassination in 1963, when American liberals took a sharp leftward turn. They began to "argue that the purpose of national policy was more to punish the nation for its sins than to build a brighter and more secure future for all."[41] Kennedy, of course, had already taken a bite of the guilt apple by creating the "Peace Corps," an outfit that presumed that college-educated American youths, who did not even know the languages of the region they served in, could greatly improve the life of natives simply by, well, being American and being there.

Kennedy hitched his African star to selected strategic nations, instructing Peace Corps director Sargent Shriver to direct American assistance to Ghana, Nigeria, Tanzania, then later Guinea and Cameroon. Historians have described the Peace Corps, formed only two weeks after JFK took office, as a "bold experiment," "an example of American idealism," or as "making a difference."[42] Of course, at the time there were already thirty-three thousand American missionaries serving in Africa—but they didn't count because they weren't from the government. Proponents soon urged the volunteers to approach their tasks with the "zeal of hardy missionaries."[43] When the Peace Corps bill was introduced through Senator Hubert Humphrey, it had the objective of spreading agricultural and industrial techniques, expanding literacy, teaching the English language, and improving sanitation and health procedures. In reality, it "promulgated the delusion that 'several hundred twenty-two-year-old liberal arts graduates, with no experience or particular skills, sent abroad for two years, could make a difference in a country's development.'"[44] Years later even Robert Kennedy admitted, "we thought we were succeeding because of all the stories of how hard everybody was working."[45] Skill sets, such as they were, did not match up with needs on the ground. In Cameroon, few of the trainees knew anything about the country; 85 percent of the volunteers were assigned to teach music, despite never having had a music course in college. New arrivals were sent to teach Cameroon history, knowing nothing about it. Nor did they have a basic understanding of vegetation, terrain, or other local conditions. A skeptical Jawaharlal Nehru warned not to be "too disappointed if the Punjab, when the [Peace Corps leave] is more or less the same as before they came."[46]

But come they did: as soon as Sargent Shriver put out word that he wanted graduates from college campuses, his phone lines lit up and operators struggled to handle the thousands of calls. When they showed up, they were nearly all white. Only 3 percent of the Peace Corps volunteers were black. Instead, prosperous whites made up the majority of volunteers (as they have for the reform movements throughout American history). As the Peace Corps became more feminized, that in itself constituted a problem in Islamic countries, which did not tolerate single, unchaperoned girls in the public sphere. In one regard, however, the Peace Corps did produce a paradigm shift in that the volunteers worked directly with the people, not with a government. This became the model for the Dev Biz. To Kennedy, the Peace Corps was spreading American culture—precisely the wrong product to be sharing according to the more radical views just a decade later. Many joined to avoid the draft. Few were cut out for hard physical labor.

Whether the Peace Corps, Tom's Shoes, or the hundreds of philanthropic entities determined to impose on the underdeveloped world their own sense of culture, the handicaps imposed by the Dev Biz at the bottom were equaled, if not surpassed, by the buckets of money being dumped on the Third World—all of it coming with strings.

When the World Bank—another creation of John Maynard Keynes—was founded in 1944, the US Congress intended it to raise money through the sale of its bonds, then to "make long-term, low-interest loans to governments for specific development projects."[47] Here was the globalist dream machine, an international money institution supposedly outside the influence of a single nation and run by multi-lateral decision making. US Treasury Secretary Henry Morganthau argued that initial loans from the Bank would encourage private capital to follow. Two factors stood out. First, since the US was the only nation capable of putting in large amounts of capital for the start-up, America would for all intents and purposes control the Bank. Second, because loans went to clearly defined projects through governments rather than individuals, the likelihood that the funds would seldom see their intended purposes was high. Moreover, on a grand scale the Bank would solve the postwar globalists' dilemma of reconstituting international trade while protecting countries from being on the losing end of that trade. In other words, it operated with what political scientist John Ruggie called "embedded liberalism."[48]

In the short term, the Bank's managers were divided on how to make their loans. This so concerned the US that most real development money flowed through the European Recovery Program (1947). As more truly undeveloped nations begged for money, the World Bank focused on development as defined as building dams, power plants, ports, and highways—pretty much the same as Britain did in her colonies.

On April Fool's Day, 1968, Robert McNamara—chief architect of the Vietnam War—assumed the presidency of the World Bank. He took control at a time when US foreign aid commitments were declining. Committed to diversifying the Bank's funding sources, he persuaded the West German banks to increase their commitments, then got the Japanese to do likewise. At the same time he drastically increased lending to poorer countries, from $847 million in 1968 to $8.8 billion in 1981.[49] With the mission statement, "Our Dream is a World Free of Poverty," the World Bank sought to increase the real standard of living in poorer nations by eliminating the "strangleholds on development."[50] For the first time, the Bank began to use phrases such as "structural unemployment" and "urban decay." McNamara promised Senegalese officials he could create a productive machine that could "banish hunger" and "abolish poverty from the earth by the year 2000."[51]

But there was already a problem brewing. In many nations GDP had improved, but the conditions of ordinary people had not. This caused many true believers to question the very meaning of development itself: in 1970, the head of the International Labour Organization called for the "dethronement of GNP."[52] Nor should it be surprising that McNamara bought into the "population bomb" theory and directed the World Bank to population control efforts, claiming in his first address to the Bank that "rapid growth of population is one of the greatest barriers to economic growth and social well being of our member states."[53] No sooner had the ink dried on drafts of his speech than the population movement flopped when birth rates began declining. (As we will later see, this hasn't stopped some of the more recent globalist panic-mongers from insisting that the earth could easily lose a third or more of its population without any negative effect.)

As was typical of so many elites who care about humanity, but really don't like humans, McNamara could remain "remarkably indifferent to the plight of those in need," as when the UN High Commissioner for Refugees asked for help in providing a water supply for a Sudanese refugee camp. McNamara declined, not finding it a proper development project.[54] The Green Revolution, he fretted, wasn't getting to the right peasants.

Ultimately, though, McNamara sided with growth over reducing poverty. His policies maintained traditional postwar bank orthodoxy of limiting inflation, reducing deficits, and supporting free trade. To that end he wielded both subtle and direct threats against foreign leaders who in his view were not comporting themselves with sufficient fiscal propriety. Predictably, this upset radicals who criticized the Bank for pressuring developing countries to liberalize their economies. (Because, after all it was reasoned, socialist and agrarian models had worked so well.)

Starting in 1975, capital flows to developing nations skyrocketed, fulfilling one of McNamara's goals. This, in turn, caused a problem for the World Bank: developing countries didn't need it nearly as much. Moreover, the 1970s oil crisis had shown the Bank to be impotent in some areas. Thus, non-financial functions—technical assistance and expertise from the elites—took on an even greater role in the Bank. It increasingly operated as a "co-financier," partnering with private capital investors. (From 1973 to 1980 the number of co-financed projects more than doubled.)

Conflict with US government policies also came to the fore. In 1970, Chile elected Salvador Allende, viewed by the administration of Richard Nixon as a threat to US interests. Allende nationalized industries and engaged in land reforms, but his socialist disruptions to the economy naturally put in jeopardy the nation's significant external debt, much of it owed to the World Bank. Nixon pressured the Bank to refuse to negotiate the repayment. When relations nearly broke down in 1972, the Bank folded and went forward with new loans. Not only did the Bank make an enemy of many Latin Americans, but the American people now questioned the organization. Congress saw it tied up in the overall foreign aid packages.

Critics weren't wrong. Increasingly it was discovered that "project" lending ended up in the hands of political parties or corrupt rulers through front companies. One such instance involved the perpetually troubled Rwanda; another involved a Nigerian project that forced peasants off their land. Most troubling were the land clearing and population relocating efforts, which appeared "successful" in the short run because production increased. A look at the Bank's lending produced troubling signs. For example, in in 1989 the organization reviewed some 82 agricultural projects approved in McNamara's tenure and found the almost 45 percent achieved an "unsatisfactory" rate of return. Production often decreased.[55] The Bank's urban initiatives actually increased inequality by increasing the value of the land and pricing poor families out of their homes. Projects that were evaluated later showed a rate of return about one-third less than estimated—"a depressing picture."[56] And all the while the external debt of developing nations rose over fivefold. After decades of failure, the Reagan administration pushed the Bank to start encouraging developing countries to get government out of their economics. By then, a great deal of damage had been done.

By the 1990s, there emerged the "Washington Consensus," which included commitment to fiscal discipline, reduction (if only slightly) of public expenditures, market-determined interest rates, liberalization of trade, and foreign investment. Once again, however, Triffin's Dilemma raised its ugly head, because to achieve the latter, fiscal discipline and reduction of public expenditures would suffer. If budgets were balanced, foreign aid distribution would suffer. Thus, the Dev Biz in itself became a component of the K Street lobbying network that distorted purely economic goals or incentives with political bribes.

The same was true with the activities of the International Monetary Fund and World Bank: nations needing money took loans; those loans came with strings. Unlike the Dev Biz that worked through NGOs and often at a local level, the IMF loaned money only to nations. Whereas the "recolonialization" via the Dev Biz sought to influence communities and localities, the World Bank and IMF wanted to force policy changes at the national level. Through "financial programming" and "conditionality," the money organizations exacted government policies that they wanted.

For example, one of the biggest "conditionality" interventions came with the debt crisis of the 1980s, where Ronald Reagan's Treasury Secretary, James Baker, introduced the "Baker Plan" for bailouts. Addressing some fifteen middle income Third World countries whose total debt came to $437 billion—again, debt to the IMF or World Bank, not specifically to the US—carrying an interest rate of 10 percent, Baker called for new loans amounting to $29 billion. The catch was this time the money would come from commercial banks, with the IMF and World Bank supplying any balance. But to obtain a Baker Plan loan, nations had to agree to "structural changes" that, in theory, would allow them to grow sufficiently to repay the debt. Those changes included such common-sense policies as lower taxes, privatization of state-owned businesses, and lowering trade barriers. This in turn permitted more globalization by allowing in foreign investors. At least, that was the plan.[57]

Commercial banks balked at handing over so much cash without more of a guarantee, and ultimately the loans from private banks and the IMF were almost equal. Growth never occurred, and the Baker Plan was deemed a failure. Interest rates for the undeveloped nations rose further. It dawned on everyone that the debts would never be repaid, resulting in the United States attempting to write off the loans as a necessary cost of retaining friendly governments. In the case of Mexico, the labyrinthine arrangements involved a menu from some five hundred banks that in various ways would reduce Mexico's debt by 35 percent. Essentially, the bankers agreed to an exchange in which they would reduce the debt in return for a guarantee that Mexico would repay the balance.[58] Under a broad new agreement by President George H. W. Bush's Treasury Secretary, Nicholas Brady, eighteen countries agreed to deals that forgave $60 billion in debt, or roughly 35 percent reduction per country.

That lasted until 1998, when a new wave of financial collapses beginning with Argentina demanded new IMF bailout money. In a statement that angered the Argentinians, but which represented the attitude of a large swath of Americans, President Bill Clinton's Treasury Secretary Paul O'Neill said "we're working to find a way to create a sustainable Argentina, not just one that continues to consume the money of the plumbers and carpenters in the United States who make $50,000 a year and wonder what in the world we're doing with our money."[59]

It would likely not shock any reader of this work to know that a) Argentina got the bailout, and b) Argentina failed to attain IMF growth projections. An independent but liberal think tank, the Center for Economic and Policy Research, found that the IMF growth projections were consistently wrong, and that the errors "were politically driven."[60]

Other assessments were equally unkind: a Heritage Foundation report in 1999 showed that of the 48 out of 89 countries that received IMF money between 1965 and 1995 had shown no economic improvement and of those 48, some two thirds were worse off.[61] A similar conclusion came from the United Nations Conference on Trade and Development: average real GDP per capita declined by an average of 1.4 percent before IMF aid, stagnated the three years after aid was begun, then declined 1.1 percent thereafter.[62] Leftists such as Richard Peet want to blame the capitalist ideology, particularly the "Chicago School" of development. But the failure of the IMF rested on more than the notion that money was a form of influence. Rather, none of the Third World states had the fundamental "Pillars" for success, regardless of how much money the IMF threw at them. Put another way that leftists would hate—they didn't have the right kind of influence coming with the money.

At heart was a question: was it better the states remained poor, or that they developed under the influence, or even control of, outside organizations? It was the devil's bargain every single entrepreneur faces when he needs capital. With money comes control. If you don't want control, don't take the silver. That didn't satisfy many borrowers, as protests broke out in Egypt (1977), Morocco (1981), Dominica (1984), Nigeria (1988), Venezuela (perpetually, but especially in 1989), and Indonesia (1998). Riots erupted when governments attempted to restrain domestic spending to pay down the debt—something every working family is familiar with—and while some protesters wanted to reject the money, most were complaining because they could not have both IMF loans and spend them any way they wanted.

In most cases, even if a ruler *had* wished to comply with austerity measures, the daunting double realities of geography and the absence of the "Pillars" of a tradition of private property and common law short-circuited their attempts. As with all the other globalist institutions, the IMF, World Bank, and others started to decline in influence in the late 1990s beginning with the East Asian crisis in 1997. That contagion soon spread to Brazil and Russia, wherein the countries had accumulated enough foreign reserves themselves they could resist IMF pressure. In 2003, Argentina told the IMF to pound sand and even recovered on its own. Communist countries already hated the IMF and World Bank

(Venezuela's Hugo Chavez called them "tools of empire"—does that phrase ring a bell?).[63] That really left only some of the poorer African countries as the remaining clients of the financial organizations.

In place of those global giants, regional lenders were created, such as the Bank of the South (2007) among Argentina, Venezuela, Bolivia, Ecuador, Paraguay, and Brazil. By that time the IMF had redirected most of its funding (and strings) so that its overall lending shrank.

The World Bank acted similarly, as a predominantly development agency oriented toward nations that were not "credit worthy." It was to assist in both the reconstruction and development of countries or economies disrupted by war or to develop productive facilities.[64] The World Bank also promoted private investment by partnering, and sought to promote international trade. (As we will have seen, the last item has become increasingly problematic in a post–Bretton Woods world.) Headquartered in Washington, DC, the Bank was an American creation.

Naturally there was suspicion that the sudden interest by the US, and the west in general, toward the huddled masses of the Third World was driven by more than compassion. Cold War alliances with the developing world were critical. McNamara's role in the Bank has already been discussed. After McNamara left—with few of the countries any better off—the World Bank shifted its emphasis toward the "social and cultural dimensions of poverty," which is to say the absence of true market structures. However, the fox in the henhouse was that economic growth could not result in too much inequality, which was precisely what capitalism in its infancy generated as some people master businesses, services, or products while others fail. As George Gilder and Thomas Sowell have pointed out repeatedly, in a burgeoning capitalist system high inequality in the early stages is a benchmark of success. Indeed, such was the Bank's *own research* in 2002.[65] The same author, however, later came to criticize unfettered global capitalism's impact on developing countries.[66]

Naturally the Bank came under attack from leftists for imposing the "Washington Consensus" on clients under the overall rubric of "paradigm maintenance." In a sense it reflected the same self-reinforcing biases found in the Marxist universities, namely that the Bank would incentivize research that supported the "Washington Consensus" that the Bank knew what was best for developing countries. Put another way, the Bank's own internal research praised the Bank's approach.

To address serious economic growth in most geographically-challenged Third World countries, which is to say, almost all of them, such things as highways needed to be constructed through jungles or forests, prompting the environmentalists to scream "eco-disaster." Such was the case with the highway to be built through the Amazon in Brazil. Subsequently, the Bank held up construction of a dam for environmental reasons. People stayed poor, but ecologically pure (which is to say, suffering from disease and absence of electricity that a dam could bring). An even greater battle ensued over a dam in the Narmada Valley in India, which displaced forty thousand with flooding. After enough pressure from activists, the Bank pulled out of the project, but India announced it would continue on its own. So was a national government coming to a conclusion about its own economic future without globalist forces acceptable to the activists? No. They engaged in hunger strikes and protests. The dam was completed in 2017.

The final block of the globalist financial construction was the World Trade Organization (WTO) emanating from the Geneva Conference on Tariffs and Trade (GATT) in the 1940s that then resulted in several rounds of trade negotiations. During the Uruguay Round, which lasted from 1986 to 1994, participants established the World Trade Organization to oversee commitment to the agreements.

There can be little doubt that on one level, the WTO and the US military brought about a half-century of general peace to the globe. Marring this harmony were wars fought primarily by the US or its allies against communism (Vietnam) and Islamic terrorist states (Libya, Iraq, Afghanistan), with an occasional squabble over old-fashioned territory (the Falklands). A miniature war between Serbia and her neighbors was squelched in the 1990s, but not until many Muslims in Kosovo had already been killed by the Serbs. For the most part, though, everyone "played nice," driven by the allure of money.

It wasn't until Americans woke up to the fact that they were not only footing the financial bills, but the butcher's bills as well, that resistance began to take shape. Those factors, combined with financial crises in the early 2000s, the continued unraveling of Bretton Woods, unsupportable US defense spending, and the birth dearth all but ended the globalist financial structure's influence. And how did this affect the United States's economy? Seventy years after the Bretton Woods agreement, the US still only received 11 percent of its GDP from exports, receiving most of its economic dynamism from its $11 trillion domestic base.

Instead, the chief disruptor on the US side of Bretton Woods has been inflation. Beginning in the 1960s, Triffin's Dilemma raised its ugly head and, apart from a twenty-year lull after Ronald Reagan and Paul Volcker managed to squash inflation, followed by Bill Clinton largely copying their policies, inflation remained somewhat tame.[67] Instead, a series of non-Bretton Woods-related policies in the American housing market brought on the sub-prime collapse of 2007–2008.[68] America's subprime mortgage crisis, of course, had worldwide implications, suggesting the old saying, "If General Motors sneezes, America catches a cold." In this case, when the US financial markets sneeze, the world can catch pneumonia.

With the banking-mortgage catastrophe came the predictable bailouts, and with the skyrocketing spending—only exacerbated by Barack Obama and Congress thereafter—inflation ramped up. When Covid-19 arrived, more bailout money injected the money supply with steroids. None of this stopped foreign aid under Bretton Woods, but it did considerably cheapen the money across the entire world structure.

Deficits and debt soared everywhere, threatening to break the United Kingdom's entire financial foundation. China experienced major real estate debt problems that are only just beginning. And as of this writing, neither the Federal Reserve in the US, nor Congress, nor the finance ministers in any foreign nations have managed to defeat inflation. (A few managed to control it.)

Financial globalism was doomed from the start by Triffin's Dilemma, but the inconsistencies of aid from organizations such as the World Bank and the International Monetary Fund and the inherent contradictions they bring added to the ultimate failure. Economic growth cannot be imposed from the outside, and the western concepts of capitalism and freedom, in the end, mean that peoples and nations must be free to fail. And so they have. The looming birth dearth in the world, combined with America's withdrawal as world policeman means that many will not only face decline, but outright de-civilization.

That de-civilization seemed to arrive more rapidly than anyone thought with a new virus that arrived out of a lab in China. Neither kings nor armies nor diplomats nor scientists nor bankers had managed to install global control of governments. Could doctors achieve what all the others didn't?

Chapter Six

Medical Globalism—Covid, Vaccines, and Lockdowns

No disease in recent memory, not even AIDS, affected the world, let alone America, as did the coronavirus of 2019. Also referred to as Covid-19 or even the China Virus, the disease became truly the first human disease deliberately misreported, misunderstood, and worst of all, mis-treated in history. For the first time, medical authorities around the world refused to critically investigate, challenge, question, or even temper official statements emanating from the World Health Organization. Health authorities worldwide quickly, and hysterically, fell in line.[1]

Whether this extremism, uniformity, and often callous disregard for common medical practices, treatment protocols, or verification came at "global" direction is, as of this date, still unclear. What is clear is that *if* there was a "conspiracy" by international elites to use a disease in an attempt to subjugate all mankind, it couldn't have been more effective. That the measures came within a hair of working as globalists would have wanted—had they indeed been in "control"—is terrifying. At the same time, it is somewhat reassuring. In the end, they took their best shot (no pun intended) and failed. Their failure was so spectacular and obvious that they likely destroyed any second chance they ever had with this particular power-grab again.

Its damage, however, was permanent and significant, harming society well beyond the number of lives it took. As Scott Atlas, one of the few in the medical team of President Donald Trump who questioned, then opposed many of the official protocols forcefully foisted on the American public, said, "the pandemic exposed grave problems with the essential functioning of science, research and debate . . . foster[ing] a climate of fear [that] inhibited other scientists and health experts from contributing to the discussion, effectively inducing self-censorship."[2]

At the most narrow of levels, the virus played a particular role in removing one of the biggest thorns in the side of international elites who ever existed. Reporter Mollie Hemmingway noted that the Covid-19 pandemic (and I shall routinely use the alternate term "China Virus" simply for variation) was "so perfectly suited to damaging President Trump's re-election that it almost seemed designed in a laboratory."[3] Evidence indeed says it was, contrary to the squeals of the media, which slowly began its retractions denigrating the idea.[4]

Even at the time of this writing, three years later, no one seems able to confirm with certainty what most suspect: the virus was created in a Chinese lab in Wuhan. From there, debate continues on whether it was accidentally or deliberately released. Congressional hearings have concluded that it was almost certain the disease itself originated in the Wuhan laboratory that received funding from Dr. Anthony Fauci and the National Institute of Allergy and infectious Diseases (NIAID).[5] Dr. Robert Redfield, the former director of the Centers for Disease Control and Prevention (CDC) said science indicated that the China Virus infections were likely the result of an accidental lab leak. Other witnesses to Congress, including Nicholas Wade, the former editor of *Science*, testified that Dr. Anthony Fauci and Dr. Francis Collins used unverified data to dismiss the initial lab leak theory.[6] The media often continued to deny the lab-leak theory, but a majority of Americans had already passed them by and accepted it.[7] Recent congressional testimony confirmed that Fauci and his cadre of associates lied and hid or deleted records related to the origins of the China Virus.[8] Researchers who tried to discredit the lab-leak evidence received more cash to study viruses.[9] And even today, Wikipedia attempts to discredit the lab leak thesis, and still pushes the "bat origins" from Wuhan "wet markets."[10] This was the first big lie.

The London *Sunday Times* went further than the theory that the China Virus was just developed in a lab. It revealed that the China Virus was developed by the "military" at the Wuhan lab.[11] "Investigators who scrutinized top-secret intercepted communications and scientific research believe Chinese scientists were running a covert project of dangerous experiments, which caused a leak from the Wuhan Institute of Virology . . ."[12]

Many pandemics, flus, and health disasters have swept through the United States (and indeed, the world) on occasions too numerous to count. Europeans, of course, point to the Black Death or Bubonic Plague as the primary medical disaster of the last thousand years. In America, the Spanish Flu epidemic of 1918–1919, AIDS in the 1980s, and the Avian flu outbreaks (2014–2015), plus the Ebola outbreak in Africa and the SARS epidemic in China that threatened to reach the US all constituted serious medical emergencies. The Spanish Flu worldwide killed fifty million, including 675,000 Americans; AIDS killed about 100,000 in the 1980s. While the numbers on the China Virus are unreliable, given the relative size of the US population in 1918 and 2023, Covid has killed only about half the number taken by the Spanish Flu epidemic. And the nation never locked down, isolated, or masked the general public in any earlier epidemic.

Few took notice, then, in December of 2019 when an outbreak of a pneumonia-like illness occurred in China's Hubei Province around the town of Wuhan. Two weeks later, the World Health Organization's country office in China was alerted. Like all the other "world" organizations, the World Health Organization (WHO) originated with the United Nations in 1948 and headquartered in Geneva, Switzerland. Its official mandate was to promote health and safety worldwide, providing technical assistance, collecting data, and serving as a forum for scientific and policy discussions that pertained to health.[13] It all sounded so innocuous, even benign. Over the years, the WHO claimed to have successfully eradicated smallpox and polio, as well as developed a vaccine for Ebola.[14] Governed by the World Health Assembly, a group of almost two hundred member states who elect thirty-four health specialists and approve budgets and funding, the WHO started a mass tuberculosis inoculation program as early as 1950, and launched a malaria control effort five years later.

For our purposes, the focus will remain more on what happened than on whether the successes claimed by the WHO (or virtually any medical community) were as legitimate as seemed. For example, Forest Maready argued in *The Moth in the Iron Lung: A Biography of Polio*, that polio stemmed from pesticides—particularly DDT—and with the elimination of those toxins polio rates were already dramatically falling before the polio vaccine was introduced.[15] Robert F. Kennedy, Jr. in *The Real Anthony Fauci*, makes nearly irrefutable claims that previous vaccine and treatment programs, including AZT for AIDS and Dengvaxia for Dengue, not only failed to stop diseases but actively agitated them or themselves were deadly. For example, in the Philippines, one place where the government actually conducted tests on the vaccines themselves, after application of Dengvaxia, autopsies performed on six hundred children led to indictments of fourteen government and pharmaceutical officials for homicide.[16] Ex-UN official and BBC correspondent Edward Hooper made a solid case for the source of HIV/AIDS as emanating from the batches of the Oral Polio Vaccine that came out of the Belgian Congo.[17]

Medical globalism had been under way for seventy years before Covid. But the China Virus provided the perfect tool for international bodies to attempt worldwide control based on a medical emergency for the first time. Three elements for this globalist control were necessary: First, the threat had to not only be real, but be so dramatically horrible that immediate, drastic action was demanded by the public. Second, the disease needed certain characteristics, namely ease of transmission, that enabled authorities to employ isolation and control at levels that were previously never attempted. And third, the threat required a solution that could only be provided by governments or international organizations (which is to say "natural immunity" had to be ruled out).

Establishing the China Virus as a horrific disease equivalent to the Black Plague involved far more than a few health officials chattering in front of cameras. Rather, it entailed the corruption of the *world's* news media and virtually all medical professionals. When the first pictures out of Wuhan descended on the world outside China, people recoiled at video of citizens being welded inside their houses and apartments, of teams in hazmat suits spraying chemicals and gas in the streets, and of bodies in the open. Indeed, the Chinese government locked down entire cities.[18] The Wuhan images seemed like something out of Chernobyl.

Information on the origins and early transmission of the China Virus remain completely unreliable because of the questionable reporting by the Chinese communist government. It is generally accepted that whether the lab-leak was deliberate or accidental, the Chinese government engaged in a coverup of deaths and the immediate scope of transmission. The information that did surface suggested the virus spread fast, with the number of cases doubling in a week, and on January 20, China reported cases in Beijing and Shenzhen.[19] Wuhan's position as a major transport and shipping hub enhanced the transmission of the virus.

As the spread of the virus gained momentum, the WHO declared the Covid-19 a public health emergency on January 30 as it spread to Italy, then on to the US. In an environment where panic could be induced easily by the media, the images from Italy were sobering, even "borderline apocalyptic," as Trump's son-in-law Jared Kushner recalled: "patients lined hallways and field hospitals as overwhelmed doctors triaged the sick and were forced to make life-or-death decision about who would receive care."[20]

Those images were quickly reinforced by purely hoaxified statistics from Neil Ferguson, a British epidemiologist who predicted that 510,000 would die in Great Britain and up to 2.2 *million* in the US.[21]

The number in the US, after three years, was half that.[22] Later, in fact, other research showed the "Failure of [the] Imperial College Modeling is far worse than we knew."[23] Others, including Fauci, latched on to the number, with some even expanding it to forty million deaths if "unchecked."[24] Fauci unhesitatingly and uncritically passed along those alarming projections to President Donald Trump.

This constituted the second big lie. The China Virus numbers were horrifically inflated because, as Dr. Scott Atlas noted, "The reported fatality rates were based only on patients who were sick enough to seek medical care *rather than on the undoubtedly much larger population of infected individuals*" (my emphasis).[25] Put another way, infected people who weren't really sick (as in showed few debilitating symptoms—who treated Covid like a common cold or mild flu) weren't counted. By the millions. That led to a massively inflated fatality rate being reported.

As these numbers circulated, professionals such as Atlas "presumed that every serious academic researcher understood the role and limitations of such models," but they quickly found their presumptions were wrong.[26] Few bothered to point out to the president that Ferguson was wrong more often than economist Paul Krugman or cable snake-oil salesman Jim Kramer, so much so that he was ridiculed as the "Master of Disaster." (Only after he had propagated disastrous lockdowns did the British government force him to resign.)[27] Robert Kennedy, Jr., who had battled Fauci over significant (some would say criminal) errors in his role in the AIDS crisis, pointed out that Fauci had his own motivations for accepting the higher number.[28] Among other things, Kennedy revealed that Fauci had significant holdings in vaccine patents, a conflict-of-interest story that would resurface constantly in the research for a vaccine and against re-purposed or therapeutic drugs such as hydroxychloroquine or ivermectin.

To Americans, Fauci was a beloved symbol of their hope in medical technology. At one point he was labeled "America's Doctor," and his approval stood at 80 percent.[29] That was in stark contrast to Trump's approval rating, which hovered in the mid-40s, meaning that in any head-to-head conflicts with Fauci, Trump would lose. Even as Fauci labeled Trump "anti-science" and claimed that "attacks on me . . . are attacks on science," Trump had the exact right policy prescriptions.[30] Trump thought masks should only be used, if at all, in close proximity indoors; wanted to reopen schools; stressed protecting those at high-risk while opening businesses and allowing the healthy to work.[31] Indeed, as the Brownstone Institute later concluded, the CDC's policy decisions "knowingly reduced the accuracy of collected data in a way that would serve their political purposes [particularly by] stopp[ing] distinguishing between dying of COVID and dying with COVID," incentivizing deaths as caused *by* the China Virus, whether they were or not.[32] With the media on Fauci's side, Trump was continually under assault. Soon that would translate into pressure for a national quarantine.

Italy, one of the worst hit European countries, became the first nation in the world to impose a national lockdown or quarantine on March 8, 2020.[33] It restricted people from moving around except for necessity—work or health circumstances—and closed numerous shops and businesses, constituting a massive suppression of human rights. On the other hand, Sweden, which had its first cases of the virus in January, did not quarantine but prohibited gatherings of over fifty people.[34] As of September 30, 2021, the death rate from the China Virus under Fauci in the United States was 2,107 per one million; in Sweden, Iran, Germany, only half that. In African countries that already permitted the use of hydroxychloroquine (HCQ) for malaria, as low as 0.86 (Tanzania).[35]

If the globalists at the WHO had provided the dynamite for a panic that would enable radical and highly unethical measures, all that was needed next was a compliant, largely ignorant, and unquestioning media. Whether it was a "controlled" media seems all the more likely in light of the behavior of so-called journalists and media sites over the next year. A National Bureau of Economic Research study later showed that not only were the majority of worldwide stories about the China Virus negative (54 percent) even when discussing positive treatment or cures, but American journalism was *overwhelmingly negative* (91 percent).[36]

As two researchers who studied journalism covering the China Virus, Michael Horning and Jim Kuypers, noted, journalists "have historically been ill equipped to report on scientific matters because they so often lack the depth of knowledge to ask the right questions about studies [and] reports . . . "[37] The narrative changed almost from day to day—wear masks, don't wear masks, the disease is virulent, the disease is difficult to contract—and in many cases reporting resembled the early days of AIDS when the public believed that HIV transmission could occur through tears or sweat. Fauci himself warned that "the possibility that routine close contact, as within a family household, can spread the disease."[38] Fauci also said that "non-sexual, non-blood-borne transmission [was] possible."[39] Given that journalists had *never* called Fauci to justify his earlier absurd comments, the Fauci-fed narrative that developed on Covid should not be surprising.

President Trump had acted rapidly. On January 29, 2020, he formed the Coronavirus Task Force that included Fauci, Dr. Deborah Birx, Dr. Robert Redfield (Director of the Center for Disease Control), as well as many political department appointees from HHS, NIH, State, and others. (Scott Atlas could not uncover how Birx exactly got appointed to the task force: he said Pence "inherited her.")[40] Most of the outside participants had no medical background; a few doctors, such as Atlas, were invited to join but from the outset, Fauci, Birx, and Redfield dominated all discussions about the pandemic. Those three shared a background of deep bureaucratic history and had spent much of their careers focused on AIDS, which was entirely different from the China Virus in every respect. They were all quite comfortable with big government.

Immediately the task force recognized the most immediate goal was to develop an adequate test for the virus. In the meantime, however, "unprecedented responses from those in power" and others coalesced on a wide variety of non-medical/non-scientifically dictated responses. As Atlas put it, "These recommendations were not just based on panic; they were responsible for generating even more panic."[41]

Trump imposed a travel ban from China in early February, despite severe criticism for being "racist." One thing immediately became clear: to the media, if President Trump said it, or believed it, it had to be wrong, and whatever Fauci said at the time—even when he contradicted himself within weeks as on the value of mask-wearing—had to be right. The National Bureau of Economic Research paper that showed China Virus coverage was overwhelmingly negative later showed that not only was American news *overwhelmingly* negative, but if President Trump was involved it was, if possible, even more so. For example, "Among major US media outlets, stories discussing President Donald Trump and hydroxychloroquine [were] more numerous than *all stories combined that cover companies and individual researcher working on COVID-19 vaccines*" (emphasis mine).[42] Where there was success, the American media saw only death and suffering. Even as China Virus cases were *decreasing* by a factor of 5.5, and new cases declining, all uncertainties were highlighted. But those same outlets never once questioned Fauci's constantly transmuting admonitions, and certainly never gave President Trump credit for the decline. Recall again that Fauci claimed a "bat" origin of Covid, claimed masks worked (after saying they didn't), and ridiculed hydroxychloroquine or ivermectin, which were already proving effective when administered early.

As Atlas put it, "almost all of the public health officials appearing in the media seemed to add to the fear and confusion."[43] Panic, though, was a key element of the globalist plan for using the virus, suggesting still again that the media and the top medical professionals were at least tacitly in compliance. Moreover, he noted that Trump's intuition—when not overridden by his political advisers—was usually correct, not only about HCQ but about testing. "Why are we testing healthy, younger people? Why don't we just test sick people?" he asked Atlas, noting that "if we test more, we find more cases. But those people aren't sick."[44]

Early, the media hewed to two major points, namely that the virus did *not* originate in the Wuhan lab (because that would make China look bad, and Trump had been engaging in a cold war with "Chy-na" as he called it) and that lockdowns, masks, and social distancing measures were beneficial (regardless of the data from Sweden). It did not help that even if journalists understood the science, they seemed incapable of explaining what "two weeks to flatten the curve" really meant. Indeed, before long, it did not even matter to so-called journalists if *Fauci himself* contradicted their template. They had the story they wanted to tell.

Jim Kuypers, a professor of journalism and a historian of the press, has provided an excellent record of media bias from its earliest days in America in his *Partisan Journalism*.[45] A wide range of journalistic standards and practices, including double sourcing with public sources for every major fact, never using an anonymous source, and always telling both sides of the story in the *most positive way they would want their story told* were blended into practices in virtually every American newsroom. When journalism schools began to change in the 1960s, reporting accuracy followed, and as Kuypers showed, there was no single event such as the Vietnam War or John Kennedy's assassination that sent it off the edge; rather journalism started a slow decline in standards during the decade. Just a single example suffices. In the American Society of Newspaper Editor's statement of principles, under the heading "truth and accuracy," the statement read: "Every effort must be made to assure that the news content is accurate, free from bias and in context, and that all sides are presented fairly. Significant errors of fact, as well as errors of omission, should be corrected promptly and prominently." Clearly anyone who lived through the Russia Hoax during President Trump's administration could attest to the utter absence of such a rule. During one call with Atlas, Trump told the doctor, "I'm sure you will teach me many things . . . But there is only one thing you'll learn from me. Only one. You will learn how vicious, how biased, how unfair the media is."[46]

Instead of following the traditions of objective reporting and multiple sourcing, journalists gravitated to the "framing theory," where the reporter began with a slant on a story and then "framed" it accordingly. Framing involves "the presence or absence of certain keywords, stock phrases, stereotyped images, sources of information, and sentences that provide thematically reinforcing clusters of fact or judgments."[47] Journalism schools focused more on telling a story than on gathering or understanding evidence. (A stellar counter-example, a reporter who understood the science of food and obesity so well that he gave up journalism to write books, is Gary Taubes.)[48]

When reporting science (and, when properly done, economics), where conclusions are *always* presented with subtleties, implications, and gray areas, the likelihood of engaging in reportorial bias grows in the extreme. Even President Ronald Reagan once quipped that he wanted to meet a one-armed economist so that he couldn't say, "on the other hand." However, anyone who has read a scientific paper knows that conclusions are carefully buffered by the limitations of sample groups and the need for more research. Virtually all refrain from stating a direct fact, but instead use terms such as "indicates" or "suggests" and contain multiple qualifiers. Liberal journalist Walter Lippmann wrote "where the issue is complex, as for example in the matter of the success of a policy, or the social conditions among a foreign people,—that is to say, where the real answer is neither yes or no, but subtle, and a matter of balanced evidence . . . the report causes no end of derangement, misunderstanding, and even misrepresentation."[49]

Such insidious practices included using silly and utterly unrepresentative terms as "undocumented migrant" instead of "illegal" (or, I would even add, "criminal") alien, "budget cuts" vs. "controlling costs," "anti-abortion" vs. "pro-life," or "single payer healthcare" vs. "taxpayer-funded healthcare." In addition to these tricks, journalists preface subjects or actions which, in their view, are undesirable with metaphors, symbols, images, and labels.

Making the false reporting and "misinformation" (a term picked up to discredit conservatives, when, in fact, research shows it applied more to liberal reporters) worse, reporters who were almost always liberal/Democrats already had biases. For example, the Brookings Institution—hardly a conservative source—asked respondents to estimate the share of deaths from the China Virus for people under twenty-four. Democrats were more likely to overstate the risks. An interesting thing occurred, however: in its own study, Brookings asked if the death rate from Covid was worse than "influenza" and ridiculed President Trump for saying so, despite no evidence in the article to that effect. Again, democrats were more likely to agree. In fact they were correct, but it had to do with context and framing.

Or consider the use of the term "flu": it had both a current and historical context. Many knew that the Spanish Flu of 1918–19 *killed more than Covid* at the time of the Brookings study.[50] In fact, as of the time of the Brookings study (December 2020), almost *twice* as many Americans had died of the Spanish Flu as from the China Virus![51] Keep in mind that we now know that many deaths attributed to Covid actually were caused by other "co-morbidities," but that the CDC overstated deaths by 72,000 through a "coding error," its euphemism for ignoring co-morbidities.[52] Then the CDC revised the deaths of children by Covid by 24 percent because an "algorithm was accidentally counting deaths that were not Covid-19 related."[53] Further study showed that the CDC removed between 40–75 cancer deaths *per week* from the record and concealed them as China Virus deaths.[54] Yet another investigation strongly suggested that *any* unvaccinated person who died of any disease was categorized as a Covid death.[55] By January 2023, sources from the *Washington Post* to the *Wall Street Journal* noted "overreporting" of deaths by the CDC and "the vicious circle of Covid Boondoggles and Bad Data."[56]

Perhaps the greatest, most damaging, and pernicious of all the failures (deliberate actions?) of the world's public health agencies was the conflation of a positive China Virus *test* with causation of death. As Dr. John Ioannidis wrote in a March 2020 article called "A Fiasco in the Making?" in which he noted "a positive test for coronavirus does not mean necessarily that this virus is always primarily responsible for a patient's demise. . . ."[57] He showed that strokes, heart attacks, bleeding, trauma, or other actors might actually be "cause" of death, but once the CDC attached the Covid designation to any patient, a mortality was immediately blamed on the virus.

Among other major flaws the Fauci/Deborah Birx approach to the pandemic was an "absurd fixation" on the number of China Virus *cases* reported vs. the number of *fatalities* from an Covid infection.[58] Ioannidis, for example, did an early serology study that found that infections were far higher than others projected, meaning deaths per case were much lower.[59] He put the actual infection rate fatality in the category of the seasonal flu. But voices such as Ioannidis's stayed muffled because, as Jared Kushner warned Scott Atlas, a task force critic of the pandemic policies, that Birx was "easily threatened."[60] A source inside the White House warned Atlas that the "task force doctors were fixated on a single-minded view that all cases of COVID must be stopped or millions of Americans would die."[61]

With the marching orders (and funding to follow) out, a "constant drumbeat from epidemiologists and others" greeted the public with a mantra based on *false claims* from the WHO:

- The China Virus was extraordinarily deadly, and worse than any other flu by orders of magnitude. (False)
- Everyone is at risk to die. (Utterly false)
- No one had immunity because the virus was new. (True, but that changed very rapidly as people contracted Covid-19 and got natural immunity)
- Everyone spread the infection. (False)
- Testing everyone was needed and all testing positive needed to be isolated. (Wrong and totalitarian)
- Masks worked. (False, proven so in multiple studies)
- The only real hope was a vaccine. (Totally false)
- Locking down everyone was essential. (Completely false)

How effective was the effort to create a hysteria? In February 2020, the *Wall Street Journal* published an article on "how many people might one person with coronavirus infect?" leading to an estimate of 40 percent to 70 percent (!) of the world's population being infected.[62] Quickly the author revised this downward, but still by not enough—but few outlets carried the revision. Similar hyperbole and sensationalism accompanied the "Case Fatality Rate," which the WHO stated as 3.4 percent, but when compared to actual data fell to about .02 percent in most of the world, and as low as .01 percent in the Scandinavian countries.[63]

Likewise, people vastly overestimated the likelihood that Covid infection would put them in the hospital. Surveys showed that 35 percent of adults said half of those infected would end up in the hospital (the correct percentage was between 1 percent and 5 percent).[64] Again, Democrats were six points higher in their responses predicting hospitalization than Republicans. How one viewed the pandemic strongly influenced the kinds of reactive measures one supported: in short, those who feared more proved much more likely to shun gatherings, get tested, or wear a mask. Those exaggerating the spread and risk to young people supported closing schools, restaurants, and other public facilities at a much higher rate than the data suggested or that common sense required.

Still, how did anyone know that any measures were effective? Against significant odds, President Trump rolled out testing in early March. But this in itself helped fuel the panic because early tests proved unreliable and thus generated more cases. A wide variety of causes that contaminated early testing results were a single bad test device in Canada, kids using cola-flavored drinks to throw off results, failure to design test equipment that could isolate Covid from the general flu, differences in results between children and adults, unexplained delays in test results manifesting, human error in taking the tests, and numerous other factors.[65] Even NPR had to throw in the towel on tests as effective.[66] By then, Dr. Jay Bhattacharya at Stanford found reported fatality rates "were grossly off-base, too high by a factor of fifty."[67]

One of the most important factors left out of journalistic reports involved the number of undetected infections, which, if they did not result in death, were never counted. On the other hand, deaths that *should* be laid at the feet of the "hyper infectionists," or, as I call them, vaxiopaths, were the deaths of despair. Again, the not-so-conservative Brookings Institution found that an additional fifty thousand people died "in a deep state of despair" in 2021 compared to the time before the China Virus.[68] This despair came from being sealed away from loved ones (especially damaging in the case of older Americans) and from being told they were just one breath—namely someone else's!—away from dying.

An equal amount of lunacy accompanied the lockdowns of schools, where, in the first 60,000 deaths, only twelve were children; in New York City, which had 15,756 deaths, only eight were children—but only one had no underlying condition.[69] Even the *Journal of the American Medical Association*, which had toed the Fauci-Birx line, admitted kids were at far more risk of dying from the everyday flu than from Covid.[70] Teachers' unions played an instrumental role in keeping schools locked down and perpetuating the hysteria. By June, out of nearly 69,000 China Virus deaths, only twelve were kids under fourteen and only ten were teenagers. In retrospect, the number of young people under thirty dying from vax-related side effects is staggering. Meanwhile Sweden, which did not lock down at all, had *zero* Covid deaths.

Liberals, by then appropriately triggered by the "hyper infection- ists," started to blame the unvaccinated for perpetuating the pandem- ic.[71] Researchers concluded "liberals . . . were more likely to scapegoat the unvaccinated (vs vaccinated), *even when presented with information challenging the culpability of the unvaccinated* known at the time of data collection (eg, natural immunity, availability of vaccines, time since last vaccination)" (emphasis mine).[72] To no one's surprise at all, Joe Biden used the bully pulpit of the presidency to blame the unvacci- nated for the "COVID-19 slog."[73]

Standing opposite the armies of talking heads that parroted Fauci's (and later, Biden's) lies, a small heroic group of independent journalists and media outlets stood firm. They suffered remarkable repression for reporting the truth:

- South African police beat reporter Paul Nthoba, after he photographed security forces aggressively enforcing the Covid-19 lockdown.

- Myanmar officials sentenced news editor Zaw Ye Htet to a two-year prison stint for his outlet's Covid-19 coverage. His crime? Spreading information that could "cause alarm or fear to the public."
- Nepal detained four journalists and beat others for their coverage of the pandemic.
- A Rwandan a journalist for Ishema TV was charged with violating the Covid-19 lockdown policy.
- In Malaysia, Wan Noor Hayati Wan Alias faced a six-year sentence for allegedly causing a public panic over a story he wrote about a cruise ship with Chinese tourists docking and the tourists disembarking in Penang.[74]

And, of course, the most powerful source for refuting Fauci's lies was Kennedy's book, *The Real Anthony Fauci.*

In sum, globalists largely succeeded in creating an international panic where only Sweden and a handful of African countries resisted lockdowns. Media and governments had combined to turn a somewhat more virulent flu into the worst epidemic since the Black Death, in the process demonizing those who challenged the narrative in any way. The threat was real, but not in the way journalists portrayed it; it was easily transmittable, but since the fatality rates had been grossly exaggerated, this factor was blown up to permit the third aspect of a globalist plan, namely, to view governments as the only institutions capable of dealing with it.

Once the WHO declared the China Virus a "Pandemic" in March 2020, governments had free reign to invoke emergency powers. Support for lockdowns went against pandemic guidelines adopted by the WHO itself, and consensus (a word that itself came to be laden with wokeism) in the epidemiological community "was that large scale lockdowns were neither effective nor desirable" against infectious diseases.[75] Indeed, Thomas Inglesby and his co-authors in 2006 argued that "negative consequences of large-scale quarantine are so extreme. . . that this mitigation measure should be eliminated from serious consideration."[76]

Yet throughout the world, most societies willingly ceded power into the hands of their governments. The "primary non-pharmaceutical measure adopted by countries . . . took the form of extreme social distancing or 'lockdowns.'"[77] One study concluded four out of five members of the Organization for Economic Cooperation and Development (OECD) adopted similar lockdown-type measures, a homogeneity of which—among such diverse countries—the authors found "striking."[78] Australia, supposedly the home of free people living in a democracy, imposed some of the most extreme measures in the world (outside of China), and ultimately ended up building concentration camps for the unvaxxed. It immediately closed its borders and did not reopen until February 2022. Even so, the Human Rights Commission in Australia focused almost entirely on the impact of policies on race and sex, not on the abridgement of human freedoms nor on the "despair" quotient that savaged mental health, especially among the young.

Likewise, Canada enacted strict lockdown policies, bankrupting numerous truckers who, from January 23–27, 2022, staged a convoy of 1,200 vehicles from western Canada along the Trans-Canada Highway in protest.[79] Lawyer David Freiheit (who goes by the internet handle VivaFrei) covered the trucker protest in Ontario. When he arrived, he "expected to see vandalism, extremism, and violence" based on news reports, but when he arrived with his camera, he found "people smiling, shoveling sidewalks," with no violence. He stayed fifteen days and recorded no violence: truckers blared their horns. Eventually, the police moved in—"literally out of *Starship Troopers*"—moving in lockstep, one step every thirty seconds, before eventually applying tear gas and pepper spray and beating "the living piss out of everyone."[80] After the fact, the Canadian government created a commission that completely justified the lockdowns and called the truckers an "occupation."

Early on, it was known that lockdowns had little to no impact on mortality, as seen in studies of different counties in the US, of different countries at a point in time, or within a single country over time.[81] Individual behavior such as taking precautions had more to do with a reduced likelihood of dying from Covid than did lockdowns.[82] Already studies showed that lockdowns imposed massive costs that exceeded any benefits by large magnitudes. Why, then, did so many countries so willingly—almost gleefully—leap to impose quarantines?

Paul Frijters and his associates in the *Great Covid Lockdown* identified three main policy responses as adopted by three broad groups: "minimalists," "pragmatists," and "Covid cultists." Japan, Taiwan, Belarus, and Senegal, among others, fell into the first group that imposed very minimal restrictions. South Korea, Ghana, Switzerland, and Sweden placed some restrictions on the public but not large-scale mandates. But the "Covid Cultists" that included Great Britain, New Zealand, Australia, Argentina, Canada, the Philippines, and the United States engaged in the most draconian of lockdown policies. Using a "maximum stringency index from January 2020 to July 2021, the authors show that the percentage of China Virus deaths since the imposition of the first lockdown hardly varied between the "Pragmatists" and the "Cultists."[83] That should not be surprising. History told us as much: Dr. John Ioannidis found that claims about the effectiveness of social distancing in the 1918–19 Spanish Flu epidemic were likely wrong because people died later and were not counted.[84] Moreover, to escape the fraudulent recording of non-Covid deaths as due to the China Virus, another researcher merely looked at all deaths during the lockdowns and found, yet again, across multiple countries those with the most stringent lockdowns reported *more* deaths.[85]

The *most* stringent quarantines, those in China, were also subjected to the most secrecy. Therefore, measuring their (in)effectiveness proved daunting.[86] Ironically, China's radical lockdown at first made "two weeks to flatten the curve" look benign. ("See? Other countries are forcing people to stay in their homes. We at least allow people to get groceries.") To those who had studied epidemics before, China's activity came as a shock: "This is the mother of all quarantines," said University of Michigan medical historian Howard Markel. "I could never have imagined it."[87] Another professor of global health law observed that traditionally governments had to gain the trust of the people, but "[these] kind of lockdowns are very rare and never effective."[88]

Similar overwhelming research exists to show that masks did not adumbrate Covid in any way, though the adherents—"maskiopaths" in my jargon—were rabid and unhinged when confronting anyone not masked. How could this happen in a rational society? Authors of *The Great Covid Panic* argued that the emotional interconnectedness of the globe had generated a contagion of its own—fear. Sweeping through social and popular media, and *overwhelmingly reinforced by the mainstream media in each country*, populations willingly and overwhelmingly supported totalitarian responses to the China Virus. Even worse, they strongly resented individuals or even countries that tried visibly different policies.

It turns out this is something of a herd behavior. It was, as Robin Koerner wrote, a "trolley problem" in which a trolley car operator of a loose train would release one car certain to kill people if it meant possibly saving the rest of the train.[89] This time, however, the herd did not know it was being manipulated by a globalist force that exerted pressure in a vast array of measures on news and social media. On June 26, 2023, the US House of Representatives Judiciary Committee issued a report on the Cybersecurity and Infrastructure Security Agency (CISA), concluding it had "colluded with Big Tech and 'disinformation' partners to censor Americans."[90] As the report noted, government actors worked with third parties to overturn the First Amendment, while censors prioritized narratives based on their interpretation of the truth.

Overall, the report found that an unaccountable bureaucracy had hijacked American communications.[91] CISA's head of censorship, Brian Scully, referred to the process as "switchboarding," which would "trigger content modification," or, in other words, would insert lies for truth. In addition, CISA funded a nonprofit, EI-ISAC, in 2020 to enhance censorship operations.[92] Frequent Twitter poster Alex Berenson found significant evidence in the Twitter emails that White House China Virus adviser under Biden, Andy Slavitt, undertook a censorship program against him. Berenson subsequently sued Biden, several White

House advisers, Pfizer CEO Albert Bourla, and Pfizer board member Scott Gottlieb for "orchestrating a public-private censorship campaign against him."[93]

Following Berenson's suit, there was a media blackout of the case. Ironically, it was a case against President Trump, *Knight Institute v. Trump*, in which the Second Circuit ruled that President Trump could not block users from his Twitter account because it was a public platform. Reporters Michael Shellengerger and Matt Taibbi further exposed this unholy connection, describing it as a "Censorship-Industrial Complex."[94] Needless to say, the US Supreme Court already found hiring mercenary organizations to do what government itself was prohibited from doing to be unconstitutional.

Predictably, the Biden regime's oppression went much further than just messing with a few Twitter or Facebook accounts. It adopted a "malinformation" campaign to "shape the political content available to the public."[95] House investigators found that state and local politicians used EI-ISAC to silence criticism and dissent, all in a much larger campaign involving the suppression of information from Hunter Biden's laptop: attempts to discredit natural immunity, hydroxychloroquine, ivermectin; any information about vote fraud; and the often deadly side effects of the vaccine.

In October 2022, the *Intercept* released the Department of Homeland Security's plans to curb speech it thought "dangerous" (an astounding descriptor, given that much of what the government claimed was true about the China Virus proved false).[96] DHS had created a "Disinformation Governance Board" (DGB) to stop "misinformation" (false—by its definition—information spread unintentionally), "disinformation" (false information spread intentionally), and "malinformation" (factual information shared out of context). Originally this DGB was so widely ridiculed it was scaled back, then publicly canceled—but in secret the government continued to pressure private platforms. This information surfaced when the Missouri Attorney General, Eric Schmitt, filed a lawsuit against government censorship, and appropriately on July 4, 2023, a federal judge prohibited the Biden administration from communicating with social media platforms about "protected speech."[97] Internal documents showed that government agencies sought to "avoid the appearance of government propaganda" by pressuring Facebook, Twitter, and other platforms to police speech for them. (Though not the subject of this chapter, it should be noted that Mark Zuckerberg of Facebook admitted that his platform had participated in blocking information about Hunter Biden's laptop that could have swung the 2020 election).[98]

Despite these statistics and studies, many of which were available to all medical professionals and politicians early in the China Virus pandemic, the three-legged "treatment" of lockdowns, masks, and vaccines nevertheless dominated policy. If viewed through the lens of a supranational power, say the World Health Organization of the United Nations, or malevolent Ernst Stavro Blofeld characters at the World Economic Forum, there would be little difference in what policies those sinister actors would have put into place than what Fauci or New Zealand's Jacinda Ardern implemented.

The question remains, "Why?" A common follow-up question was, "Aren't these countries [referring to Canada, Australia, New Zealand, and the Western European nations] *democracies*?" And that answer is yes, but not bottom-up democracies. As Mike Allen and I argue in *A Patriot's History of the United States*, the first two "pillars" of American exceptionalism established a bottom-up religion (Protestantism/Puritanism) as the foundation for the colonies and England gave us common law, a bottom-up political structure. The United States was, and remains, the *only nation in the world to have such bottom-up structures in place at the time of its founding*. Thus, Australia, New Zealand, and Canada—three of the most vicious prosecutors of the lockdown/vax/mask unholy trinity— were all either Anglican (with top-down governance and not truly "Protestant" because the Church of England wasn't protesting anything except Henry VIII's inability to get a divorce) or Catholic. Likewise, all three were under the British Dominion system, which directed authority from the top down.

In contrast, though some would say not enough, the United States adopted a "federalism" approach whereby states could impose their own laws regarding lockdowns and masking. Some, such as Governor Kristi Noem's South Dakota, never locked down. Others, such as New York, Minnesota, and Oregon mandated lockdowns but allowed rioters and Black Lives Matter protesters to fill the streets any time they wished with no repercussions. Nevertheless, there were significant differences in the American response at the state level—which came through CDC "guidance" but never mandates—and those of other countries. Trump had appointed Vice President Mike Pence in charge of the Coronavirus task force in February.[99] Pence, Fauci, Deborah Birx, and the CDC's Robert Redfield met with Trump, but they first greased the wheels with Jared Kushner, who warned Trump of their guidelines. "They may seem draconian," Kushner said, "but we think they could save thousands of lives."[100] When they recommended the "Two Weeks to Flatten the Curve," Trump said, "That's it? . . . I thought you were going to ask me to call in the military to make people stay in their homes. We can't do this forever, but people will tolerate this for a few weeks."[101]

Despite all those who died needlessly from the China Virus, it could be argued that America dodged a bullet, for while no national quarantines had ever been imposed on the public, such precedents existed in the world of animal quarantines, and dated to the late the earliest days of the Republic. According to historians Alan Olmstead and Paul Rhode, Congress passed the first quarantine legislation in 1796 which directed federal agents to assist state and local officials, often in ports.[102] Little else was done until the 1870s after yellow fever outbreaks among humans in the South prompted Congress to establish the National Board of Health to act where local rules were lacking. That represented "a significant extension of federal powers because it provided for federal regulations of railroads . . ."[103] Debates over animal and human health often occurred in Congress on the same day and addressed the same Constitutional issues. Concern for regulatory reform came mostly from populist farmers and Southerners. During inept attempts by the city of Chicago and the state of Illinois to wipe out a cattle disease CBPP (Contagious Bovine Pleuropneumonia), precedents were set, although usually the mere threat of a federal quarantine forced states and localities to quarantine their animals until the extinction of the disease.

What the newly created Bureau of Animal Industry, which became the tip of the spear for these quarantines, showed was large-scale government medical interventions were possible with animals. The policy history implied that such large scale interventions could translate to human diseases, but with the caveat that they survive the court of public opinion. Olmstead and Rhode, again writing of animal epidemics, noted "finding the appropriate level and means of governance was vitally important."[104] However, determining the "appropriate level" proved difficult with a media entirely compliant to the daily prognostications of Dr. Fauci. Eventually individual Republican governors in Georgia and Florida soon opened their states' businesses back up, while the tyrannical Democrat governors of Illinois, California, New York, and Michigan kept their states in prison mode.

Of course, one could find exceptions to the partisan norm. Ohio's Governor Mike DeWine embraced the lockdowns as warmly as any Democrat. He apparently paid no penalty for it and was reelected. Other elections, however, suggested that Brian Kemp in Georgia and Ron DeSantis in Florida, who both opened their states for business (Kemp on April 8, 2021, DeSantis later that month) fared well in the subsequent elections. But Governor Doug Ducey of Arizona, who had kept his state locked down despite major protests from small businesses, found he had a toxic name among voters when he explored running for the US Senate in 2022. At any rate, the research suggested that no aspect of quarantines had made any difference in death tolls.

It is important to reiterate that from the outset Fauci, Birx, and Redfield had adopted an unattainable and irrational goal of stopping the infection entirely, with zero "cases." A reasonable and sane strategy would have been to focus on the most vulnerable and let everyone else—more or less—alone. Thus their recommendations to states always took on the aura of an impossible goal.

Worldwide, after the economic impact on poorer nations set in, the WHO itself turned on lockdowns. In October 2022, the senior envoy on the China Virus sent a note to the Director General saying "We in the World Health Organization do not advocate lockdowns as a *primary* means of controlling the virus. We may well have a doubling of world poverty by next year . . . [L]ockdowns have one consequence that you must never ever belittle—and that is making poor people an awful lot poorer" (emphasis mine).[105]

A similar lunacy laced with panic involved the push to force people to wear masks. Initially, Fauci insisted the healthy had no reason to wear masks. In February 2020, he said, "in the United States, there is absolutely no reason whatsoever to wear a mask."[106] Just three weeks earlier he had argued that "asymptomatic transmission has never been a driver of outbreaks."[107] Indeed, the National Institutes of Health's own website admitted that mask wearing did not even reduce viral infection in hospitals. Some two dozen studies showed there were, in fact harms to *wearing* masks, including respiratory and immune system illnesses. The clincher was that the CDC's own data showed 85 percent of those who contracted Covid were wearing a mask.[108] Again, Fauci admitted in March 2020 that a mask's only value was in "making people feel better."[109]

If the lockdowns and masks later proved a nullity at best and deeply damaging at worst, what about the third pillar of the CDC plan to stop the virus—the vaccines? Here, Fauci and many others among both the medical and political elites had direct financial ties to patents (in the case of doctors and researchers) and pharmaceutical shares (in the case of politicians). The NIH paid roughly $32 billion in tax dollars annually in research grants to pharmaceutical companies, but its income stream of private royalties remained hidden. Fauci had profited from drug patents for decades, and finally NIH documents surfaced showing Fauci and his supervisor Francis Collins received multiple royalty payments.[110] While no exact sums accompanied Fauci's more than twenty royalty payments, his annual 2020 income (on a government salary of $456,000) was $1.7 million.[111] (Fauci claimed to have donated his payments to charity, but records are nonexistent.) But one source, Justia Patents, showed that Fauci already had at least thirteen AIDS-related patents, some associated with his failed and deadly AZT drug.[112] And how far Fauci's roots into the NIH funding went may remain murky, but the NIH itself had joint ownership of the Moderna China Virus vaccine and sued Moderna when the pharmaceutical company was slow kicking back its share, finally paying NIH $400 million in 2023.[113] And whatever Fauci got, it paled next to the $40 billion pocketed by the pharmaceutical companies.[114]

It must be kept in mind that virtually *all reporting related to Fauci* except for a handful of small, independent citizen news outlets and organizations such as Robert Kennedy's Children's Health Defense was being guided, manipulated, "fact-checked," and even removed from major sites due to the documented government censorship noted above. The very same "fact checkers" who attempted to cover up Fauci's role were often those cooperating willingly and enthusiastically with the government, particularly major news outlets like the *Washington Post*, the *New York Times*, and sites such as Facebook. Thus the very people and sites supposedly "debunking" Fauci's financial gains were the ones illegally paid to do so.

Nor was it just Fauci who was subject to corruption by funding. One of the early researchers into ivermectin in fact was funded by the WHO and thought he was originally looking for a drug to repurpose against the pandemic. When he discovered the benefits of ivermectin, he was told he could not make public statements or interviews. He was forced to retract his early papers supportive of ivermectin which had found a massive reduction in mortality by using it. Put another way, the drug companies and the WHO were using researchers to "identify" useful drugs for the purpose of eliminating those cheaper alternatives.[115]

Partly as a path out of the lockdowns, President Trump sought a solution through a vaccine. Trump's generation had grown up with vaccines that were safe (the miracle cure to polio) and seldom associated with autism or other side effects. As a businessman, finding solutions came naturally, while simply waiting on natural immunity or nature to "take its course" ran against his action-oriented nature. Again, keep in mind that Trump's medical experts were operating from the position of stopping *all* Covid cases, not treating the sick.

Urged on by Jared Kushner, his son-in-law, Trump looked to the Manhattan Project or the moon landing as programs where government resources and organization could achieve monumental goals and "condense time" as one historian of the atomic bomb program put it. Could trials be fast tracked? In May 2020, President Trump announced project "Warp Speed" to accelerate a Covid vaccine research and production that it could be available in less than a year, and in December, Operation Warp Speed produced its vaccines.[116] In between came a number of decisions that later proved questionable and ultimately foolhardy.

At the time, Trump took great pride in delivering the vaccine, and over the ensuing months almost 82 percent of Americans willingly or unwillingly took "the jab" as it was derisively referred to. (Over 50 percent of Americans took at least one booster as well). To his credit, Trump never mandated receiving a vaccine, though US government employees and the military all were required to take it. Many resisted and fought in court over religious objections, and eventually the Supreme Court upheld the legality of the US government forcing armed service members to receive "the jab."[117] At almost the same time, though, the Court struck down mandates from the government on private businesses.[118]

As many predicted, the combination of fast-tracking the vaccines combined with the indemnity from harms provided by Congress allowed the pharmaceutical companies to churn out vaccines without proper testing, or concern over either efficacy or side effects. And as Robert Kennedy noted, "Tony Fauci dictated a series of policies that resulted in far more deaths, and one of the highest percentage COVID-19 body counts of any nation on earth."[119] Fauci quickly upgraded his estimates of how many Americans would need the vaccine to ensure "herd immunity" from 70 percent in March to 80–90 percent in September based on *polling* that indicated rates were rising—but not actual data.[120] Later, even as then President Joe Biden was lapping up

Fauci's policies, the doctor himself admitted he could cite no scientific justification for his policy of Covid vaccinations.[121]

One of the first things that Fauci and his press allies did was to ignore or discredit VAERS, the Vaccine Adverse Event Reporting System, which was already showing significant and serious side effects from the vaccines. VAERS had in fact *undercounted* vaccine related injuries, sometimes by 99 percent.[122] Over time, the VAERS reports would be one of the best indicators of the widespread side effects of the vaccines.

While Fauci ram-rodded Trump, then found a willing supplicant in Biden, he and the media embarked on a dedicated mission to shift epidemic protocols away from early treatment and natural immunity to lockdowns, masks, and vaccines. Those measures included such "repurposed" drugs as the malaria treatment hydroxychloroquine and ivermectin. Dr. Peter McCullough pointed to peer reviewed studies that showed that early treatment may have averted up to 80 percent of the China Virus deaths. But Fauci's cabal—empowered by the media and with its near-total grip on information given to Trump—discredited alternative treatments and natural immunity. In essence, due to Fauci's guidelines, "a whole generation of doctors just stopped practicing medicine."[123] Indeed, the situation became so mind-bogglingly ludicrous that people thinking they had contracted Covid were turned away from their general practitioners' offices and told instead to go to the emergency room, thereby making the "overwhelming of the hospitals" a self-fulfilling prophecy. As McCullough noted, "not a single medical center set up even a tent to try to treat patients and prevent hospitalization and death. There wasn't an ounce of original research coming out of America available to fight COVID—other than vaccines."[124]

Many alternatives were available, the most successful of which were hydroxychloroquine (HCQ) and ivermectin. HCQ had been dispensed widely in Africa as an anti-malaria drug, known as the "Sunday-Sunday" drug. Obviously it posed a threat to the $48 billion China Virus vaccine project. After all, who needed a vax if an over-the-counter or easily prescribed therapeutic would keep someone out of danger? President Trump endorsed the drug on March 19, setting off Fauci's disinformation campaign.

It is critical to understand that, as a therapeutic, the timing of the use of HCQ became essential: most trials waited until too late in the disease process for HCQ to be effective. Dr. Harvey Risch, who conducted the most comprehensive study of HCQ by May 2020, noted that evidence against the drug used too late in the cycle were irrelevant, and that an French researcher in March 2020 had published a report on successful treatment of patients with HCQ, which in experiential instances was confirmed. Risch's study published two months later concluded that an HCQ "cocktail" was that early use could prove effective.[125] A study conducted in 2023 found a higher survival rate of hospitalized patients who took HCQ.[126] However, the greatest impact of HCQ came when administered immediately upon diagnosis of the China Virus.

Kennedy recounted the astounding deceptions the WHO and the Bill Gates Medical Foundation went through to discredit HCQ, including administering borderline lethal doses and delaying treatment, *as proven by minutes of the Gates Foundation's own meetings.*[127] This brings us to what Bobby Kennedy called "*Lancet*gate," wherein a Gates-supported study was published in the *Lancet* that portrayed HCQ as ineffective and dangerous.[128] Yet that study, and one in the *New England Journal of Medicine*, relied on data from Surgisphere Corporation, which was a "medical education company" (not a research lab) that claimed to have analyzed data from six continents regarding Covid; both journals republished that data.[129] So armed, the media immediately jumped on the "HCQ as ineffective" framing—which, of course, buttressed their deeper mission to undermine and sabotage President Trump. Researchers Michael Horning and Jim Kuypers found that across the board the media ran with the framing of HCQ as a "dangerous drug that was harmful if used by those who have COVID."[130]

For example, CBS said "Malaria drugs *pushed by President Trump* as treatments for coronavirus did not help and were tied to a greater risk of death and heart rhythm problems in a new study" (emphasis mine).[131] "Hydroxychloroquine does not help COVID-19 patients, and indeed may increase deaths, according to a large, international study published Friday in *The Lancet*."[132]

Even the more reliable sources such as *Breitbart* or the *Wall Street Journal* repeated the lies. *Breitbart*, without mocking President Trump, repeated the falsehood: "Chloroquine and hydroxychloroquine offer no clinical benefit for people with COVID-19 and might cause serious heart-related side effects, according to a study published Friday in *The Lancet*. People with severe illness caused by the new coronavirus, SARS-CoV-2, treated with either drug—either alone or with an antiviral medication—were up to twice as likely to die than those in the control group . . ."[133] The *Wall Street Journal* also echoed the general conclusions: "Antimalaria drugs didn't help patients fight Covid-19, while raising the risk for heart problems and death."[134] Horning and Kuypers provided at least seven additional examples of media framing and erroneous information based on this single study.[135]

Communications expert Jim Kuypers noted that much of the China Virus reporting contained a trick called "sandwiching," in which the journalist would start with a summation that supports their view, presents briefly the "other side" (though for reasons discussed in the note, this is almost never the actual "other side" of the case), then ends with statistics or additional quotations that support the original summation (i.e., the reporter's viewpoint). Even when not necessary, journalists would include Trump as the middle section and sandwich two contradictory paragraphs or sentences around him, particularly with regards to his positions on Covid.

Then came the retraction. On June 4, 2020, the authors of the *Lancet* study voluntarily retracted it based on questions about the validity of the (suspect) database. A key to the ten major outlets' retractions, though, was that elements of the *Lancet* study were wrong, but *not that in fact hydroxychloroquine could be beneficial*. In other words, they assassinated HCQ, then admitted there was no reason to do so. But the body was still dead. In no way did media outlets suggest that their claims of the alleged ineffectiveness or even dangers of HCQ were wrong.

Similar approaches were taken to delegitimize natural immunity (treating it as though it was a non-factor). But possibly the worst case of journalistic malfeasance came with the remedy called ivermectin, a drug with a track record of success against parasites, including round-worm, hookworm, and others. Indeed, the WHO included ivermectin along with HCQ on its inventory of "essential medicines."[136] Beginning in 2012, however, many studies found that the drug also inhibited many viruses as well. Three months after the China Virus hit west-ernized countries, Australian researchers found that ivermectin could SARS-CoV-2 in hours, and subsequent researchers found it inhibited Covid-19. Peruvian doctors adopted it in May and their China Virus loads fell dramatically.[137] Many other doctors reported similar results across multiple countries. Like HCQ, ivermectin worked better sooner rather than later, but it still had positive effects. Even the WHO's own research showed ivermectin significantly reduced death.[138] And, as Kennedy found, "nations whose residents have easy access to iver-mectin invariably see immediate and dramatic declines in COVID-19 deaths."[139] In Uttar Pradesh, India, where large-scale prophylactics and the therapeutic use of ivermectin was introduced, saw death rate 1,000 *times* lower than the US. Utter Pradesh has a population nearly two-thirds that of America.[140]

By itself (like HCQ), ivermectin posed a threat to both the inter-national pharmaceutical industry and, more specifically, to the vax-happy Dr. Fauci. All it took to ensure that the media accelerated its lies was for President Trump to endorse ivermectin. Then journalists swung into action. Upon learning that ivermectin had proven an effec-tive dewormer in horses, *Business Insider* hysterically warned that peo-ple were "poisoning themselves trying to treat or prevent COVID-19 with a horse de-worming drug." The AP intoned there was "No evi-dence Ivermectin is a Miracle Drug Against COVID-19," and even the FDA, in one of the most astoundingly stupid posts ever, posted on its website, "You are not a horse."[141] It did not matter that drugs were multi-purposed all the time. Antibiotics were used on animals *and* humans. Needless to say, countless men thanked researchers for discovering that Viagra worked on organs other than the heart!

The war against ivermectin—which could have nullified the vaccine tyranny—kicked into high gear when Fauci started berating the drug ("it could potentially have toxicity"—a statement that wise people might have applied to the vaccine itself).[142] Jake Tapper flat-out lied about emergency rooms in Mississippi and Oklahoma being filled with poison calls due to ivermectin,[143] and AP chimed in saying 70 percent of calls into the Mississippi poison control center were for the drug, when in reality they were for normal drug overdoses. The Gates Foundation weighed in. When podcast star Joe Rogan said he beat the China Virus using ivermectin, social media erupted with attacks.[144] Even the once counterculture *Rolling Stone* obediently towed the CDC/Fauci line on ivermectin, repeating the lie that emergency rooms were filling up with ivermectin overdoses.[145]

All this hysteria was normal, right? Even if the journalists were incompetent or biased in telling their stories, there was no sinister machination behind the disinformation about the lockdowns or the vaccines, was there? After all, what was the "data"—the holy grail of so-called "science"—saying? Steve Kirsch followed the VAERS data, which told a brutal story: China Virus vaxxes killed an estimated one person per thousand, accounting for over 675,000 dead Americans.[146] Kirsch, who has become a one-man clearing house for China Virus vax data, noted that the "blood issue" in the UK spiked immediately after the vaccines were rolled out; that US civilian labor force disability claims soared after the vax; that the vaxxes likely caused over 25,000 new cases of multiple sclerosis; and that Apple Valley Village Health Care Center saw a *ten times* higher China Virus death rate *after* it introduced vaxxes.[147] Peru declared a health emergency after a case explosion of "vaccine side-effect" linked to Guillain-Barre Syndrome;[148] The *European Journal of Heart Failure* reported that one person in 35 who received the Moderna vaccine showed signs of heart damage.[149] Rochelle Walensky, Director of the CDC from 2021–2023, knew there were "breakthrough infections" with the vaccines in January 2021.[150]

Still other sources confirm vax-related harms: "Moderna Spikevax Trial Data Show Serious Adverse Events and Death," and "IgG5 Increases with Repeated mRNA Vaccines: Linked to Disease."[151] After almost 130 billion doses worldwide, there wasn't a single vaccine label displaying side effects.[152] Another vaccine critic who has relentlessly gathered vaccine-harms data, Dr. Peter McCullough, found that data from Japan and Germany revealed that all-cause mortality was up after the China Virus vaxxes.[153] Brownstone Institute, a critic of the debate suppression, noted "as time went on, it became very clear that some of the informational claims that had been made to convince people to get 'vaccinated,' especially by politicians and media commentators, were false."[154]

As of this writing, the immunity wall of the pharmaceutical companies had just started to show cracks. A nurse injured by the Covid-19 vaccine headed to trial against her former employer.[155] Whistleblower Brook Jackson's case involving the Pfizer vaccine proceeds, arguing that the company falsified data, unblinded patients, and was slow to follow up on adverse effects.[156] And Covid researcher Steve Kirsch argues that litigation is now our "best path forward."[157]

What we have discussed were merely the *vaccine-related damages*. Economic and social carnage from the lockdowns and masking greatly expanded the body count. A former chief medical officer in the UK said the lockdowns "damaged a generation," and that in preschools children "haven't learned how to socialize or play properly, they haven't learned how to read at school," and admitted she and her colleagues "didn't plan" for the social and emotional side effects of lockdowns.[158] Harms seemed so obvious in *July 2020* about the lockdowns that even the World Bank issued a report that up to 100 million people could be shoved into extreme poverty.[159]

We now know, however, that journalists, news outlets, and social media outlets were strong-armed to censor China Virus posts that ended up being true.[160] At least, that was their excuse when in all likelihood they would have willingly done so—as Twitter did. From December through March 2023, billionaire Elon Musk, who had purchased the social media site Twitter, released a trove of internal documents to journalists Matt Taibbi, Bari Weiss, Alex Berenson, and others.[161] A shocking level of big tech-government collusion emerged under the Biden administration, wherein Democrats and federal officials routinely demanded Twitter take down an posts they objected to.[162] According to Taibbi, the files told of a "Frankenstein tale of a human-built mechanism . . . that had grown out [of] control of its designer," revealing an overwhelmingly left-wing employee base that facilitated censorship and bias.[163] In addition to outright locking accounts (including that of this author, at the time with 125,000 followers), Twitter engaged in "shadow-banning," wherein accounts would have posts hidden or "retweets" and "likes" blocked. Ultimately President Trump himself was banned—an unprecedented step in American media history. Equally important, though less relevant to the story of the China Virus, the story about the laptop of Biden's son, Hunter, which contained clear evidence of foreign bribery and infiltration into the vice president's own family, was shut down. The FBI routinely reported tweets to the company's "safety team," and monitored accounts.

However, one of the most egregious violations of free speech and worst examples of journalistic malfeasance came in the Covid debate, where doctors who challenged Fauci and/or the CDC's "guidelines," such as Harvard Medical School epidemiologist Martin Kulldorff, had their expert opinions labeled "misleading."[164] As one reporter, who had access to the Twitter files revealed, "Information that challenged [the government's position on Covid] such as showing harms of vaccines, or that could be perceived as downplaying the risks of COVID-19, especially to children, was subject to moderation, and even suppression."[165]

Yet it was the pro-vaccine "side" that perpetually generated the most falsehoods. Joe Biden said "The vaccines are safe. I promise you" and "You're not going to get COVID if you get the vaccinations. We are in a pandemic of the unvaccinated."[166] Fauci added: "The vaccines are safe and effective."[167] Nothing could have been more ironically perfect than the 2023 headline, "Vaccinated Outbreak at CDC Conference Bigger than Reported."[168] And the CDC did finally admit that a large portion of those who died of the China Virus had at least *four* co-morbidities.[169]

Whereas Elon Musk reopened Twitter (now called "X"), restored most banned accounts, and lessened censorship of comments, and whereas Mark Zuckerberg appeared to backtrack from Facebook's censorship with the "the-government-made-me-do-it" excuse, YouTube has gone the other direction with a "long term vision" for "medical misinformation policies."[170] The site claimed it would "remove content that contradicts health authority guidance on the prevention and transmission of specific health conditions," that it would "remove content that contradicts health authority guidance on treatments [including] unproven remedies," and that it would remove content that disputed the existence of specific health conditions," such as denying people died from COVID-19, despite the fact that evidence is becoming overwhelming that such is exactly the case.[171]

It should go without saying that these kinds of challenges to "health authority" are precisely how medical science has advanced, and that on multiple occasions "health authority" has been egregiously wrong. Most people know about the case of Soviet doctor Trofim Lysenko, who rejected traditional genetics in favor of his own theories. A darling of the Soviet Union, which not only adopted his food policies but prohibited any competing theories, Lysenko played a key role in the "Harvest of Sorrow" that killed upward of twenty million people in Russia.[172] A similar story about the authorities having the wrong answer came at the turn of the century, when studies started to show that the mosquito could be the leading transmitter in malaria. In the United States, Walter Reed in 1901 confirmed the mosquito transmission theory—which ran counter to the "health authority's" views that malaria was transmitted via dirt. The issue became more than an academic exercise when President Theodore Roosevelt's Panama Canal Commission deadlocked over which theory to adopt in clearing the Panama Canal Zone, Roosevelt courageously decided against the "health authority" to side with Reed, saving countless lives.[173] A far different outcome emerged from the campaign by researcher Ansel Keys in the late 1950s and early 1960s to reorient Americans away from proteins, fats, and meat, and toward more carbohydrates. He succeeded in gaining controlling influence over the American Heart Association in the midst of to gigantic studies (almost fifty thousand subjects) the AHA sided with Keys in demonizing proteins and fats. When the studies were actually completed, though, they found *no correlation* between a protein-heavy diet and heart disease, and shortly other studies found the exact opposite, that *carbohydrate-heavy diets* were correlated with heart disease.[174] Or, to sum up rather bluntly, the "heath authorities" often do not know what they are doing in some of the most important health areas. Moreover, research literally changes within a period of a few short years.

So where does this leave us in our history of globalism? Was the China Virus man made? Absolute conclusive proof awaits, but a "yes" answer seems warranted. Was it accidentally or deliberately released? As of 2023, no one knows the answer to this question. If a "plan" by globalists, how did they fail so badly to impose worldwide restraints and control, and indeed in America, even total nationwide control? We should also ask if the China Virus was a dry run at a newer, more deadly globally controlled medical emergency.

An interesting aspect of this question involves reporter Tracy Beanz, researching CDC data. She found a "dramatic spike" in "influenza like illness" in some states as early as November 2019.[175] She also discovered that the US military had participated in the 2019 Military World Games in . . . wait for it . . . Wuhan in October 2019. Moreover, when the military traveled through Washington to other destinations, a spike in flu-like diseases appeared. Beanz's analysis had previously asked the same question she asked of Washington, "Why Italy?" The answer was that Italy had a large Chinese immigrant population and had just entered into a new economic partnership with China. When China Virus broke out, the mayor of Florence, decrying racism, urged his citizens to "Hug a Chinese."[176]

In fact, China early on had sought to blame the US military for creating and spreading the virus.[177] While the reverse was true, Beanz's revelations meant that it was likely far more Covid cases had existed than were measured, earlier than were thought, that it was already present in China, and that more people were surviving or not even treating it as anything but the flu.

The timing is key and debunks the notion that the virus came from Chinese eating bats or other animals from a "wet market." Quite the contrary. In August 2019—just weeks before the first Covid infections appeared in Wuhan—a war game called "Crimson Contagion" concluded. Many of those involved in the China Virus participated, including Fauci, Redfield, and Health and Human Services Secretary Alex Azar. Unfortunately, Robert Kaldec, the central planner and the administration's Disaster Response Leader, who had written papers on using epidemics to institute tyrannical rule, oversaw the war game. Trump had been rightly concerned with the rise of Communist China as a global threat and had approved the exercise. Crimson Contagion focused particularly on mobilizing state and local responses to a pandemic, which used a "novel influenza" that emerged from China.[178] How much Trump was informed is yet to be determined. Already the military were unconstitutionally keeping secrets from the president, whom the brass despised.[179] Nevertheless, the subsequent report revealed that clearly the "war game" involved a "virus outbreak originating in China to spread quickly to the United States and overwhelm the nation."[180]

Then, in mid-October 2019, Bill Gates used his web of foundations to prepare "decision makers for the mass eviction of informed critics of the vaccine industry from social media."[181] As Robert Kennedy documents, Gates then personally organized a training and signaling exercise for government biosecurity bigwigs, including specific simulations of a *coronavirus* pandemic. Among the participants were members of the World Bank, the World Economic Forum (WEF), the CDC, and even the Chinese government, plus a representative from Johnson & Johnson. It was this event that led WEF director Klaus Schwab to term it the "great reset."[182]

Known as "Event 201," Gates's war game practiced several psychological warfare techniques for controlling official narratives, silencing dissent, and forcibly masking a large population. Most important, it used the disease to impose mass vaccinations. Of course, as Kennedy pointed out, no one discussed therapeutic measures, natural immunity, or otherwise fortifying the immune system. Nor was there discussion of civil rights, the dangers of authoritarian government or the dangers of drugs themselves. Oddly, Gates later claimed the simulation didn't occur.[183] Gates and his associates, though, apparently aimed for the stars: the reality came far short. Instead of the sixty-five million deaths the team planned for, Covid only killed a little over 10 percent of that number—and recall that *all* of the China Virus deaths are in question as to cause, given that anyone who died from almost any other cause was listed as a Covid death.

What is clear is that Gates, members of the US government's medical, military, and intelligence communities, and the WHO collaborated (some might say conspired) to deal with a "potential" situation that, in fact, had already started in China.

Two final questions remain: why did President Trump so willingly go along with the lockdowns, and what is the future of medical globalism? To the first question, there are multiple explanations. First and foremost, those in charge at the CDC and NIH, namely Collins, Redfield, Fauci, and Birx had settled on the foundational point of stopping the spread of "cases," not in allowing natural immunity among the healthy to develop and to treat the most vulnerable. The "zero case" approach became canon, and from there policies were misguided at almost every level.

In his book *Breaking History*, Trump's son-in-law Jared Kushner argues that it was his own organizational genius in bringing all the right experts to convince the president. Trump literally changed his position in a week's time. An explanation much more favorable to Trump has been offered by Jeffery Tucker, whose analysis of the timeline shows that on March 10—six days prior to the March 16, 2020 edict—Trump met with a members of the national security team. Tucker theorizes those national security officials, including members of the military, "let him know a highly classified secret."[184]

What did they tell the president? Tucker argues they laid out a virus that was "something far more threatening and terrible" than a traditional virus and *that it came from a research lab in Wuhan.*[185] This was significant for several reasons. Trump already distrusted China because of economic issues. Second, the briefers almost certainly produced selected information from "Crimson Contagion" and from Event 201. Xi Xinping, they explained, had engaged in drastic measures because of the lethality of the new virus, and that America should follow China's example. More important, they likely suggested that thanks to those exercises, a vaccine had been in the works and could be available in months, not years. And the *coup de grace* in convincing Trump? Pence had already outlined the "federalism" argument which appealed to Trump's federalist instincts, thus assuring the president that the states, not "Big Government," would dictate policies. Moreover, as a classic delegator, once Trump put Pence in charge of the Task Force, as Scott Atlas observed, Trump's participation declined significantly.

But Trump soon had questions. As Tucker wrote, "it only took a few weeks for Trump to become suspicious about what happened" and that he swung between believing he was tricked and believing he did the right thing (a point Kushner reinforced). Only after Dr. Scott Atlas outlined the con to him did Trump conclude he needed to stop talking about it. And while he has substantially buried the topic in his rally speeches, according to insiders Trump still believed he saved a lot of lives with the vaccine.

Globally, we can conclude a few things. First, despite having more than sufficient preparation to install their plan, the globalists, the WHO, Bill Gates, and others only achieved a relatively short-lived regime in which they were the "health authorities." Even armed with media-induced panic, overwhelming media support, censorship, and big tech "misinformation" campaigns, enough Americans and enough nations worldwide refused to play along for more than a year. In America, states were reopening and de-masking within months.

While the "maskiopaths" and the "vaxiopaths" continued to try to shame fellow citizens, the public had had enough. Sweden never locked down. Most African countries never imposed severe Covid measures of any sort.

Typically, the globalists concluded that they simply lacked enough power to impose their will on the class of "slaves" and "serfs" as WEO adviser Yuval Harari termed them. Round two would require more authority. Enter the amendments to the 2005 International Health Regulations and a new pandemic treaty called CA+.[186] The new WHO pandemic instruments would:

- Expand the definitions of pandemics and health emergencies
- Change recommendations from International Health Recommendations to mandatory instructions
- Increase the director's ability to independently declare emergencies
- Set up intensive surveillance processes in all nations
- Grant a wide new range of binding powers, including border closures, travel restrictions, and quarantines

The Treaty itself would set up a WHO-directed "governing body" to oversee the process.[187]

There are many hoops this "treaty" must jump through to become a reality, including support of at least 50 percent of the member states, and, in the United States, the fact that any treaty must be approved by two-thirds of the Senate. Currently, even with a Democrat majority in the Senate, that seems remote.

But clearly the elites—having failed in their first effort at medical globalism—have plans for others on the horizon. However, now nations other than the United States have seen the destruction waged by lockdowns; the damages from the vaccines are slowly surfacing in scientific literature; and a somewhat rightward turn seems to be occurring worldwide (see, for example, recent elections in Slovakia, New

Zealand, Australia, Holland, Argentina, and Italy). In short, for now, the world seems to have adopted the "fool me once" mentality. Polls in America show that over 80 percent of the public will never take another Covid vaccine.

Stymied once again, the globalists had the final ace up their sleeve in the form of a new world religion, with its holy sacraments of abortion and climate change. It is the ninth inning, and the spiritual globalists now came to the plate.

Chapter Seven

Spiritual Globalism, Celebrities, and Climate Change

P aul Robeson, a famous black singer in the 1930s, probably became the first well-known American celebrity to be associated with protests. His rendition of "Ol' Man River," from the musical *Showboat*, won him fame around the United States. During the Spanish Civil War, however, Robeson changed the lyrics to the song and inserted an entire, additional uplifting verse of his own. Although Robeson performed benefit aid concerts during World War II, shortly thereafter he was associated with leftist causes and even traveled to the Soviet Union.[1]

Other than Robeson, however, celebrities tended to stay away from politics over the next forty years with good reason: movie stars and singers had to appeal to the broad populace. Or, as basketball star Michael Jordan said, "Republicans buy sneakers too, right?" Movie stars remained movie *stars* in large part because they kept their mouths shut, not just about politics, but about any controversial issues.[2] To use another now-forgotten business saying, "The customer is always right."

The Vietnam War began to change this celebrity status, most notably when Jane Fonda, then at the height of her career, went to North Vietnam and sat on the seat of a Vietnamese anti-aircraft gun used to shoot down Americans. Singers had perhaps been ahead of the curve in folk-music protests with performers such as Peter, Paul, and Mary, Bob Dylan, and Joan Baez. Even then, though, as Kenneth Bindas and Craig Houston showed, nearly all the anti-war protest music during the Vietnam War came *after* public polls shifted against the war. Far from leading the way, musician/celebrities were followers.[3]

A new cause, though, seemed to even supersede war: "global warming." Later called "climate change" because the evidence did not confirm a warming planet, early "global warming" advocates were pure watermelons—green on the outside, red on the inside. At first they were simply goofy. The great Rush Limbaugh, however, took them seriously from the get-go, warning in the early 1990s that news stories about the dangers of "SUVs" (sport utility vehicles, or vans) had an agenda connected to the global warming movement. Those early SUV-crusades failed, largely because the part of the population that used them the most, urban white women, had no interest in giving them up.

But the new global warming hysterics soon gained a major cadre of proponents among the celebrity class. Actor Ed Begley Jr. even had a television series that featured his totally green lifestyle. Later, Leonardo Di Caprio would take the lead as one of the most recognizable advocates for "green" lifestyle and technology—all the while jetting around the world in his private plane.

Early in the movement, so-called green advocates went after children, beginning with *Captain Planet and the Planeteers*, a cartoon show that aired on Turner Broadcasting System" from 1990–1992. Villains were always evil corporate polluters, but never the Chinese or Indians (who were, and remain, the largest polluters on earth).

By the early 2000s the evidence had so challenged—and often debunked—the notion that the earth was continually heating up due to human activity. Subtly "global warming" became "climate change." After all, it is absolutely true that the climate changes all the time and has for thousands of years. Greenland used to be green with vineyards planted there. Routinely Roman artifacts appear in the "disappearing" glaciers in southern Europe, revealing that two thousand years ago, Romans lived there.

A masterful analysis by Guy Mitchell detailed the positions of many, if not most, of the think tanks and websites that reflected the general "consensus" of scientists.[4] One stands out in shifting its position—the Helmholtz Association in Germany, which in 2017 admitted that the effects of climate change varied significantly and that it sought to make scientific results available to the public. Their mission changed two years later when the Association said definitively that "climate change is real and is predominately caused by us humans."[5] Likewise, the French Academy of Sciences and the US National Academy of Sciences insisted humans were at fault for changes in the earth's climate, but based whatever research they had on the flawed Intergovernmental Panel on Climate Change.

A few held out. The British Royal Society has not taken clear positions on human-caused climate change. In 2017 it noted that over "hundreds of thousands of years, slow, recurring variations in the Earth's orbit around the Sun, which alter the distribution of solar energy received by Earth."[6] And the Chinese came to exactly the opposite conclusion, saying the rate of global mean surface temperature "was reduced from 1998 to 2013."[7] Further, Mitchell shows that almost all hysterical news releases avoid providing actual proof, using phrases such as "likely" or "virtually." Most important, the IPCC models "contain hypotheses that have not been proven, such as the assumption that an increase in carbon dioxide concentrations in the atmosphere causes and increase in water vapor concentration which triggers the [global warming] mechanisms."[8]

More than any other cause in recent memory, even perhaps including Civil Rights, celebrities have adopted climate change as their single most important issue. Why? To some extent our answer lies in the decline of religion, particularly of Christianity, in the lives of today's celebrities. Few attend church, even fewer are vocal or public about their faith. With the exception of specific Christian genres, the music and film industry are devoid of depictions of faith except to show ministers (particularly Catholic priests) as perverts, deviants, and pedophiles.[9] (One exception: it is still entirely acceptable to portray *black* people in worship.) An absence of faith that God has the earth's future under control, and that He laid out a specific roadmap on how things end, has left at least one generation not only faithless but also hopeless.

Without a faith background, a new religion easily insinuated itself onto younger generations. It has strongly associated itself with a pagan worship of the earth. Shrouded in the language of "caring about the planet," the new church of Gaia offered people a way to "become involved" supposedly outside of partisan politics. Billionaires such as Bill Gates jumped behind the green agenda. How could anyone be opposed to "saving the earth" or want dirty air or polluted water?

Senator Al Gore of Tennessee had adopted the environmental movement as his central issue when he ran for president in 1992. He lost to Bill Clinton, who later won the presidency, and became Clinton's running mate, and then, vice president. Gore's entire "global warming" movement—as it was then still called—was structured on his 1992 book *Earth in the Balance: Ecology and the Human Spirit.*[10] Generally referred to as *Earth in the Balance*, Gore warned that "humankind's assault on the earth" left the planet with only ten years to survive. Just as Vladimir Lenin drenched his rhetoric in violent phrases such as "goad," "compel," "states of siege," "flame," "leap," attack," "sheets of steel," and his favorite word, "exterminate," so too did key words and phrases adorn Gore's hysterics.[11] His favorite term was "crisis." There was a "grave crisis," an "environmental crisis," an "ungodly crisis," a "deep crisis" a "catastrophe in the making"—must have missed that one—a "crumbling ecological system," "destruction of the earth's surface," a "destructive cycle," and an "ecological holocaust."[12]

It would be a good time to recall that the book came out in 1992, and that it is now thirty years later and the earth is still here. It would also be worth noting that in modern writing, authors on the left especially have bastardized the word "holocaust" to mean anything that in their eyes is damaging. (My former mentor Robert Loewenberg wrote a powerful article depicting the trivialization of the Holocaust as an aspect of modern idolatry. When Loewenberg wrote in 1982 he had already identified the demonic roots associated with the early environmental movement.)[13]

Overall, as one reviewer put it, *Earth in the Balance* was a "cunning warrant for the establishment of the equivalent of world government" through global agreements that would require all nations to work in concert. Never in Gore's work (nor in that of any other environmentalist) is it spelled out exactly how any "world government" would force India or China, the world's worst polluters, to comply without a nuclear war.

By the early 1990s, two key aspects of the new "green" movement were apparent. First, it demanded a "crisis" much the way the atomic scientists had developed their countdown-to-Armageddon clock for nuclear war. Every green spokesman invoked a specific number of years the world had left. For example, the darling of the green movement, Greta Thunberg, said in 2020 that the earth only had "eight years left" to avert global warming.[14] Actor Leonardo DiCaprio in 2022 said we "literally" had only eight years left (or nine, depending on the setting).[15] DiCaprio had first used his 2016 Oscar speech to urge action on climate change, saying "If you do not believe in climate change, you do not believe in modern science or empirical truths."[16] Keep in mind this is an actor, not a scientist, instructing people on "modern science" and "empirical truths." But metaphorically speaking, the *Titanic* hadn't sunk yet and DiCaprio still was shouting from the bridge that "Climate change deniers should not hold public office."[17]

Actress Meryl Streep, in a series called *2046*, portrayed the "last whale on earth."[18] Actor Mark Ruffalo said "Climate change is the greatest threat to our existence in our short history on this planet. Nobody's going to buy their way out of its effects."[19] John Cusack did a disaster movie *2012*: ending his career was probably not the disaster he had in mind. Congresswoman Alexandra Ocasio-Cortez, who presumes herself to be a celebrity, said in 2019 the "World will end in twelve years" if climate change isn't addressed.[20] (So as of 2023, we're down to eight years according to her, four according to Thunberg.)

Celebrities clearly had played their role, but the media joined in, adding its bassoons and timpani to the crisis orchestra by citing scientists and public officials. For over fifty years the United Nations' environmental spokesmen have played off the same sheet music:

- 1972, the UN's "environment protection boss" said "We have ten years to stop the catastrophe." In the Old Testament, that would have qualified him for a stoning as a false prophet.
- A decade later the next head of the UN environmental program told the *New York Times* "an environmental catastrophe as irreversible as any nuclear holocaust" would hit the world by 2000. Oops. Must have missed that.
- Apparently his colleague's death-date was too late, so another UN environmental official moved the End-of-the-World clock up a year, saying that by 1999 global disaster would see "nations wiped off the face of the earth [and] crop failures." As best I can tell from my *Atlas of the World*, the nations of 1999 are still here, though many by different names.
- Unable to generate enough concern, yet another UN official weighed in, saying in 1990, "We shall win—or lose—the climate struggle in the first years of the 1990s." Since none of his policies were adopted, and we're still here, he also seems to qualify for a little Old Testament, er, discipline for a false prophet.
- Not to be outdone, yet *another* UN climate spokesman said that if there was no action by 2012, "that's too late." I guess, then, we ought to party like it's 1999.
- Oblivious to the fact they had moved enough goalposts for every NFL stadium, in 2019 the UN, yet again, warned that we only had eleven years left to prevent "irreversible damage" from climate change. Apparently providing dates that people could check easily—at least before memory loss set in—was proving daunting.
- Still other predictions were that Britain would be plunged into a "Siberian" climate by 2020—which almost did come true, but only because of British sanctions on Russia in the Ukraine

War and their subsequent green energy policies that drastically diminished their domestic energy. Somehow, I don't think failing wind farms and exploding lithium batteries were quite what was meant by that comment.[21]

- One shocking exception was Bill Gates, who in 2023 saw "a lot of climate exaggeration" out there and said "The climate is not the end of the planet. So the planet is going to be fine."[22] Gates apparently had sensed that hysteria wasn't working. He had not, however, changed teams.

Why is it that "global warming/climate change" elicited such a response from celebrities and then was embraced by schools, universities, Hollywood, and the media? And indeed, how is it that individual celebrities such as Gore or Leonardo DiCaprio thought they could "save the earth?—an "aspiration [which] suggests a degree of self-importance that borders on megalomania."[23] In September 2021, pop singer Camila Cabello wrote an "open letter" to CEOs of fourteen major media companies urging them to back Joe Biden's climate agenda and legislation. It said, "the plan . . . will protect communities form climate change through investments in clean energy, clean transportation, and infrastructure upgrades . . ."[24] Signed by Shakira, Lady Gaga, Justin Timberlake, Dua Lipa, Cate Blanchett, Sean Penn, Hugh Jackman, Don Cheadle, Shawn Mendes, Selena Gomez, Billie Eilish, Jimmy Fallon, and predictably DiCaprio, the letter was touted by Jimmy Kimmel and fellow late night shows under the rubric "No Planet B." Late night host Stephen Colbert got it halfway right when he said that the shows were as likely to stop "climate change" as Gal Gadot singing "Imagine" was to stop the China Virus.[25] Reality was that if the *sun* or other timeless planetary factors changed the climate, there was nothing any human could do about it, good or bad.

Prince Harry and his former-star wife Meghan Markle joined the September 2021 "Global Citizen Life" concert in Central Park. According to the Global Citizen Life mission statement, it was to "call on world leaders, major corporations, and foundations to combat "catastrophic [there's that word again] climate change" and to address the "climate needs of developing countries."[26] Although we will examine this in detail later, it should be noted that the "climate needs" of "developing countries" apparently aren't the same "needs" as the rich West, because "developing countries" such as India, China, and African nations were voracious polluters. Virtually all coal-pollution in the world comes from China. More on that soon.

So, again, why did celebrities attach themselves to this particular issue? Some of it has to do with the growing role of celebrity overall in modern culture. As one study put it, the role of celebrities as communicators of issues such as climate change is "an outcome of a political environment increasingly influenced by public relations and attuned toward the media's representation of political ideas, policies, and sentiments. Celebrities act as representatives of mass publics [sic], operating within centers of elite political power."[27] A new "achieved celebrity" has replaced "ascribed celebrity" (as in kings), but there is now a "new aristocracy of fame."[28] Celebrity status, in fact, because "a desacralized highway to transcendence," intellectual speak for a means for people to think of themselves as gods.[29]

Modern celebrities made a transition into public philanthropy and do-gooder-ism (or as one expert called it, "celanthropy") in the 1990s with Bono, Brad Pitt, Angelina Jolie, Annie Lennox, Bob Geldof, Sting, Oprah Winfrey, and Nicole Kidman joining various causes. They were welcomed as spokesmen because in theory celebrities could speak basic truths that politicians and business leaders avoided.

Mind you, while research supports the notion that celebrity endorsements can sell *products*, the proportion of people influenced by celebrity endorsements remains around 30 percent.[30] In 2016, Hillary Clinton had every major celebrity in America supporting her, even to the point that aging rocker Bruce Springsteen played a concert for her the night before the election—and still lost to Donald Trump. Like reporters, celebrities' views are highly *unlikely* to influence anyone's positions, according to a poll in 2018, where only one-quarter of adults said celebrity opinions are effective in influencing how they voted.[31] Republicans were even less susceptible to Hollywood's endorsement siren songs, by 7 percent. One study found younger people were "cautiously positive" about celebrities using social media to push positions, but nevertheless were skeptical.[32] Another study found that while endorsements could be effective, they largely varied depending on the type of celebrity (national vs. local).[33] Celebrities expand their "concern" brand through a "penchant for the commoditization of everything including . . . care and concern for the environment."[34] They "frame for audiences the emotionalized problems and solutions to global environmental change."[35]

Yet such "scholarship" itself falls into its own bias trap, failing to ask why celebrities embrace the highly questionable claim of whether "climate change" (as defined by human-caused alteration of the earth's climate, vs. normal, natural, centuries old changes out of human control) as opposed to challenging the assumptions themselves. Or, why don't we see major celebrities attacking the unproven notions of climate change based on the estimated massive damage pro-climate policies would bring?

What author Mike Goodman called *Celebritus politicus*, this group of elites have been situated and also worked to situate themselves as a stylized form of the neo-liberalized governance of the problems of environment and development.[36] Goodman noted that simultaneously the celebrities seek to engage in "heroic individualism" while on the other hand they collectivize their responses through mass appeal and through both "fame-seeking" and "fame-utilizing" behaviors. They embody contradictions as individuals who are the "true citizens of the world" creating their own "Porto Davos."[37]

Celebrities indeed have the ability to generate spectacle—visual, exuberant, theatrical. The present day's celebrity culture differs vastly from that of just thirty years ago, when celebrities were generally viewed as possessing a high degree of virtues, including prudence, modesty, humility, and sobriety. Even reporters played along, covering up Babe Ruth's binges, John Kennedy's assignations, or Liz Taylor's drunken domestic fights. All that changed with the 24/7 news media and the arrival of cell phones and social media.

In past decades, celebrities and especially movie stars especially remained out of reach; hence when they appeared within feet of ordinary people at a red carpet event, they became familiar for one of very few times in their careers. Today, ordinary people can become familiar with celebrities without ever having even seen them in person through relentless image management, reality shows, and aggressive public relations agents. Moreover, the news coverage of the day emphasized maintaining the "mystery" of celebrities, whereas the newer demands of the modern news media emphasize lives of crisis, risk, and extravagance. Paparazzi show us the most intimate details of celebrities, including semi-nude starlets on vacation on a remote island, out-of-shape actors between movies, slovenly or make-up-less actresses with their kids or shopping; and couples engaging in public spats. All of that is made available in tomorrow's *Sun, UK Daily Mail,* or *National Enquirer.*

Celebrities' ability to generate spectacle actually concerned some. One environmentalist worried it could distract from the real environmental issues being scrutinized. Or, complains one source, celebrities "render climate change as monetized and meaningless media performances."[38] To put it terms Rush Limbaugh would have used, they engage in symbolism over substance. Worse from a realistic point of view, they continue to superficially reinforce the very notion that human-caused climate change is possible and deadly.

Why does anyone listen to celebrities? Ironically it may have nothing to do with causes and the socialistic world view them embrace, but rather the fact that celebrities often reflect and validate concepts of social mobility and political ascendancy of ordinary people. Virtually none of the celebrities who lecture us on "global warming" ever graduated from college. The list of non-college celebrities includes Richard Branson, Bill Gates, Michael Dell, Tom Hanks, Oprah Winfrey, Madonna, Jim Carrey, Jake Gyllenhaal, Prince Harry, Katy Perry, Leonardo DiCaprio, Demi Moore, Jessica Simpson, Whoopi Goldberg, Anne Hathaway, Jay-Z, Maya Angelou, Claire Daines, Jessica Alba,

Hillary Swank, Russell Simmons, Britney Spears, Drake, Lady Gaga, Kim Kardashian, and Rihanna. Without seeking to, scholars have explained the role of the political leader, such as Donald Trump, as somehow "embody[ing] the sentiments of the party, the people, and the state" as having become aligned with the role of the celebrity "who must somehow embody the sentiments of an audience."[39] Status of celebrities as non-politicians actually enhances their trustworthiness, again reinforcing one of the prominent advantages Donald Trump had over Hillary Clinton in 2016.[40]

What drew the climate change globalists to celebrities was that above all celebrities excel at manipulating people's *emotions* through song, film, literature, etc. And while celebrities proved exceptional at employing guile, media persuasiveness, and clever tugging of heartstrings for policy purposes, they themselves were largely uneducated and thus *themselves* were easy to mold and manipulate. The public endowed them with "privileges that are not given to the majority."[41] With climate change, their special status protected them from critical or skeptical challenges in the public sphere. Who wants to argue CO_2 with Camilla Cabello?

Ronald Reagan was the first modern master that used this celebrity advantage for political change. In his televised speeches, for example, he always looked at people rather than the teleprompter because of his excellent script memory. He employed humor or a story (for storytelling remains one of the top advertising methods) to make a point or deflect a question, and always employing uplifting rhetoric.[42] He perpetually had stories from his Hollywood days. It is ironic that Reagan succeeded where the cabal surrounding John Kennedy failed to turn Camelot into a lasting political force.

Modern environmental campaigns that employ celebrities often do so in the context of consumer practices, urging moral activity within the marketplace. "Buy green," for example, still operates within the larger construct of capitalism, a feature that drives radicals crazy. As two leftist authors wrote, it contributes to "the moral authority of a hegemonic market-led governance of sustainability."[43] This conundrum enters an entirely new level—and for conservatives, one that is much more entertaining—when the old "White Man's Burden" is again tacitly applied to celebrity activists when it came to development projects, particularly in Africa. Here, one could think of Tom's Shoes or Angelina Jolie's African ventures, or other such do-gooder projects addressed in chapter five. Those campaigns, complain leftists, trace the lineage of such portrayals back to colonial narratives about Europeans traveling to the "dark continent" to enlighten the backward locals.[44] Leftist scholars complained that such images of white celebrities in Africa subtly promote notions of white superiority and rationality as opposed to irrational African subjects.[45] A conundrum, no? How do you employ (mostly) white celebrities for Third World projects without them being, well, white?

Increasingly the news media has relied upon public relations agencies for content, in turn elevating the role of celebrities within news stories themselves. Turning celebrities into "mobilizing agents" helped raise awareness and then (their sponsors hoped) shape public policy. Celebrities played the role of a leader through whom large numbers of people can be reached for a particular group or cause. That leader then is filtered through the support apparatus of lobbying groups to the general public, a process that entails an army of publicists, bodyguards, chauffeurs, voice coaches, yoga or health instructors, physical trainers, and others whose sole job is to make the celebrity leader look and seem appealing.

Consider the great actor Marlon Brando, a devout activist, who nevertheless grew (literally) so physically unappealing he had to send an Indian to make a speech on his behalf about Native American rights at the Oscars. Brando personally lost much, if not all, of his celebrity clout by, bluntly, eating himself out of celebrity status. A star who is no longer appealing doesn't have much celebrity market value. (In recent times, think of actor Brandon Frasier, who stood on the brink of megastardom, only to allow injury and food sink his career until he found a role that emphasized obesity!) As the author of *Fame Attack* put it: "Before stars are known to us they are *prepared* for public consumption.

Questions of hairstyle, skin tone, scent, dress, political values, social beliefs and anger management are sifted by experts."[46]

One of the first to recognize celebrity status was Edward Bernays, who saw the influence potential of motion pictures. Bernays came to develop press campaigns for President Calvin Coolidge and actors Al Jolson and Ed Wynn. Bernays, the nephew of Sigmund Freud, challenged the notion that universal literacy enhanced democracy, noting that people achieved just enough of a level of literacy to be subject to propaganda, but "quite innocent of original thought."[47] To Bernays, the most important elements of celebrity were not those traits inherent in what the person did, but those related to media placement and representation.

A media-driven celebrity machine for endorsing political issues, however, entails four major problems. First, celebrities, unlike (supposedly) scientists or some politicians, are deeply attuned to the market and cannot engage in excessive radicalism lest their brand fall or be fatally damaged. What makes them useful for spreading propaganda also makes them extremely open to rapid backlash. While they indeed play a role in bringing attention to issues, the public does not usually trust them as spokespeople for scientific issues. But with proper "framing," celebrities indeed *could* and have been turned into "authorized speakers" for climate change.[48] At least for a while. More recent research found that Americans, Brits, and Australians saw celebrities as undermining the saliency of climate change arguments. It turns out that converting people with no background in science and usually with no college degree into "experts" on a highly contentious scientific issue is tougher than people thought.[49]

A second dilemma celebrities have found is that to dramatically engage younger audiences, more hyperbole is needed; yet the more terrifying the "harms" associated with global warming, the higher the levels of hopelessness that are generated within the youth themselves.[50] Put another way, the more effective the celebrities were at scaring kids to death over climate change, the less likely kids were to do *anything*. Celebrities were scaring them into *in*action.

Thirdly, for celebrities to be effective spokesmen, advocates had to, well, *show the public*. They had to be seen. However, climate change imagery rarely invoked celebrities' images. Scholars working in the field of celebrity impact have considered Leonardo DiCaprio's documentary *Before the Flood* (2016) as exceptionally effective, viewed by sixty million people. On the surface that indeed appears impressive, until it is contrasted with the "docudrama" about Jesus, *The Chosen*, which now has been seen by 312 million viewers as of 2022 alone.[51] Nevertheless, the DiCaprio documentary exemplified a new use of celebrities called "After Data," as in "after the scientists/economists failed to convince people of the 'crisis' we'll send in the celebrities." Or, as *Hollywood Reporter* wrote reviewing *Before the Flood*, "maybe movie stars can sway public opinion more effectively than tightly reasoned activist docs full of hard data. . . ."[52]

Even within the film, however, DiCaprio was shown to be a hypocrite, as he admitted to having a larger "carbon footprint" than most people—given his private jets and constant international travel—and was confronted by an American Indian conservationist about America's energy consumption (which, by the time of President Trump, fell below that which we produced). One advocate for the film claimed the producers wanted DiCaprio to be "everyman"—but he absolutely wasn't. Indeed, watching a multi-millionaire megastar traipse around Sumatra or the Arctic only reminds ordinary people who must work normal jobs that he is anything *but* "normal." DiCaprio's role, according to the director, was to "meet the experts and make the experts more palatable."[53]

Climate change activists also worried that if the experience of celebrities in humanitarianism is a model, their efforts are only affecting other elites . . . who already are believers.[54] Consider that after nearly forty years, Tibet still isn't "free," despite the efforts of actor Richard Gere. Research may in fact be avoiding a rather crucial question: Do activists only get engaged when they operate in societies already drifting toward their point of view? It's the old rock and roll question, namely when did protest music actually appear? The answer as I noted, was only after the public had already come to the anti-Vietnam War position.

Our look at aid in developing countries suggests that the proposition celebrities follow, rather than lead, is true. Now-passed great comedian Sam Kinison once, in dark humor, joked about activists for food relief to Africa *filming* starving children instead of feeding them: "Give her a *SANDWICH!*" he shouted at the audience. Bob Geldof's Live Aid concert for Africa raised over $150 million immediately—but the accounting for how that was spent has been murky. In the meantime, it caused a backlash. One African writer said "Live Aid led to the patronising 'save Africa' industry. We don't need a musical about it." It created, Moky Makura wrote, "the false narrative about a broken continent plagued by poverty, conflict, corruption and disease . . ."[55]

"[S]hifts in celebrity fronted-climate media are quite astute . . . that has come to bedevil larger scale, immediate solutions to the climate conundrum."[56] Politically, it is quite possible that celebrities increase voter turnout among the "yout" (to quote *My Cousin Vinnie*) but do they incentivize follow-up—active participation in a party, voter registration, donations? With climate change, have the celebrities' efforts led to regular contributions to Greenpeace, or more activism? It seems not. Constant, nearly hysterical appeals to save the planet are jarred by the simple observation that the water level at Plymouth Rock or the Statue of Liberty hasn't moved an inch, causing appeals to fall on deaf ears.

A fourth and final issue for celebrities involved the double-edged aspect of fame itself. On one side of this, celebrities, as we have seen, possess an aura of entitlement which can create interest, even trust. Yet at the same time it generates resentment over their ability to adopt children when others cannot, to go wherever they want with special access when others can't, and to have access to high echelons of political, scientific, even military power. (Think of what would happen if an ordinary person with a camera walked into the Pentagon and wanted the navy to put on exotic maneuvers in F-18s as Tom Cruise could.) In a much darker edge, malevolent, evil, and often mentally deranged people such as the Columbine killers acted predominantly out of a quest for fame.[57] Over time, however, this fame notoriety has *decreased* the "legacy effect," because the public has "become habituated to apparently random mass and serial killings," and while the outrage is remembered, the assailants are not.[58]

For those celebrities the media values and wishes to promote, it has been argued that a person's "fifteen minutes of fame" can be extended, perhaps indefinitely. No better example exists than Madonna, who has effectively morphed her image through four decades of music. Some analysts claim that with proper marketing and support, celebrity status can be perpetuated indefinitely.[59] This also explains why mass-shooters are so quickly forgotten: no one is going to willingly extend their fame.

Our modern society developed a term for this celebrity value-posing: virtue signaling. It may be that the Overton Window has moved to the point that among the young, hip, and elites "climate change" is a reality, but at a deeper level it may also just as easily be the "expected thing to say," as has occurred with the homosexual and transsexual movements.

When it comes to the globalists, "climate change" became the perfect instrument to force a one-world government and celebrities their perfect propaganda vehicles. After all, if the earth itself is at stake, then no single nation could be allowed to block efforts to save it, and no one could make the case faster than those individuals already well-known. This phenomenon came to fruition with the United Nations' Paris Agreement, which set out "a global framework to avoid dangerous climate change by limiting global warming to well below 2°C and pursuing efforts to limit it to 1.5°C."[60] Obviously ignored by this mission statement were such key questions as, "What if the earth, via its relationship with the sun, is naturally warming?" "What if there are benefits to a warmer earth?" "What if humans have no role whatsoever in accelerating or retarding such warming?"

The entire Paris ideology was based on the notion that even if other aspects of human life, including pollution, were improving, "we still have to change our current lifestyle dramatically because our way of life is now changing the climate and causing global warming."[61] Beginning with the European Union's member states, the Paris

Agreement was ratified in 2016 and included "close to 190 parties," Under Barack Obama, the US announced its intention to join, which it did in September 2016, despite the fact that technically as a treaty, the Senate had not even debated it—let alone ratified it. One of President Donald Trump's first acts was to announce the United States would withdraw, though it could not do that until the day before the election in 2020.[62] Immediately after his election, Joe Biden announced the US would rejoin.

Biden went further than the "Nationally Determined Contribution" (NDC) to reduce greenhouse emissions, which were voluntary, non-enforceable, and submitted every five years. Instead Biden proposed a complete, and utterly unattainable, complete decarbonization of the power sector by 2035 and economy-wide net-zero greenhouse gas emissions by 2050. As had Obama, Biden planned a wide range of attacks, including shutting down the Keystone XL pipeline that Trump had approved, placing tariffs on countries not meeting "climate objective" (i.e., China, which Biden deliberately did *not* want to punish), and having the federal government push electric vehicles, wind power, and solar power. Biden (or his minions, who likely ran the entire administration) created new initiatives and regulations in the Department of Energy, the Department of Agriculture, and even the Securities and Exchange Commission.[63] Obama created the Green Climate Fund to subsidize energy projects to the tune of $3 billion and used the State Department to bypass Congress in supporting third world countries begging for money under the auspices of "climate mitigation."[64]

Such silliness defied comprehension. As of 2021, some 80 percent of America's energy came from petroleum, natural gas, and coal, all of which emitted carbon dioxide. Coal and natural gas supplied two-thirds of the US electricity needs.[65] The economic impact of the proposed goals was staggering: by 2035, it would cost the US *annually* 400,000 jobs and see the GDP fall by $2.5 trillion. An average family would lose $20,000 a year in income with such regulations.

When Biden signed on to a policy of making a transition to a full green grid by 2050, it constituted a potential act of national suicide and at the same time of utter fantasy. Cambridge professor of engineering Michael Kelly calculated the absurd requirements of a "net zero" emissions program by 2050. Merely "greening" residences, apartments, and houses for heat would cost between $20 and $35 *trillion* dollars. Then there were transportation costs, which would require an increase in the US energy supply to maintain battery support at 2023 levels (i.e., not even allowing for growth). But that doesn't even include all the transport or specialized types of heating that cannot be done electrically as with, for example, steel production. To get the power grid decarbonized and 60 percent bigger—as demanded by the new net-zero requirements—the US would have to add 120,000 miles of transmission lines to its existing 200,000 high voltage lines. But it's the local distribution lines where the real expense lays. There, 5.5 *million miles* of local lines would have to be upgraded with another cost of $6 trillion. Even before getting to other, real-world costs (and/or the *increased* cost of power after companies pour all this money into them), the price tag was somewhere between $26.6 trillion and $36.6 trillion.[66]

None of these costs take into account the phenomenal expense of the materials needed to make the electric grid, which would only increase with the new demand. (Think of any project, ever, that the federal government has done in which costs came in lower than expected.) But possibly the most challenging (and impossible) hurdle would be the number of engineers required to attain even these numbers. The UK engineering firm Atkins estimated that a $1 billion project in the electric sector over thirty years needed twenty-four professional engineers and one hundred more skilled tradesmen. Scaling up to the requirements Kelly listed, America would need 300,000 college engineering graduates and over 1.2 million skilled tradesmen, full-time, for all thirty years.[67] (As of 2023, American colleges only graduated 145,000 engineers a year—in all sub-disciplines of the field, such as hydro, metal, structural, mechanical, nuclear, and so on: *electrical* engineers only constitute 14 percent of all engineers.)

Finally, Kelly noted, there was the issue of "intermittency," which simply meant wind and solar don't work all the time. They only work when it's windy and sunny. What do you do when it's neither? The answer was that the massive backup for "net zero" with hydrocarbons would require an additional *eighty times* as many non-wind/solar power plants as we have today at a cost of hundreds of trillions of dollars. Net zero isn't a fantasy, it's a nightmare. Kelly argued it would require a "command economy" to even come remotely close to the net-zero goals by 2050. I disagree. Command economies throughout history have been *less efficient and less productive*, and thus whatever cost or whatever personnel numbers he has estimated would have to be in all likelihood doubled with a command economy. If the US spent every single penny of the government's money for twenty-seven years, it would barely cover one-third the cost of net zero in the most optimistic of scenarios. Still another study said that by 2040 the requirements for "green energy" would be 50 million miles of new transmission lines, or more than all the transmission capacity built in the entirety of human history.[68]

Meanwhile, the world's largest polluter, China, continued to build coal plants, and its coal production in 2020 was the nation's highest since 2015.[69] Some of the other nations' commitments were almost humorous. India committed to emissions reductions that were less than what the country would achieve if it made no changes at all, and Russia, the fifth-largest emitter of CO_2, sent in no plan for reductions.[70] Combining all the reductions by nations that signed the pledge and submitted goals acceptable to the Paris gurus, the Universal Ecological Fund noted that the impact would be practically undetectable.[71]

It was thus no surprise that President Trump said the Paris Accord was "unfair at the highest level to the United States."[72] That was by intention. The hidden agenda of all "climate agreements" is to punish wealthy western nations, using "climate" as a sort of weapon of redistribution to the poorer countries—who create more pollution. It was never about the environment. It was always about capitalism, or, more accurately, how to stop it. That is seen in the pronouncements coming out of the World Economic Forum and its leader, Klaus Schwab, whose goal is to reduce populations, globalize governments and economies, and end economic growth for all. To the WEF, people being better off automatically means the climate is worse off.

Hence, beginning in the 1990s, the WEF and President Bill Clinton began a dedicated effort to restructure the West's energy and transportation sectors around "green" energy. As Guy Mitchell in *Global Warming: The Great Deception* notes, global warming was "a fraudulent hypothesis developed to promote climate change research and to advance a socio-economic agenda. It has no basis in scientific principles or facts."[73]

Using celebrities to advance the cause constitutes one arm of the globalists' strategy. Money constitutes the other, mostly in the form of subsidies for green projects. Elon Musk, who had developed cozy relationships with both Obama and Trump, had opened his Fremont, California assembly lines for his electric Tesla automobiles during the China Virus lockdowns. However, Biden left Musk out of an announcement ceremony in August 2021 where he revealed a plan to make half of all new passenger vehicle sales electric or hybrid by 2030. After a long "honeymoon" between Musk and the government, Tesla was on the outs because his auto company was not unionized—yet another contradictory policy of the Biden energy plan.[74] Tesla also used its own charging stations, which could not be accessed by any other electric car. Musk called federal support for charging infrastructure unnecessary, and Tesla itself had thirty thousand charging station nationwide.[75] In August 2023, Musk won, as Ford and General Motors announced they would use Tesla's charging technology, making Tesla the de-facto standard in the US.[76]

Tesla had achieved much of its popularity only because government subsidies made the ultra-expensive cars somewhat more affordable. It seemed entirely possible his strategy was to first, gain control of the EV market itself by demanding an end to subsidies, then, once the competition was eliminated, return to a "need" for subsidies to stay afloat.

As for charging stations, even the vast numbers planned were dwarfed by gasoline stations. As of 2023 there were more than 145,000 gas stations—but it must be remembered that at each of these, there could be as many as a dozen actual pumps, and at almost all there were at least four. Thus the "real" number of "gas stations" available to drivers was over 400,000, whereas charging stations almost always included no more than four. Moreover, as of 2023, it took *four hours* for the CEO of Ford to charge his Ford F-150 truck to only 40 percent![77] Even then, a genuine test of such a vehicle would be to require it to get you someplace in 15–24 hours, thus prohibiting charging times of over a few minutes; would not provide you with easy GPS access to the closest charging stations (so you would have to "hunt"); and would keep you from driving to a Tesla charging station with your Ford! Charging times are routinely more than twenty minutes, meaning that the lines behind those four chargers would back up at an unsustainable level. Indeed, an apples-to-apples comparison of someone who had to drive to a meeting or a convention would require an EV driver to leave *days* beforehand.

Opposition to electric cars (EVs) was not limited to the United States. In reaction to EVs, truckers have modified their diesel engines to increase their horsepower and their pollution output. One company selling such "defeat devises" had to pay a $1 million fine for breaking environmental laws, but if those laws work as well as the laws against radar-detector "fuzz busters" worked? Fuggedaboudit. Since 2014, "rolling coal" as it's called has become a standard protest against electric cars. There is not only anxiety about range and recharges, but also about job losses, about China's attempt to dominate the EV market, and to the overall legitimacy of "global warming" concerns itself.[78] And the issue literally heated up further during Hurricane Idalia when flood waters, coming into contact with electric cars, ignited multiple fires.[79]

In nation after nation, the green dreams of wind power and electric cars smashed headfirst into reality. America's auto industry is a case in point. In September 2023, the United Autoworkers went on strike because much of their pay increase was being redirected to electric vehicles, whose division at Ford was losing $4.5 billion. Yet Ford's CEO insisted that he would not back off "investing" in electric Fords. That term was interesting, because much of the "investment" was coming from Uncle Sam. While the auto industry "finds itself . . . cranking out new electric models . . . car dealership lots overflow with electric cars that consumers have proven reluctant to buy."[80] It was also worth noting that sales of the electric Ford F-150 had "dropped off a cliff" in 2023, down by almost 50 percent.[81]

Once the globalists got behind electric cars, they became "weaponised as a political tool," and most accept that Biden's unattainable goal of having two-thirds of the car market to be electric by 2032 is a disaster in waiting. The fight over banning gas or diesel cars in England has damaged the administration of Prime Minister Rishi Sunak, who declared himself on the side of the motorists. One would add, "for now."

Climate insanity was associated with a lack of knowledge about the environment, according to one study.[82] That explains simultaneously the dumbing down of schools and the catastrophism that dominates "climate change" talk. It also underscored Bernays's theory that Americans had received just enough education to think they were smart. Or, as Ronald Reagan used to say, "It's not what you don't know that hurts you, but what you think you know that's wrong."

As seen in chapter five, even celebrity philanthropy was accompanied by a range of problems. Many of the stars' "contributions" looked tarnished when exposed to deep investigation. Madonna contributed to building an academy for underprivileged girls in Malawi. Then an audit in 2011 showed that the school had never even been built and that there were grand salaries for employees and lavish expenditures on cars, and even a golf course.[83] Not only did the executive director, Philippe van den Bossche, resign, but some eighty of the charity employees sued Madonna for unpaid salaries and non-payment of benefits. Madonna also *loaned* the organization over $11 million, which she viewed as an act of charity. In similar fashion, during the Johnny Depp-Amber Heard divorce case, it was revealed that Heard claimed she had "given" $7 million to charity, when in fact she had only "pledged" it and actually given very little. She insisted at trial that "pledged" was the same thing as "gave."

Even when celanthropy doesn't involve outright fraud or deception, the record is clear that most donations—which, in the US, are all tax deductible—were eaten up by the bureaucracy. For example, the Justin Timberlake Foundation distributed a grand total of $32,000 in 2006, while spending $146,000 on travel and other costs. Tyra Banks's TZONE Foundation that same year paid $35,000 in salaries and distributed only $32,000. Some outfits, if run directly by the celebrity, could be extremely generous. David Letterman's American Foundation for Courtesy and Grooming had an overhead expense of just $25! Steve Martin's foundation gave away $399,000 on an overhead expense of just $329. But Rosie O'Donnell's All for Kids Foundation, while giving away $2.9 million in grants, ate up another $1.9 million in overhead.[84]

Nothing came close, though, to the 2010 report of the famous 1985 Band Aid concert, which was one of the first big celebrity events. The BBC wrongly claimed that 95 percent of the money raised ended up in the hands of Ethiopian rebels, but ultimately the project's own field director in Ethiopia admitted that between 10 and 20 percent ended up in rebel hands.[85]

Celebrity status itself didn't come without a cost. Celebrities lived on average *thirteen* fewer years than the average American. One analyst of celebrity culture cited much higher death rates from cancer, accidents, influenza, cirrhosis, suicide, homicide, and ulcers.[86] Celebrities also had to live with the knowledge that their behavior always motivated some individuals to act in similar fashion. For example, following the coverage of a Viennese celebrity's suicide, there was a 43 percent increase in attempted or actual suicide in Austria.[87]

While certainly not all celanthropy goes to fight climate change, that is by far the most dominant issue in celebrities' talking points. And it's a hoax. As of 2022, NOAA (the National Oceanic and Atmospheric Administration), which is the central organization tracking "global warming" found that the land surface temperature has only recorded a .01 degree increase in *the last 140 years*.[88]

It should be obvious to anyone (and certainly those who believe in evolution) that the earth's core temperature has changed many times over the centuries. Thus, even if there were significant changes going on, it would be, well, natural. But the ARGO Float program, which measures ocean temperatures, has found temperature change to be nonexistent. Oceans cannot even absorb long wave infrared photons from the sun below a depth of 100 microns, or that of a human hair. So even if all the CO_2 molecules caused sun rays to be radiated downward (and they don't: only about .2 percent is absorbed), it would still be non-detectable.

Attempting to stop a non-problem, globalists at the UN's Intergovernmental Panel on Climate Change embraced a completely unscientific approach to the role of carbon dioxide in the atmosphere. The UN's models, as have those of other "climate scientists," have routinely produced results that exceeded reality. As we have seen, all efforts to demonstrate the efficacy of such models through "back testing" have failed.[89]

But it's not only the tests that have failed. So have the treaties. The Kyoto Protocol saw CO_2 emissions *increase*. The Paris Accord, from which President Trump smartly withdrew, did not have an enforcement mechanism, likely because China and India couldn't be forced to comply. As Guy Mitchell wrote in *Global Warming: The Great Deception*, the "real purpose of the climate treaties is to perpetuate the trading of carbon credits to enrich global investment firms," and, I would add, to transfer money from wealthier nations to poorer ones.[90]

Then there is the "97 percent of the world's scientists agree" that there is man-made global warming. This in itself is a total myth, and a lie. It is, however, sufficiently woven into a fabric of falsity that it requires explanation. The percentage stemmed from a *letter* published in *Environmental Research Letters* in 2013 called "Quantifying the consensus on anthropogenic global warming in the scientific literature," by John Cook.[91] Yet the letter itself said that after analyzing almost 12,000 climate abstracts from 1991–2011, the author found "that 66.4 percent of abstracts expressed *no position on Anthropogenic Global Warming*" (emphasis mine).[92] The letter went on to say that only 32 percent endorsed global warming," and of *those 97.1 percent agreed on human causation.* Which is to say that two-thirds of the world's scientists, as reflected in the scientific literature, disagreed with the human-caused global warming position.

Such blatant lies naturally led to some politicians hedging their bets with even more ridiculous comments. Former US Senator Tim Wirth said *"Even if* the theory of global warming is wrong, we will be doing the right thing [acting as if it is right] in terms of economic policy and environmental policy" (emphasis mine).[93] Or the Canadian former minister of the Environment: "No matter if the science *is all phoney,* there are collateral environmental benefits. . . Climate change [provides] the greatest chance to bring about justice and equality in the world" (emphasis mine).[94] Jonathan Schell, the famous anti-nuke activist, had written in *Discover* magazine in 1988 that regrettably scientists were "ethically bound" to the scientific method, so activists such as himself had to "offer up scary scenarios, under simplified, dramatic statements, and make little mention of any doubts we might have. . . . Each of us has to decide what the right balance is between being effective and being honest."[95]

Academic journals, which took to backing the global warming thesis, acted as gatekeepers to contradictory evidence. Patrick Brown, at Johns Hopkins University, said he had to omit key data on wildfires *not* being caused by climate change in order to get his piece published in a prestigious journal.[96] As noted in our discussion of the China Virus, researchers dependent on government grants often provide the answers the government wants to hear. Even beyond that, as John Ioannidis noted, "There is an increasing concern that most current published research findings are false," most notably because studies use extremely small samples to make broad claims and may often "be simply accurate measures of the prevailing bias."[97] Add to the researchers' bias the bias of the journals themselves, and genuine science that questions everything is out the door. This was evident during the China Virus, where studies on the death/injury effects of the vaccines were all but prohibited.

As just one example, an early paper done on the effects of pollution by Stephen Schneider, which later became part of his book *Global Warming*, received great attention in the *New York Times*. There were several problems, most notably that he took pollution readings— well, where there *was* pollution—overestimating the effects of CO_2 by threefold. Most of the earth was not subject to the same pollution as the locations where he took samples.[98] And our earlier discussion of Neil Ferguson's original panic study over the China Virus had modeling errors that were "far worse than we knew."[99]

Not only were directly contradictory voices squelched, but overall research tended to be "less disruptive." Despite the fact that the volume of new scientific and technological knowledge witnessed an "exponential growth" in the last few decades, progress in fact slowed in several major fields.[100] A study of over 45 million papers and patents found that the unveiling of truly new knowledge or genuine scientific advancements was slowing. In other words, researchers were increasingly reluctant to unveil new discoveries that might be controversial, cost them research funding, or result in ostracism.

A distrust in facts and suspicion of authorities for obvious reasons fueled a decline in Christianity and Judaism, a central goal of the globalists. A godless people are both more easily agitated and at the same time more easily depressed. Jean Twenge's generational research showed a continual rise in anxiety or depression among younger Americans correlated to their growing use of social media and falling levels of religious observance.[101]

Declining income—or perceptions of declining income exacerbated unhappiness. By 2010, five times as many whites in the lowest fifth of income were unhappy compared to those in the top fifth.[102] Unhappiness among non-white non-college educated working class Americans "swelled after 2000, especially after 2010."[103] At the same time, a search of the terms "self-esteem" and "self-focus" skyrocketed.[104] Adulthood came as a shock to generations raised on such pablum, to the point that by the time America got to the Millennial generation, a new term, "adulting," was created to describe a transition to boring but necessary grown-up activities. Mowing one's lawn is simply not "fulfilling" or a job most people loved. Predictably, the use of narcissistic phrases has skyrocketed with the "self-esteem" movement.[105]

Another factor feeding the discontent was the role of perceptions energized and magnified by social media. One measurement of discontent used the metric, "the difference between expectations and reality."[106] Or as Twenge observed in her generational research, "If people had an unbiased view of others' income, their subjective views would line up with their objective views . . . Instead, social media and TV showcase those at the very top of the income distribution [or those who appear to be at the top] giving a skewed view of others' income."[107] The result was a larger group of people who believed the system wasn't working and thus proved more susceptible to programs offering government aid to "offset" the inequality in the system. In fact, Millennials (for example) were not falling behind, and in terms of actual wealth per capita they were building wealth at about the same levels as all other generations.[108] Millennials had the misfortune of starting their working lives right at the trough of the 2007–08 depression, but since then they have tracked nearly the same as others.

One of the most important, but least discussed, factors in the skepticism over authority, logic, and despair has been the loss of faith. Younger generations had increasingly lost their religion, and with the diminution of faith came even more helplessness and vulnerability. A combination of poor perception of wealth and lack of religion led to fewer children. By 2021, large percentages of all younger Americans said they did not want to have kids, although in 2023 the birth rates started to rise some in an "unexpected increase in US fertility rates."[109]

Virtually every measure of happiness—especially of people under twenty years of age—showed a marked change after about 2010. This had two major causes. First, as researcher Jean Twenge pointed out in her mega-study of surveys, almost every downward trend coincided with the introduction of iPhones and iPads. *This occurred even as adults were becoming "more happy."*[110] Another study found that more liberal teens were worse off in their attitudes than conservative (one might add, "faith based") teens.[111] Teen girls were particularly susceptible to high levels of sadness, according to the CDC.[112] Most experts, including Twenge and Jonathan Haidt, identified social media particularly was damaging to young females.[113]

One could not ignore the "Obama effect," however. Right after Barack Obama's reelection, sharp and shocking changes occurred in the satisfaction related to a number of problems, most notably race. The percent of those dissatisfied with the state of race relations shot up after Obama won his second term. The conclusion was inescapable. Initially many Americans had hoped Obama would make a positive change, but within just four years they found he had caused race relations to collapse.[114]

Other research has pointed to a second, strong non-political influence in younger people's disillusion and gloom, namely the constant drumbeat of negativity, particularly regarding "climate change" that young people are indoctrinated with on a regular basis.[115] Constant "catastrophism" destroys faith, confidence, and happiness. Young people cannot constantly be told the world will end in ten years and expect them to plan for an entire life. Even if the claims were true, there would be little benefit in catastrophism.

Young people are to some degree malleable and are largely unaware that the World Economic Forum and the UN saw climate change as the tip of the spear for a larger anti-human movement. For the first time, the goal of such international organizations was not to increase material prosperity for those currently on the planet or who will be born in the near future, but to "cap and curtail it."[116] The WEF's goal was not even to manage scarcity, but to outright *cause* it. In the attempt to impose the climate change mentality on the world, the UN, WEF, and climate groups (as seen earlier, spearheaded by celebrity shaming) have targeted multinational corporations through the "ESG" (Environmental, Social, Governance) movement. This has been labeled by author Carol Roth "World War F"—a "financial world in which you are 'F'd.'"[117] It is an international effort to redistribute wealth on the most massive scale in human history.

To some degree it worked. As of 2017, the most commonly owned asset for most Americans was a home (26 percent). But the near hyper-inflation of the Biden years drove interest rates to over 7.3 percent, pricing many younger people out of homes. That was on top of the great crash of 2007–08 where almost five million people lost homes to fore-closure.[118] That was followed by a nine-year period of underbuilding, when new houses added were about 5.6 million units short of what was added in the 1990s. Compounding these problems, corporate America, led by Starwood and BlackRock, have entered the home-buying market, while AmericanHomes4Rent has now competed with private renters. Corporations were now competitors to ordinary Americans seeking housing.

Using primarily climate change but aided and abetted by other "social justice" nostrums, this new world war, far from being about one nation controlling the territory of another, is about globalist world leaders and their governments trying to control mass populations via control of their currency, housing, food, and medicine. Those aligned against the people are obviously government forces, social justice claims, namely that many were unfairly dispossessed in life of wealth or status or education, form the background of the second tentacle seeking to redistribute wealth.

Fortunately, the new globalist climate change agenda involving distortion of facts, to make people less trusting of institutions, and to create a catastrophic cloud of defeatism—making people "less happy"—simply wasn't going to work. Reality is that the "green revolution" is not only impossible as currently framed, but is radically stupid. For example, governors begged Joe Biden for more subsidies, as by 2050 the US would need "Thousands of wind farms," included farms over all of Illinois, Indiana, Ohio, Tennessee, and Kentucky to meet energy needs.[119] Inflation and "insufficient subsidies" challenged Big Wind. What went unstated was the fact that, like almost all "green" projects, subsidies were needed because the market had no use for Big Wind.[120]

Was this all part of a globalist movement to deprive people of property and ownership of everything? The World Economic Forum and its lackeys at Wiki insisted that no one at the WEF ever said in the future "you'll own nothing and be happy." Rather, it was contended, the original video from which this phrase originated in 2016 featured an essay by a Danish politician Ida Auken who had envisioned a network of technology, including stoves, refrigerators, and other appliances hooked up to one giant international provider that would remotely fix problems. Auken's essay, "Welcome to 2040. I own nothing, have no privacy, and life has never been better," became "You will own nothing and be happy."[121] Reaction to the statement, which swiftly and widely circulated during the pandemic, was such that the WEF had to back-track. It quickly pointed out that its 2030 framework included individual ownership and control over private property.[122]

As former Congressman Thaddeus McCotter wrote, "the first goal of the collusion between the WEF and the apocalyptic climate cult is to convince the upper and middle classes of the wealthiest industrialized nations that diminished expectations are virtuous."[123] Keep in mind Twenge's research that showed Gen-X and Gen-Y (or the "iGen" as she called it) prioritized "making a difference" or having idealistic goals, especially from their jobs. This, in turn, produced among Boomers high levels of poor mental health, depression, and suicide as work turned out to be, well, work.[124]

Another attempt at forcing proper virtue (as the elites deem it) involved the use of digital currency and/or a "social credit system," where totalitarian governments can reward or punish citizens whose behavior comports with their goals. China is attempting at present to implement such a system, though so far it hasn't gotten much further than applying it to some businesses. That in itself may be a blessing, because China's economy is on a downward slide. Some say it is entering crisis levels. Social credit scoring definitely won't make the Chinese companies more competitive.[125] Among the "crimes" that can lower your credit system score were "loitering," spreading "fake news" (i.e., anything the government didn't like), and even cheating when playing video games (an extremely important pastime in all of Asia).[126]

Naturally, the World Economic Forum sought to horn in on any program that gave elites more power, beginning with the "Alternative Credit Scoring" system. Originally conceived (or so stated) as an organization for the "underbanked"—as in people whose credit history is so bad no reasonable person would lend them money—the ACS data includes rather normal records of asset ownership, utility payment information, and other routine reports, but also social media posts and location data (i.e., Orwellian stuff).[127] In America, Joe Biden already set up a "Disinformation Governance Board," a laden term which actually means "A Disinformation Purveyance Board." As the *Wall Street Journal* noted, the policy was all about people, and the people Biden would empower to "govern disinformation" would not be trustworthy in the least.[128]

A key component of any international credit system would be a "digital identification." The China Virus provided a unique test run for such a device with a vaccine card, which more or less flopped. As seen in the chapter on medical globalism, while the elites came close to locking down much of the planet, in the end they failed. It may have allowed them to steal a presidential election, but the backlash both against the vax itself and against lockdowns was so severe that in 2023 when a "new variant" of Covid appeared and authorities again made noises about masks and lockdowns, resistance appeared so quickly and strongly that multiple universities had to rescind their vaccine edicts. The masks never did make a comeback.

Social credit systems interacted with globalist dreams of population reduction and destruction of the family in another way, however. The transsexual movement, which had been virtually nonexistent in 2000, took off after the *Obergefell* decision on homosexual marriages. Few paid any attention to it at first. Surely no one could take seriously that men so deeply believed they were women they would chop off their genitals, much less that *anyone* would allow such procedures on children. Yet by 2023, California was enacting laws taking children away from parents who interfered with their "gender identity."

Overall the trends embodied an assault on masculinity—not just in the United States but worldwide. The problem grew so serious that even Communist China found it necessary to teach masculinity to boys.[129] American schools increasingly sought to allow children to "change their gender" while at school without parents' knowledge. Gender ideologues came to see parents and families as a major threat to "trans-genderism" and sought to keep curricula and school events secret from parents.[130] Of course, activists issued calls to "Abolish the family."[131]

Globalism's dark spiritual side was seen in its push for "sexual rights" for children, an effort that undermined parental rights and involved grooming. Three groups—the International Planned Parenthood Federation (IPPF), the World Health Organization (WHO), and the United Nations have promoted new programs to emphasize children as "sexual beings" with their own sexual rights apart from maturity. Those efforts sought to advance transgenderism and abortion in a "very well-funded" and coordinated program as a part of the "2030 Agenda for Sustainable Development."[132] Social credit systems were tailor made for such authoritarianism.

With the transsexual movement and credit systems, "ownership" of children entered a new phase. It included fights between parents and teachers over what was being taught during the remote learning periods of the China Virus lockdowns. Biden's regime responded in 2022 by attacking the "Moms for Liberty" parental activist group as "terrorists" under the Patriot Act.[133]

Many of the shadows cast over America in the twenty-first century were common to the rest of the world. A "birth dearth" had been underway for decades. A combination of birth control measures, rising affluence, and a nearly global resistance to large families, combined with China's "one child" policy, had caused a steady decline in birth rates. In the West, especially in the United States, the women's movement had spearheaded an effort to downplay (or even demonize) childbearing, leading the US birth rate to hit a record low in 2019. Experts warned that America faced a "demographic time bomb" that stood to be fast-tracked by the Covid (or China Virus) pandemic.[134] By 2021, states such as California had already started to face demographic calamity with a birth rate barely half of what it was in 2000.[135]

A "growing prevalence of singledom among America's rising generation of women" became "one of the most potent forces in politics."[136] (Even Europe, with state incentives for motherhood, had failed to raise birth rates.) Unmarried women tended to vote far to the left of the electorate and on average proved far more enamored of big government. At the same time the surging rights and homosexual movement de facto worked against traditional families. By 2023, 30 percent of women under twenty-five considered themselves lesbians (contrasted with only 5 percent of women over sixty years old).[137] This was a "sign of a deeply decadent culture . . . a culture that lacks the wherewithal to survive."[138] Not only were traditional, normal families under attack, but the decreasing number of stable family models made it more difficult for young people to see what they were like.

If it feels like there is something deeper, something much more sinister in all these attacks, there is. The globalists have always acted on a larger spiritual level. Usually they keep it hidden, but in recent years they have become more flagrant in flying their true spiritual colors. Mind you, this is nothing new. But what is new is the degree to which the global elites now seem to flaunt their disdain for Christianity, Judaism, and traditional spirituality.

Since the Congress of Vienna, with its recreations of the Napoleonic Wars in ceremonies and its endless balls, to the party atmosphere of the Versailles Conference, globalists have always infiltrated their celebrations with heavy doses of Greek gods and paganism. Those, however, were always carefully accompanied and adorned by Christian imagery for balance. No more. Now paganism and Satanic imagery have taken center stage. The opening ceremonies of some of the largest projects would be (pun intended) illuminating. For example, at the opening ceremony of the Gotthard Base Railroad Tunnel in Switzerland—which seemed to be less about opening a tunnel than opening a portal to another world or dimension—a group of clerics (including a Muslim) "bless" the festivities. A cadre of people dressed in orange construction-type suits march in with work helmets, all to the primal beating of drums, marches up to a massive screen upon which there is superimposed a cliff. The "employees," starting one at a time, then five at a time, try to "climb" the cliff with the assistance of cables. One at a time, they fall off. Earth worship, Gaia-ism, Baphomet, and Egyptian gods are all displayed on screen. Finally all five fall off at which point all of the rest of the "workers," at the foot of the cliff . . . begin to strip off their clothes down to their underwear.[139]

If you're wondering what nudity has to do with a train, you and I are probably on the same page. But the scene got more bizarre: suddenly a type of gas appeared as the semi-naked bodies writhed in front of a new image on screen, namely that of a circular "eye" to another place. (On screen in the "eye" were more naked bodies, of course). The "writhers" then roll down the ramp to the bottom while, crawling one atop another's shoulders, other "workers" begin to again scale the "mountain" on screen, where a picture of an asteroid-type object appears, "killing" the workers. But they are quickly replaced by three women in long flowing angelic type robes in front of a portal to outer space, while the semi-naked "rollers" walk back in white.

Just when you think perhaps something pure or good might come from this scene, a man dressed as a goat-god comes out dancing, screaming, and barking like a dog as all the other participants simulate screaming. Beetle-like creatures take over for the "workers" trying to ascend the screen as multiple eyeballs appear. Traditional Swiss horn-blowers heralded the goat-god who selects one of the white-clad women. Replacing all the people wearing white now are people covered in grass from head to toe. All—those in white and those in grass—now worship the goat-god (who hasn't quit screaming the entire time).

The "workers" had died for the commune, as all threw off their clothes to return to Sodom. No one opposed the symbolic devil (the goat-man) while all the celebrities and officials nodded in approval. Interestingly—perhaps fittingly—in August 2023 there was a freight derailment inside the tunnel that closed it for months.[140]

The CERN Hadron Collider, which even Elon Musk labeled "demonic technology," has yielded the "God particle."[141] In front of CERN is a statue of Shiva, the Hindu god of death or emptiness. Just as concerning was the recently installed statue dedicated to former US Supreme Court Justice Ruth Bader Ginsburg outside the Appellate Court in New York City. The gold statue looks incredibly satanic, with horns and tentacles, and many call it "Medusa."[142] The Strasbourg Parliament building in France is not only based almost exactly on the Tower of Babel designs, but the "Woman on the Beast" sculpture outside of the Council of Ministers in Europe is straight out of the Harlot in Revelations. This isn't a good thing![143]

Such images, ceremonies, and statues did not occur by accident, or without major individuals in power knowing what they were about. They weren't "accidents." They were clear, overt, in-you-face statements of the globalists and their anti-Christian/anti-God agenda. The entire climate change movement was an attempt by man to control the planet (and nature) itself. What was remarkable was that the forces behind these movements are now comfortable enough coming out of the demonic closet. Yet just as they thought they had succeeded, the entire globalist fabric began to unravel before their very eyes.

Chapter Eight

Globalism in Decline

I n April 2022, US District Judge Kathryn Mizelle struck down the federal (Covid) surgical mask mandate for riding airplanes or being in airports or while riding mass transit.[1] Videos showed captains making the announcement on panes as passengers exultantly ripped off their masks and celebrated. Of course, Mizelle was accused of being an "activist Trump judge," and big-government/globalists everywhere all but went into mourning. Suddenly those who had lived by judicial activism, colloquially speaking, died from it. Big government was good only when it ran in the progressive/globalist direction. Dr. Anthony Fauci—"Dr. Fallacy" to critics—complained that only the Centers for Disease Control, not a judge, had the capability to make medical projections and recommendations, a position completely in opposition to what had happened over the previous year and for over a century.

This simple act, long overdue, in some ways marked the first shovel of dirt on globalism, the burial rites, as it were, over the authoritarian cadaver. It was precisely that unconstitutional and illegitimate expanded authority they had used to eliminate Donald Trump as president. Under sweeping and coordinated globalist Deep State actions, they had imposed emergency controls in an attempt to control, contain, and regulate almost every aspect of human life, from whom people interacted with, to where they went to school or traveled, to whether they could work out or go to a bar. It prompted former president Barack Obama to whine about "disinformation" at Stanford University where he claimed that there was "information sanity" in the age when people received all their news from only three broadcast networks . . . which largely the elites controlled. No wonder he liked it so much.[2] In earlier times Obama's own speech would have been considered "disinformation," but instead of regulating it, people would have ignored it as rubbish.

Judge Mizelle was only one of many who had started a revolutionary and grassroots-level pushback against the globalists and elite control. In January, a more important and wide reaching—but less theatrical—decision had come from the US Supreme Court in *NFIB v. OSHA*, which invalidated the China Virus vaccine mandate for companies that had at least 100 employees.[3] It came in many forms, and in many cases was already well under way. The same month that Mizelle's decision rocked the Biden administration and the WHO, an equally momentous event occurred in the private sector, when billionaire and entrepreneur Elon Musk purchased the social media site Twitter. Declaring himself a "free speech absolutist," Musk vowed to restore banned and shadowbanned accounts (including my own, which he did!). Promising to restore Twitter to a more "neutral" forum, he was attacked roundly, as "free speech" had been seen by the progressives and globalists as a code term for extremism, anti-vax sentiments, white nationalism, and fascism.

When the *Washington Post* expressed alarm that such outlets needed regulation to "prevent rich people from controlling our channels of communication," it unwittingly described itself, owned and controlled by a multibillionaire.[4] Indeed, across the board, advocates of government regulation (as they always had in the past) were merely seeking to protect their own monopolies over their domains. Lunatic comments such as those of Elizabeth Warren ("For democracy to survive we need more content moderation, not less") or Max Boot ("we must pass laws to . . . promote algorithmic justice . . .") boggled the imagination.[5] No one had yet suggested that anyone championing limits on free speech begin with their own drivel.

In a historical context, it's hard to overstate the revelations that Musk's takeover of Twitter produced. Musk began to open the "Twitter Files," as they were called to journalists. Those files encompassed and connected "every major political scandal of the Trump-Biden era."[6] An "unholy alliance" between big tech and the Deep State was "designed to throttle free speech [through] censorship and propaganda."[7] The "Twitter Files" went back to before the 2020 election and revealed policies of shadowbanning (restricting views through algorithms), banning, and suspending any dissident voices, including that of President Trump himself. Twitter propaganda and disinformation also struck any commentary that ran against the government's official line on the China Virus or Hunter Biden's laptop.

Matt Taibbi, a journalist allowed to examine the Twitter Files, wrote that they showed "the FBI acting as a doorman to a vast program of social media surveillance and censorship, encompassing agencies across the federal government . . ."[8] Hunter Biden's laptop, which had been dropped off at a Delaware computer store for repair in 2019, was a treasure trove of insider asset-buying by foreign interests. It revealed that he was making tens of millions of dollars from foreign companies, mostly for introducing "business" associates to his vice president father. One executive from Burisma, a Ukrainian energy company, flat-out asked for "advice on how you could use your influence" on behalf of the foreign company. Yet Twitter suppressed the story, removing links to a *New York Post* story that laid out the corruption and added warnings saying those posts might be "unsafe." Twitter also locked the accounts of the *Post* or anyone sharing the stories.[9]

What Musk's public release of the Twitter files showed—along with mountains of documentary evidence obtained through Freedom of Information Act lawsuits, Congressional investigations, and state attorneys general—was that these actions were not those of low-level haters, but came from the very top levels of the company's top censor with the government propagandists cheering Twitter and other repressive platforms on. As of this writing, a major suit from the state of Missouri against Joe Biden continues to wind its way through the

Fifth Circuit involving the Biden administration "threatening social media platforms over spreading misinformation."[10] To date the court has upheld all the suit's request and defeated all government challenges. FIRE, an outlet for free speech, called it "an important victory for freedom of expression."[11]

Biden had muzzled the media not just over so-called "misinformation" regarding the election and the China Virus, but also had squelched any discussion of his corruption involving briberies while as vice president in connection with deals set up by his son, Hunter. In that regard, though, he hardly needed any help: the news media obediently went along with the narrative that Biden was clean by stifling and suppressing *all* mention of Hunter and his corruption during the election. Later, the numbers came out—but steadily escalated, with first revelations suggesting the Bidens got $11 million, then $13 million, then $24 million.[12] The Ukrainian prosecutor, whom Biden *on video* clucked about having gotten fired, gave proof of Biden's bribes.[13] It got worse. As the media tried to firewall Hunter away from his corrupt father, new documents showed that Chinese business partners sent $250,000 directly to Joe Biden's Delaware home![14]

Peter Schweizer has well documented the sleaze in his book *Red-Handed: How American Elites Get Rich Helping China*, but there was corruption involving Biden well beyond just the bribes flowing from China.[15] Nevertheless, Biden's corruption is not the focus of this work, but rather how that Mt. Everest of dirt was buried during an election to protect Biden by the globalists and their media allies. Even then, the media had to slowly admit the corruption existed, was real, and if even by omission admit they lied to elect him. Only eighteen months after Joe Biden was ensconced in the presidency did the "news" media slowly begin to admit the bribery and coverups as a result of an investigation by Senate Republicans who released details. And only then did media outlets grudgingly admit that not only had Twitter and other sources buried the Hunter Biden story, but that indeed it might have had an impact on the election. (Over half of Americans made aware of the laptop story said they would have changed their vote in 2020. If true, a 13.5 million shift easily would have handed the presidency to Donald Trump.)[16] The FBI had arranged for Twitter executives to receive secret clearances so the FBI could "share" intelligence about possible threats to Biden.

The back-channel's real purpose not only involved getting Biden elected, but to stop any questioning of the fraudulent election after the fact. At both Twitter and YouTube, merely using the words "fraud" or "vote fraud" were grounds for removal (as occurred with me). It got worse: Twitter executives, under the watchful eye of the FBI, determined that President Trump's use of the words "Make America Great Again" were inflammatory—a slogan he'd used for six years. Overall, investigator Matt Taibbi found that the FBI and Twitter maintained a "constant and pervasive" contact that turned Twitter into a subsidiary of the Bureau.[17]

Censorship in Trump's first election in 2016 with another social media giant, Facebook, which had been fooled by Trump's media genius, Brad Parscale, who managed to use the site to Trump's great benefit. Joel Pollak and I documented this in our book *How Trump Won*.[18] Then, came the entire web of media lies regarding the Russia Hoax.[19] While it's impossible to separate out the worst offenders, the *Washington Post* was the most unrepentant, and was even exposed by *Columbia Journalism Review*, which wrote "At [the] root [of new antagonism of the press] was an undeclared war between an entrenched media, and a new kind of disruptive presidency, with its own hyperbolic version of the truth."[20] When the *Post*'s and other outlets storylines "were authoritatively undercut, the follow-ups were downplayed or ignored."

Then came press manipulation of the China Virus information, which indirectly damaged Trump. Social media platforms had allied with the Centers for Disease Control and the Food and Drug Administration to stymie, suppress, or outright eliminate any criticism of the government lockdowns, its mask mandates, or the Covid/China Virus vaccines.[21] Of course, the critics were right in every respect. Lockdowns yielded no positive constraint on the virus; the vax itself was proven ineffective at best and deadly at worst. And masks? By

January 2023, a survey of twelve different studies on masks found "little or no difference to the outcome of influenza-like illness" from the China Virus.[22] (For example, heavily-masked California had a higher cumulative death rate per 100,000 than did Florida with its much older and more vulnerable population.)[23] Likewise, writer Steve Kirsch in May 2021 became one of the first to point out that the deaths from the vaccines had exceeded those of deaths with the virus itself.[24]

It took a while to slow the globalists down through courts, but a slow drip of breakthroughs began when in January 2022 the US Supreme Court ruled against the Occupational Safety and Health Administration's mandate for businesses to force employees to be vaxxed.[25] Likewise, the Supreme Court in *Groff v. Dejoy* said that no employer could deny a religious objection to taking the China Virus vaccine unless it presented "substantial increased costs in relation to . . . the particular business."[26] That was a bar higher than almost any company could claim. In essence, the court system had protected businesses—even those which wished to comply for political reasons—from their own government and even themselves.

The courts were just getting started. In 2023, a New York Supreme Court judge ruled that the governor and the state had overstepped their authority when mandating the China Virus vax for healthcare employees, which was not included in the state's public health law.[27] An Arizona court declared illegal an Arizona legislature law passed during the pandemic that protected hospitals and doctors from Covid-related suits. Many in 2023 expressed concern that the Biden administration would attempt another pandemic-type lockdown and indeed, for a moment that seemed possible when several universities announced new vax and mask rules. Then, within a month, most had rescinded those out of a public backlash. The era of the mask, it appeared, was over, and even the Germans gave up on their mask mandates for public transportation.

Courts could be useful brakes against government tyranny, and the war against the Covid measures provided powerful evidence that globalist plans had suffered significant—albeit delayed—defeats. These were just little signs that the most obvious aspects of globalism were under attack and in retreat. Another key area where the globalists began to see major casualties came in the war against climate tyranny. There, the reaction came more swiftly than with the China Virus. For example, as of 2020, the UK appeared to have "unstoppable momentum" toward its "net zero" CO_2 emissions based on the Climate Change Act of 2008.[28] UK's prime minister Rishi Sunak ignored the net zero ban on new airports, and as the *Telegraph* put it, is "finally standing up to the green blob."[29] Sunak placed himself "at the tip of the climate spear" in a major address to Parliament in which he firstly rolled back the ban on the sale of diesel and gas-powered cars by five years—though even that seemed completely unobtainable—secondly by delaying costly proposals to phase out oil and gas broilers, and thirdly by scrapping a new tax on meat.[30]

From the UK to the coasts of the USA, there was resistance against putting up new wind farms. That came at a time that new research was suggesting that *entire states* like Illinois would have to be completely covered in windmills to generate enough electricity for normal needs. Germany desperately pushed a regional mass-transit pass scheme and no one played. "The vast majority of the 11 million subscriptions sold so far have gone to longstanding public transit users," less than one-tenth of what the German climate-whiners had hoped.[31] Likewise, Germany's plan to force 15 million people to drive electric vehicles by 2030 "remains very far off" (as in only one million electric cars were in use by 2023).[32] German attempts to compel Germans to transition to heat pumps (which would have rendered many prewar German buildings uninhabitable) were mostly blunted, while their desperation for energy found them dismantling a wind farm for a coal plant![33] Globally, spending on wind and solar, while it totaled over $4 trillion, was dwarfed by spending on hydrocarbons.[34]

Climate activists became even more frenetic and crazed in their "solutions," openly advocating cutting down trees that posed a "danger."[35] Scots were "astonished" to find that over *fifteen million* trees were felled to develop wind farms.[36] But just weeks later, Biden announced a program to spend $100 million to advance "tree equity," arguing that planting more trees would reduce crime.[37] Meanwhile the "green" solutions looked worse by the day. Germany's health minister announced a plan to "combat heat" by calling old people to remind them to . . . drink water.[38] And that came on the heels of an idiotic and expensive "Corona-Warn-App" that Germans refused to use.[39] Perhaps the most lunatic of the climate "solutions"—and one with horrific implications for the health of the planet—naturally came from the Biden administration with a study to block the rays of the sun.[40] Although offered in jest, at this rate it will not be long before some globalist Einstein insists we can just move the sun to a more desirable location.

Electric bikes ("E-bikes") showed a distinct likelihood of bursting into flames from their lithium-ion batteries, so much so that authorities began to consider regulations—the first step in banning them altogether.[41] Jackson Hole, Wyoming, a woke city, bought eight electric buses for its transit system, but none of them worked and the company that made them went bankrupt.[42] Solar is showing major ecologically disastrous side effects as well: Merely cleaning the dust off solar panels was drying up ground water, while hailstorms could lay waste to a panel field in minutes.[43]

Most of all, the insanely, almost other-worldly, costs of going green and "net-zero" are coming into focus. It's not a pretty picture. That may be why the *Epoch Times* noted that a series of new scientific studies mean the "era of 'unquestioned and unchallenged' climate change claims is over."[44] And the people said . . . Hallelujah.

From one end of the globe to another, reality is slowly dawning on elites that attempts to limit, let alone eliminate, fossil fuels are not practical in the slightest. In July 2023, Patrick Pouyanne, CEO of TotalEnergies, laid out the facts to CNBC, namely that modern society has daily requirements of 80 percent oil and gas. At best only 10 percent comes from so-called low-carbon energy. Failure to invest more in oil and gas will cause prices to soar to $150 a barrel.[45] While this might be perfectly acceptable to elites, we have seen a price ceiling resistance at about $5 a gallon, and even in California prices aren't allowed to get too far above $6 a gallon for fear of popular revolt. Biden only avoided such a revolt by digging deep into the Strategic Petroleum Reserve, which he drained by 46 percent.[46] Add to this the fact that the Biden administration was actually creating *roadblocks* for so-called "clean energy" and the upshot was, we will all be using gas and oil for a very long time.[47]

News, however, continued to roll against the eco-lobbyists: Italy admitted its wildfires were not caused by "climate change" after catching the arsonist; Greek fires were caused by two arsonists; and summer fires in Vancouver were likewise caused by an arsonist.[48] These and many others began to challenge the mantra that wildfires were the result of "climate change." Nor did it help the messaging when over 1,500 scientists and professionals signed a declaration that there was "no climate emergency" in 2023.[49] Average people seem to have had enough as well: in London, where "green" spy cameras were set up to levy fines on polluters and reduce traffic, people have destroyed or stolen over 800 of the devices.[50] A British poll found that only 25 percent of the public favored the government's timetable for moving to electric vehicles, and were strongly exerting pressure on the government to rethink its timetable . . . which it did.[51]

Another major battlefield, that of convincing children they were born the wrong sex, has tilted slightly against the globalists. Sweden banned so-called "gender affirming care" on minors (i.e., child mutilation). The US public viewed with alarm the fact that the number of trans surgeries tripled in the US from 2020 to 2023, including over 1,200 procedures on kids eighteen or younger.[52] Red states moved into action and began shutting down such clinics, rendering nearly 25 percent "inactive" due to bans in twenty states.[53]

Individual US states followed suit. Revulsion at the so-called "trans" movement grew so intense that it cost Anheuser-Busch almost $30 billion in lost sales as its premier brand, Bud Light, tanked following an April 2023 ad for the beer featuring a man posing as a woman, Dylan Mulvaney. Sales fell 25 percent and distributors gave up hope on the brand ever recovering.[54] By summer of 2023—the peak of beer season—Anheuser-Bush started layoffs related to Bud Light, and on the Fourth of July the company was giving away beer.[55]

Bud Light's struggles, plus those of uber-woke Starbucks (which had refused to allow rainbow so-called "gay" flags to fly at its locations) reflected another active battlefield where the globalists were slowly losing—DEI ("Diversity, Equity, Inclusion"). This front had involved a mass infiltration over the past two decades (if not more) of wokesters who pressed radical racial, ethnic, and gender quotas and advertising campaigns to corporate America.[56] Yet repeatedly these values clashed with corporate profits. Ordinary Americans were puzzled: shouldn't capitalist companies be all about profits, not messaging? Americans think so. Gallup found that nearly 60 percent wanted companies out of politics—a number that grew during 2023.[57]

It is necessary to take a moment to understand how this came about. In his classic book, *The Visible Hand*, Alfred Chandler, Jr. described the rise of the managerial hierarchies in American business.[58] Entrepreneur owners such as Andrew Carnegie, John D. Rockefeller, and James J. Hill found that their companies grew so large that one person could no longer control them. That was particularly true of the railroads, which, as Chandler noted, were the first industry to transform due to the speed of the trains, the scope of the funds needed, and the size of the operations crossing state lines. A professional managerial class arose by the late 1800s in almost every industry that had replaced the founder-owners. Some iconic companies such as Ford or Disney stayed in the hands of the founders for years, perhaps even through a generation, but eventually even they succumbed to the managers' control.

A second shift then occurred: managers eschewed large risks involving potentially much larger returns for safety. Spooked by sharp stock price falls, they were never reassured by significant price increases. To use the old Wall Street dichotomy, they appeared to operate more out of fear than out of greed. Thus virtually all of American industry, in almost every field, became somewhat risk averse (far more than the owner-founders). Innovation slowed. One study found that of the top fifty major technological breakthroughs of the twentieth century, *not one* came from the industry leader in the field—despite major "R&D departments." For example, going back to non-railroad overland transport in the late 1800s, it wasn't Wells Fargo, Overland, or Butterfield stage companies that invented the automobile, but a Westinghouse employee; it wasn't a balloon manufacturer who developed the first airplane, but bicycle makers; the slide rule company Keuffel did not invent the electric calculator; and IBM, which had 85 percent of the *world's* computers, did not invent the PC.[59] The list goes on: Sony, whose "Walkman" dominated portable music with the cassette tape player, was eclipsed by Apple, a computer company, with its "iPod."[60]

Why is this important? Because this pattern illustrates the dangers of the stagnant managerial hierarchies. Those hierarchies not only wormed their way into business (not just here, but virtually worldwide) but law, education, and government, creating a new "administrative man," a composite figure who is well off, but not wealthy; who is older and fairly withdrawn; has low levels of interaction with "ordinary" people outside his bureaucracy; and who tends to live in a city.[61] In government, this new administrative man acted as a cog in a largely mindless bureaucracy—which globalists envisioned as the new government, for it is unresponsive to voters and at times nearly omnipotent.

The weakness of this new administrative man was revealed, ironically, in Covid, which was to some globalists their golden moment to impose the new administrative state worldwide. It came very close to totalitarianism in some places—Australia, New Zealand, Canada. As one writer put it, "State power wishes to be free [i.e., unfettered, uncontrolled], in the same way that water wishes to flow downhill."[62] The administrative state temporarily gained control in matters of free speech, movement, and even science itself, before the counterattack struck.

While business worldwide was subjected to a shift from the "production men" to the "finance men," liberal universities increasingly turned out plenty of graduates to fill the ranks. Armies of non-entrepreneur "bean counters" entered corporate America focused first on finance and accounting. But by the 1970s, a new mutant variant of this group arrived in the form of "Human Resources" and marketing graduates. As they entered corporate America, the marketing graduates especially—with their adeptness and facility with statistics and focus groups—soon gained control over the "finance men."

Equally adept at statistics, but armed with new, powerful marketing tools such as polling and focus groups, the marketing departments (aided and abetted by Human Resources, who grew their ranks with similarly minded people) replaced the investment and accounting dominance within corporations. CEOs, who had little specific knowledge of the customers and who, by the 1970s, had been focused overwhelmingly on stock prices, were easily persuaded by the new DEI-oriented marketeers who argued that companies should be appealing to less wealthy but numerous younger, hipper customers. They convinced the CEOs—again, with their facility with statistics and marketing reports—that companies could create a whole new generation of consumers and, more important, *that they did not need their older consumers anymore.* In fact, most of those younger consumers had little brand loyalty at all, and certainly nothing like that of the older consumers they cast aside.

Utilizing hip-hop stars, entertainment icons, professional sports celebrities, and even social-media creations (such as the Kardashians), marketing departments soon had entire companies convinced that "diversity" was essential for success and that "climate change" and LGBT messaging not only was wise but needed to dominate the entire branding of products. This, they insisted, would result in greater sales and market share even if it ran contrary to the tastes and buying habits of their customers. They didn't bother to add, "even if it ran contrary to the tastes and buying habits of *most* of their customers."

The Bud Light fiasco was one of the first notable examples of a company losing all connection to its customer base. when the company used a transgender internet "influencer" named Dylan Mulvaney to sell the number one-ranked beer in America. A grassroots outrage quickly drove Bud Light off shelves and out of bars. Overall sales dropped by almost 25 percent in a month.[63] Many think it was much higher, and certainly Bud Light not only lost its top spot as America's most sold beer, but soon it wasn't even in the top ten in some regions.

Other companies, however, witnessed a similar backlash, though they often attempted to explain away falling brand popularity or sales declines as due to other (mostly unrelated) factors. Disney Corporation is one of the clearest examples of a marketing department capturing not just the CEO but a majority of the board. A once "family friendly" company, Disney had soon developed a reputation as a haven for homosexuals and transvestites, to the point that it became a vocal critic of a new law that banned the teaching of sex to small children in Florida's schools. Calling it the "don't say gay" bill (which it was not), Disney's CEO criticized the legislation publicly, which in turn led Governor Ron DeSantis and the state of Florida to review and attempt to revoke Disney's special dispensations for the Reedy Creek Development board that ran all the Disney properties under special tax breaks from the state. As of this writing, the fight over Reedy Creek was still ongoing, but if Florida wins, it will have deep cost implications for all the Disney properties in Florida.

Disney thumbed its nose at moviegoers as well by turning out half a dozen "woke" iterations of long-time Disney animated favorites such as the *Little Mermaid* and *Snow White and the Seven Dwarfs*. Disney's box office failures, compounded by often catastrophic new releases of traditional money-making series such as *Star Wars, Indiana Jones*, and the various Marvel comics movies, further financially slammed the company. *Indiana Jones and the Dial of Destiny*, in which an aging Indy perpetually needed saving and help from an aggressive, masculine female, crashed so hard that a small independent film made for $15 million, the *Sound of Freedom*, about child trafficking, overtook it at the box office after just a couple of weeks. Between 2018 and 2023, Disney turned out multiple movies that not only failed to make a profit, but lost significant money, driving the company's stock down to lows it hadn't seen in over a decade. (Some put the three- or four-year losses from Disney flops at over $1.3 billion.) Worse, in a development that would have had Walt rolling over in his grave, by 2023 nearly half of America had an unfavorable view of the company, with nearly one-quarter saying they had a *highly* unfavorable view![64]

Some of the wokeness in corporate America would soon de facto be rolled back as a result of a Supreme Court case in June 2023 that struck down affirmative action programs in college admissions. This had major ramifications for using anything but pure merit as a measurement for granting admission to college or a job.[65] Corporate America was already being hit with suits accusing companies of reverse racism. For example, Starbucks faced a $25 million settlement with a woman who was fired because, she said, she was white.[66]

This backlash arrived just in time. DEI fascism had become laughable as a black DEI college director was fired for not being the "Right Kind of Black".[67] Despite colleges stubbornly pushing DEI, those jobs were drying up in corporate America.[68] Nothing was more heartwarming than to see that Ibram Kendi, one of the leading racists in America, presided over a mass firing of almost half of his employees at the Center for Antiracist Research at Boston University. Not only was DEI imploding, but it appeared Kendi had been accused of mishandling grant funding.[69]

Concerns about the pernicious influence of DEI prompted the states of Florida, then Texas, to entirely dismantle its university-level DEI.[70] The state of Tennessee began to go even further, considering cutting off all federal funding for education.[71] With a model legislation in hand, many other states were expected to abolish DEI as well.

DEI had advanced under the overall rubric of "multiculturalism" and "diversity" as being healthy. American CEOs, led by their HR departments, embraced this with a mania. So desperate were American companies to show they were not racist that in the wake of the George Floyd death, just *6 percent* of new S&P jobs went to white applicants![72] An emphasis on "multiculturalism" spread across all of corporate America, even as the concept of multiculturalism itself, however, was increasingly (and finally) being seen as a problem. In September 2023, the British Home Secretary Suella Braverman declared that multiculturalism had "failed" in England and that it was "toxic," threatening the "security of society."[73]

Braverman wasn't alone. At the spring 2023 G20 meetings, India's Prime Minister Narendra Modi said "multilateralism is in crisis today," and that "global governance has failed."[74] India, one of the two largest polluters on the planet, of course shifted the blame to the "rich nations" and even "global warming" for its troubles, but the underlying message was clear. India was not going to toe the line to any multiculturalist garbage.

This foreshadowed the end of globalism itself. CEO Morris Chang of the Taiwan semiconductor giant TSMC said "globalization is almost dead."[75] Free trade, he added, is also almost dead and neither were likely to come back. Larry Fink of Blackrock and Howard Marks of Oaktree warned that the decoupling may be permanent. Fink urged companies to reevaluate their supply links, and Marks said the pendulum of globalization was swinging back to local sourcing—as he put it, "the safest and surest."[76] Charles Kaye of Warburg Pincus agreed that the security provided by the US military for decades had provided a certain "oxygen" for globalism—just as Zeihan observed—but with the death of Bretton Woods, there was much more on-shoring and re-shoring. The investment organization Shroders warned that structural inflation had emerged, signaling the "end of globalization" even beyond the current economic cycle.[77]

Whereas for half a century the protection of the United States had enabled a temporary era of low inflation and high growth, Triffin's dilemma eventually kicked in, resulting in slowing growth with simultaneously higher inflation. This "caught [international bankers] by surprise."[78] Bankers were able, temporarily, to fight this process with lower interest rates, with the period described by the Bank of England's governor Mervyn King as the "nice decade."[79] And it was nice for some, while it lasted.

Where offshoring kept inflation low in the United States for almost two decades, where the price of durable goods fell by 40 percent for Americans over a twenty year period, the same offshoring led to the hollowing out of American manufacturing—precisely the issues Donald Trump highlighted in his 2016 campaign. But since the 2007–08 financial crisis, world trade grew more slowly than GDP. That slowing was accelerated by Europe's reliance on Russian energy and American dependence on China's supply chain.

In 2016, concerns about the impact of low-wage immigration resulted in the United Kingdom leaving the European Union in what was called the Brexit. That was followed by the election of Donald Trump and his Make America Great Again program in the United States. However, these were just the appetizers for the main meal of anti-globalism. Then came the China Virus pandemic, with shortages of drugs and other items deemed critical to fight the virus, followed by an equally powerful shock when Russia invaded Ukraine in 2022. The West responded to Russia's invasion with sanctions that led Russia to cut off all oil and gas deliveries to Europe. Russia quickly redirected its exports to China and Mexico.[80] To date, Europe still has not recovered. A new word entered the European vocabulary, "friendshoring," or only setting up offshore manufacturing facilities in friendly states. Nevertheless, between the China Virus and the Russian invasion of Ukraine, there was a dip in international trade in goods and services. When measured as a share of GDP, imports have never recovered.[81]

Another economic measure—that of labor markets—has been distorted by the tidal wave of illegal criminal invasion of the US under Joe Biden. A massive inflow of migrants, which once would have suggested growth, actually represents the further collapse of local economies and lowering of wages.

Global supply chains, especially in semiconductor chips, which were located predominantly in South Korea and Taiwan where the Chinese could easily sever them constituted a threat to American national security. In July 2022, Congress passed the CHIPS for America Act that included investment incentives for chip manufacturing in America.[82] That was more old-style Democrat-type spend, spend, spend. In fact, Trump's trade war with China had an effect in reducing trade with China in the targeted categories. While some argued that this merely opened the door for others to trade with China, "national security" was showing up increasingly in discussions of China and trade in publications.[83]

Apple, as an example, found it difficult to quickly relocate much of its manufacturing base due to the absence of roads, infrastructure, and education in places such as Vietnam. The problem, of course, is that

Vietnam's suppliers are in China. Indeed, re-shoring to fully developed areas such as the US may be the only final answer. However, decoupling with China was having profound effects on the Dragon. Direct investment in China dropped sharply, from 4 percent in 2011 to just 1 percent in 2023, and in total dollars it has dropped by $100 billion.[84] Indeed, the drop from developed democracies is sharper, from $35 billion in 2014 to just $16.3 billion in 2023. So the expected "decoupling" has already started.[85]

During the heyday of foreign investment in China, the Chinese government used the open processes to steal western technology and transfer it to state domestic competitors. Many multinationals figured this out and determined that was a bad deal for them. Inevitably, however, as each of the "producer/supplier" countries got wealthier, the labor costs rose (just as they eventually did in Europe by the 1970s). Thus the "China dividend" disappeared . . . but soon, too, did the Vietnam dividend and the cost savings of doing business anywhere else. Then came export controls from the West, President Trump, and a general anti-China attitude that developed in the United States.

From China's perspective, though, they had already stolen as much as they could and embarked on new changes in espionage law to make sure none of *their* technology returned to the West. They "spooked foreign executives by questioning staff at consulting firm Bain & Co.'s Shanghai office" (Mitt Romney's company), launched a "cybersecurity review of imports from chip maker Micron Technology, and [detained] an executive of Japanese drugmaker Astellas Pharma."[86]

Where, exactly, China stood within the globalist structure has become murky. Many Americans viewed China as part of the globalist system, while in fact the Dragon remained clearly on the sidelines. In the 1980s many corporate leaders salivated at a mass new market for American and western goods, aided and abetted by products made for the west by cheap labor. Western investment poured into China. But Chinese leadership never saw itself as the world's workshop. Rather, low wage production provided a very short-term steppingstone to skills (and outright intellectual property theft) that would enable China to enter the US/European high-value production sweepstakes. Globalists thought they were playing Xi Jinping; it was Xi playing them. This was especially obvious in the area of "climate change" agreements. Whereas India begged off citing its own poverty—while increasing its annual coal production by 80 percent—the Chinese literally thumbed their noses at the world, building the longest coal transporting railway in the world (1,141 miles) toting 200 million tons of coal annually.[87]

And China was not entirely opposed to decoupling. China started an information lockdown, decreasing its release of increasingly negative economic data, then moving full throttle to access information about Chinese companies. For example, data coming from Wind Information Company, based in Shanghai, had dried up.[88] As Chinese economic reality grew dimmer, the Chinese took realistic analysis of their situation to be negative opinions or even outright propaganda. Tyrants usually do treat truth as propaganda. Therefore, signs of Chinese economic coercion have increased, and not just with western powers but with regional competitors such as South Korea.[89] Those were not signs of growth and control, but of weakness and fear. Even the once reliable (to China) US Chamber of Commerce in April 2023 released a statement on "Concerns Over PRC Investment Climate."[90] Likewise, growing approval for a war to take Taiwan within China also suggested the Communists cannot get what they want through peaceful coercion.[91] Meanwhile, youth unemployment in China raced to a record high.[92]

So strong was the decoupling movement that, as always, liberal globalists at the *New York Times* had to take the edge off by re-labeling it "de-risking."[93] As more war talk from the Chinese Communist government over Taiwan loomed, one expert suggested the most likely outcome for US companies would be for US companies continue making goods in China for Chinese customers, but moving all other production facilities out.[94] Expectations were that semiconductor and display work would move to Taiwan and Japan, but a truly risk-averse policy would be to simply relocate them entirely to the US or other western nations. After all, Taiwan and Japan could—in theory—become a "part" of China, although with considerable bloodshed, destruction, and economic disruption.[95]

Then there was the Chinese Belt and Road initiative in 2013, which terrified many, who thought it meant the final phase of China's international economic imperialism. They shouldn't have worried. Instead the Belt and Road initiative became a debt trap for poorer countries, but it has also succeeded in partially bankrupting China, which has spent (according to the Council on Foreign Relations) $1 trillion on the project.[96] China intended for Belt and Road to loan money to countries so *they* would build the infrastructure using . . . Chinese contractors. Projects were poorly planned, and construction badly executed. In Myanmar, the Chinese tried to boot peasants off their land and build pipelines, sparking massive protests.[97] In Pakistan, after investing billions of dollars, the Chinese were under attack from locals.[98] After building a massive new port in Sri Lanka, the Chinese found nobody wanted it and continued to use the traditional port of Colombo.[99]

Even when the Chinese built stuff, it wasn't good. The "biggest infrastructure project ever in [Ecuador], a concrete colossus bankrolled by Chinese cash," the Coca Codo Sinclair hydroelectric plant, has developed so many cracks it could break down altogether.[100] Pakistani officials shut down the Neelum-Jhelum hydroelectric plant after cracks were discovered there. A Chinese-built hydroelectric plant on the Nile is three years behind schedule and has suffered breakdowns. Cracked walls in a housing project outside of Angola have locals complaining.[101] Even a success story, Indonesia's high-speed rail, which is only eighty-eight miles long, had massive cost overruns.[102] The latest threat to the Chinese Belt and Road initiative is IMEC, or the India, Middle East, Israel, Jordan, EU program of ports and roads to link the Middle East to Europe.

But Belt and Road lending had collapsed even before the China Virus pandemic, leaving the borrowing countries with boatloads of debt. Borrowers aren't happy: the loans were pushing many countries to the brink of insolvency, including Pakistan, Kenya, Zambia, Laos, and Mongolia.[103] Neither failed states nor angry citizens make suitable allies. And, for the record, when the West did this process, it was called imperialism.

Beyond those major obstacles, if China sought to "reset the world," according to author Noah Smith, major hurdles to that notion existed. First, China is a direct competitor (née enemy?) of the United States and is not merely a cog in a supply chain. China's very success in moving up the "value chain" meant that rather than just supplying the US with low-cost stuff the US didn't want to make, now it is direct competition with our top industries, including the auto industry.[104] "Made in China" no longer means lavish American profits for the shareholders but little for employees: now it means that profits, executive salaries, even the very existence of corporations are at risk.[105]

China, not Russia, was attempting the "great reset" in 2015 when the Chinese economy was still growing. It worked so long as "rich people in rich countries were benefitting from the China gold rush. . . ."[106] The Europeans already saw the train coming and have begun to abandon free trade with China, investigating dumping, especially in connection with electric vehicles.[107] And China's growth did slow down—and that hasn't even really taken into account the massive real estate bust looming over the country.[108] Whereas in 2015—its peak—China's exports of goods and services as a percent of GDP reached a whopping 35 percent, now it has crashed back to 20 percent.

The *Wall Street Journal* noted in June 2023 that "China's recovery Is in Real Peril Now," and "China's Economy Faces Drag from Debt Purge," as Chinese urban households already had a higher debt load as a percent of disposable income than American households.[109] Real estate, long the mainstay of Chinese consumer confidence, started to fail as asking prices in financial hubs such as Shanghai fell.[110] In July 2023, it was announced that China was officially in default on over a trillion dollars in debt to US bondholders.[111] Evidence that things were seriously crumbling in China came when Xi held a meeting with "experts" to save the economy. He was told the problems were systemic in communism, an answer he likely did not relish.[112]

As the allure of China diminished, foreigners left. Chinese scholars warned the situation demanded "serious attention."[113] Nations around the world began issuing warnings about China's risks.[114] Europeans started to wake up to the sinister and deceptive deals they had cut with the Communists.[115] And it didn't help that India's commerce chief said that India's "heart" was closer to the US than China on trade.[116]

A critical element of globalist dreams involved not only subordinating western economies and cultures under their umbrellas, but forcing others to bend the knee as well. That did not go well either. Russia's Vladimir Putin simply refused to play and to one degree or another ignored globalist goals. Israel's Benjamin Netanyahu likewise refused to suborn Israel's sovereignty to global demands. The other major outlier, India, operated substantially outside the globalist framework. India's Prime Minister Narendra Modi, presiding over the fastest growing economy on earth, paid lip service to globalist objectives (particularly on climate change) and India's policy showed virtually no compliance at all.

Thus, an arrangement that looked quite "global" just twenty years ago, involving Russia, Western Europe, the United States, India, and China and which posed the threat of global control at the hands of the WEF came apart at the seams, with three of the major players no longer working with the West and the US and a counter alliance called BRICS (Brazil, Russia, India, China, Saudi Arabia) forming. Whether nations trade with the US and western Europe or not, it is clear that nations themselves were making trading decisions—not the people at the WEF. Indonesia, for example, announced it just would not export its minerals, causing a "hot global fire" of ire from the IMF, the World Trade Organization, and the EU. Indonesia told them to pound (hot) sand.[117] China, which as we have seen was not to be trusted, restricted exports of gallium and germanium—rare metals that were critical strategic resources, used to make infrared optics, solar cells, and compound semiconductors.[118] And whether an alternative "reserve currency" develops out of BRICS is immaterial: the vaunted Bretton Woods structure is gone in all but name.

Even within the "establishment" press, there is an admission that Bretton Woods is passé. *RealClearPolitics*, one of the leading outlets for leaking the deep state's views, now has realized that the end of American Hegemony is at hand—but it is "not the end of America."[119] Where has this disintegration of Bretton Woods and the reluctance of the US to be world policeman left us? The US remains in a position of quasi-leadership, and still has the potential to be world leader. As things now stand, with Joe Biden at the helm, allies and enemies understand that to a large degree they are on their own.[120] The US National Intelligence Council's *Global Trends 2040* laid out five scenarios for the next twenty years, with 1) China as a global leader but not dominant; 2) competitive coexistence between the US and China; 3) "separate silos," a world without globalism results in spheres of influence; 4) revolutionary change after a global environmental crisis; and 5) a renaissance of democracies, with the US leading a free world. Author Niall Ferguson, while preferring the final outcome, sees "separate silos" as the most likely.

Another indicator of the weakness in the creaking globalist structure came in the fractures caused by Russia's invasion of Ukraine. At first, the West, in knee-jerk fashion, launched a fusillade of sanctions aimed at debilitating the Russian economy. Those had minimal, temporary effects, and within a year Russia had restructured all its energy sales to China and other countries.

One of the main objectives when the West waded into the war was to (in warped western thinking) force Vladimir Putin out as the Russian president. But the war—certainly at first—only solidified his grip on Russia. Meanwhile sanctions backfired, costing much of Europe substantive losses in manufacturing due to higher energy costs and destroying national budgets. Germany's economy slowed dramatically. At the front, the Russians, perhaps at some cost, nevertheless took the objectives they wanted then forced the Ukrainians to attack them like Meade at Gettysburg. By September 2023, NATO warned that Ukraine needed to prepare for a "long" war. Some might say, "perpetual war." And as of late 2023, the US House of Representatives stood in open revolt against providing more funding for Ukraine, even to the point that the Speaker of the House, Kevin McCarthy, was removed because members suspected he had cut a secret deal with Democrats and with Majority Leader of the Senate, Mitch McConnell, to provide more funding.

The Ukraine war also again exposed the globalist's influence and control over the news media in western nations. Even this near dominance, however, has caused an unexpected problem; for people who simply couldn't get their news outside of the so-called "mainstream media," a growing number of people started to ignore the news altogether.[121] Faith in virtually all key globalist institutions diminished around the world. In the US, Gallup showed that three-fifths of the population lacked faith in the federal government.[122] Younger people, in fact, were more optimistic in poorer nations where they were not bombarded by state propaganda in perpetual news cycles.[123]

What may play an even greater role in ending globalism are the words and goals of globalists themselves. Chief among these promoters is the economic adviser to the WEF, Yuval Noah Harari, known to many anti-globalists as the "false prophet" of a globalist apocalypse. One of the reasons for Harari's infamous position as the "prophet" is that he seems obsessed with God, Christianity, and the Bible—or, at least, obsessed with debunking them. In June 2023 he called for an AI program to rewrite the Bible to create "religions that are actually correct."[124] "Just think about it," he added: a "holy book is written by an AI." Of course, that in itself would make it *un*holy. Regardless, a wise man once said that when someone tells you who they are, believe him. Harari, Soros, and WEF chairman Klaus Schwab repeatedly tell us who they are: mini-antichrists. We should believe them.

Although in retreat, we are now seeing the effect of the program "Global Leaders of Tomorrow," a program the WEF started in 1992—coincidentally the same year Agenda 21 and Sustainable Development were foisted on the world. Those new leaders are quite visible today in people such as Canada's Prime Minister Justin Trudeau, Pete Buttigieg, Bill Gates, Richard Branson, Bono, and former President Barack Obama. Not all plans of mice and men work out. Vladimir Putin was one of those young leaders who has now left the reservation. Others included Angela Merkel, who did her best to destroy Germany, but who left a current polity there far less enamored of the Agenda 21/WEF goals; and Emmanuel Macron, who has embraced the climate goals but who had to tiptoe away in the face of "Yellow Vests" and striking truckers.[125] (As of this writing France is in the throes of a massive insurrection by immigrant Muslims, which was always a tinderbox waiting to explode.)

Everything Harari and Schwab said is an attempt to eliminate or minimize God and the human expression of God through individuality (i.e., an attack on the very essence of Judaism, "God is One"). They intended to do this through "transhumanism," or the "next step" in the human evolutionary process that permits humans to manipulate enhancements through machines and computers. As Harari wrote in his book *Sapiens*:

> There is only one historical development that has real significance. Today, when we finally realise that the keys to happiness are in the hands of our biochemical system, we can stop wasting our time on politics and social reforms, putsches and ideologies, and focus instead on the only thing that can make us truly happy: manipulating our biochemistry.[126]

His claim that "our actions aren't part of some divine cosmic plan, and if planet Earth were to blow up tomorrow morning, the universe would probably keep going about its business as usual" is precisely a testament to a "divine plan," namely that human happiness isn't the measuring stick of the universe and that he simply *doesn't know* what would happen because by *his own scientific method* he cannot prove it.[127]

Harari's own website states "History began when humans invented gods, and will end when humans become gods."[128] Author Patrick Wood, editor at *Technocracy News and Trends*—someone quite familiar with the new "transhuman" movement—said of Harari, "The level of evil we are dealing with here is so intense that most Christians and con-servatives have no idea how deep it goes and will frankly have trouble believing it."[129] The very essence of transhumanism was to devalue life and all accomplishments or achievements associated with it. That, in part, is why the WEF and Harari are so desperate to get people to not only stop behaving as people, but as *men and women*. Humans, said Harari, "are now hackable animals that *will* be reengineered" (emphasis mine). Or, "previously government surveillance was above the skin, now it's going under the skin." Or, "The free will to choose who we vote for or what we buy in the supermarket . . . That's over."[130] "Humans," he added, "are acquiring powers . . . and the power to re-engineer life."[131]

All the God of the Bible managed to create, he states, were "organic beings, all these trees and giraffes and humans—they are just organic. We are now trying to create inorganic beings. . . Very soon we will be beyond the God of the Bible."[132] No one mentioned to Harari that all of the building blocks he, or anyone else, would use to go "beyond the God of the Bible" were not created by him—but by the God of the Bible.

In keeping with this de-humanization and attack on the individ-ual, the WEF said that all fashion would be abolished by 2030 and that humans would be forcibly limited to three choices of clothing—a uniform, in essence.[133] Klaus Schwab said "in the fourth industrial rev-olution the winners will take it all, so if you are a World Economic Forum first move, you are the winners."[134]

Schwab forgot one thing: the people, not just in the US, but around the world, still have a voice and have awesome power. They began to use it. At the national level, states began to reject globalists—not just Putin and Hungary's Viktor Orban, but Holland, where a WEF-backed government failed, Paraguay, where patriots chanted "Paraguay has Triumphed, Jesus has Triumphed" in defeating a WEF election coup; Chile, which triumphed in a Constitution vote in an "earthquake in Chilean politics"; and in Italy where a far "less global-ist" Giorgia Meloni had come to power.[135] Holland's farmer's party has surged during the government collapse.[136] Slovakian elections produced a populist victory with Robert Fico.[137] It appeared as though a populist would win the Argentinian elections.

Other strong pro-nationalist leaders such as Benjamin Netanyahu in Israel, Jair Bolsonaro, and Donald Trump in the US were temporarily removed. Netanyahu is back; Trump has a good chance at coming back. Many of the new nationalist leaders have combined into the anti–Bretton Woods/anti-globalist BRICS. BRICS nations had a combined wealth by 2023 that was greater than that of the G-7.

Across the board, green parties and the representatives of the hideous lockdowns were collapsing. New Zealand, whose Jacinda Ardern was one of the most authoritarian of the lockdown prime ministers, saw her country elect "the country's most right-wing government in a generation," handing Australia back to conservatives.[138] Greens suffered stinging defeats in Hesse and other German provinces.

As techie/futurist Joel Kotkin noted, "Once-confident globalists failed to pay attention to three critical issues: the continued importance of the material realm, the crucial role of demographic change, and lastly, the importance of culture."[139] George Gilder, certainly brilliant, nevertheless once thought he won a debate about "Manufacturing Matters," held up a copy of a book by that title, and pointed out that the manufacturing costs of the book comprised a tiny part of the book's price. The rest was "intellectual" and service—editors, designers, marketers, etc. What Gilder left out was the fact that the energy and electricity that enabled all the other 95 percent plus of the work *could not be replaced*. An editor is incompetent? Fire him. A graphic artist is unsatisfactory? Get another. But if the power supply or the food supply to the company fails, everyone else's services are irrelevant. A primacy of manufacturing, and more important, of basic resource extraction and production operates at such a fundamental level that it seems to drift out of the consciousness of the elites.

As Kotkin points out, very few non-western nations imposed sanctions on Russia during the Ukraine invasion; and most are buying more Russian raw materials than ever before.[140] Some argue that the Russian economy was outperforming Germany's.[141] India has built coal plants like they were on sale and even promised to resist the "carbon imperialism" of the eco-west.[142] Needless to say, fossil fuel use continued to grow, and for transportation and shipping such as airplanes and ocean-going container ships, anything other than fossil fuels is an utter impossibility.

On a micro scale within the United States, thanks to federalism, we are likewise seeing a severing from globalist ideas. The six fastest-growing southern states—Florida, Texas, Georgia, Tennessee, and the Carolinas—added more to America's GDP than did the northeast.[143] One key to de-globalizing the mindset of voters is to get them out of big urban hellholes, but also supposedly clean hives such as Silicon Valley and, of course, the national sewer, Washington, DC. A University of Chicago study found that half of those in Silicon Valley could work from home.[144] Decentralizing the large hubs—especially moving people out of the DC hive mentality—has the impact of, at least partially, forcing college-educated and higher-income people into daily contact with people outside their financial and educational bubble. As Charles Murray noted in *Coming Apart*, during the early parts of the twenty-first century it was possible for people in parts of Washington, DC to *never* interact without someone in his income, class, and educational status in the course of a week if he did not get his own coffee or take in his own dry cleaning.[145]

This de-globalization at the micro level is occurring through two avenues, one political and one demographic. In the political arena, President Trump had already started moving bureaus and agencies out of Washington, DC. (My concern was that he was moving them to state regional power hubs like Wichita, whereas I would have favored New Mexico, Scottsbluff, Nebraska, or the gas station near Pigs Knuckles, Arkansas.) De-bubble-izing the bureaucrats would not instantly change things, but it would slowly begin to increase the interactions between the appointed gods of the administrative state and the peons. At the demographic level, however, the shift is already under way. Manhattan's number of babies born over the last decade dropped 15 percent, a trend that is replicated in most major urban areas. The number of households with children in suburbs or "Exurbs" is three times higher than in urban areas.[146]

Although in elections from 2016 to 2020 it appeared that temporarily Democrats were gaining a foothold in the suburbs, mostly through their pro-abortion positions, internal trends nevertheless worked against that shift continuing. For example, 70 percent of metro area employees live and work in the 'burbs, and trips within the suburbs or between suburbs are double the amount of commutes to a central business district downtown.[147] Prime family areas were growing at a rate *over seven times* faster than other areas.[148] Nor was this "white flight," as Latinos accounted for nearly half this growth.

Meanwhile, Zillow found that "the great re-shuffling" was afoot, where there was a preference for larger homes in less dense areas (up from 53–60 percent between 2019 and 2021). It was, said builder Robert Schottenstein, "a flight to safety and security."[149] That was in large response to the new "doom loop" of crime, particularly murders and mass lootings, occurring in major cities.[150] As of mid-2023, one-third of woke Seattle's residents were considering leaving.[151] Even though some CEOs, such as Amazon's Andy Jassy, threatened people who didn't return to the office with their jobs, remote work was now viewed as an entitlement, or "the New Signing Bonus."[152] Remote employees left in drove.[153] But businesses themselves had started to flee the big doom loop cities: New York alone lost $1 trillion in Wall Street business as firms abandoned the Big (Rotten) Apple.[154] Moreover, the rise of these exurbs meant more private driving and less public transport. Big cities dominated by leftist, usually globalist mayors, have nothing to offer.

The collapse of these leftist/globalist cities was exacerbated by the most leftist president in history, Joe Biden, whose open border policies drove New York City to the brink of collapse and left the governor of the state of New York begging for closed borders. (A common response was: "I'll believe it when you endorse Donald Trump and support his Wall.") New York City attempted to shuffle the illegal criminals off to upstate counties, but they were blocked.[155] Already in a genius move, Governors Greg Abbott of Texas and Ron DeSantis of

Florida had re-shipped many of the illegals to New York, Chicago, and even Martha's Vineyard. By doing so, they were engaging in a "reverse Cloward-Piven," by collapsing the blue-city governments under their own liberal promises of welfare.

Do the globalists understand it is over? There is evidence that even some of the demons at the WEF know that the latest attempts at world government have failed. A WEF official admitted that neither the China Virus nor the climate jihad had sufficed to establish a world organization—why not try a "water crisis?"[156] They certainly were right about the vax: although according to CDC statistics over 82 percent of the US public took the first vax, only a little over 50 percent took a booster. Now, new polling shows more than half won't ever take another.[157]

Meanwhile, one of the central villains in the push for globalism, George Soros, seemed in retreat by 2023. First, his Open Society Foundations cut at least 40 percent of their staff after Soros handed over control to his son, Alex.[158] The Foundation was viewed as "retreating" from Europe as part of a new "strategic direction," which could easily be interpreted as . . . *losing*. Soros said the quiet part out loud. He fears a Trump victory in 2024 will end globalism.[159]

Regardless of who wins the 2024 election, there were major structural changes afoot that worked against elite world views. New data on degree completions showed that the humanities have absolutely crashed since the pandemic. Majors in history, English, and religion are down to half their 2020 levels (keeping in mind that overall college attendance is dropping steadily, down 4 percent in the last few years alone).[160] More people majored in computer sciences than in all the humanities put together. America and western Europe produced a glut of educated elites that suddenly couldn't find jobs—or found jobs they thought were unworthy of their talents—and thus turned to leftist politics out of disappointment. Law school enrollment in particular plunged. Elite magazines such as Condé Nast went into long term decline, even before the 2008 recession and the China Virus.[161] Three out of five information industries suffered long-term decline, some precipitous (such as newspapers). But overall the number of job postings with humanities disciplinary associations fell in everything except Classical Studies—which were a tiny fraction to begin with.[162]

Even (finally) public service jobs flattened and tailed off some after 2008. So did K-12 teaching—most notably after the skyrocketing numbers of homeschooling parents took their kids back from schools. In 2022 I interviewed the heads of the two major homeschool convention organizers. One estimated that homeschooling had doubled, to around ten million. The other suggested that those numbers were low because they did not count homeschooled children who attended a public school for a single class/activity, from archery to band to athletics. He put the number of US homeschooled students at twenty million.

Those realities clashed with a revolution in rising expectations, leading economists to argue that such constantly rising expectations contribute to bubbles.[163] Put simply, if a trend goes on long enough, people expect it to continue, and get angry if it doesn't. This notion has, some researchers think, contributed to social unrest as it leads to rising inequality, despite the fact that everyone is better off.[164] It also has led researchers to develop a new theory of happiness itself, namely "Reality minus Expectations."[165] Constant propaganda by media and the self-esteem industry succeeded in convincing post-Boomers that work had to be enjoyable, and, more importantly, meaningful.[166] Even the great Rush Limbaugh used to urge people to find what made them happy as work.

This is not possible. People's talents are rarely suited to what would truly "make them happy." It was often joked in Hollywood that every actor wanted to be a singer, and every singer wanted to be an actor. A simpler truth is that work is, well, *work* and by its very nature (and the commandment of God), wasn't to be "fun." Occasionally someone will land in a field where they literally "love their work." Truly Rush was one of those people. Those individuals are very few and far between.

Our society—and the world—seems to be in the middle of a great reset, but not the one Klaus Schwab had in mind. Polls have been showing that Americans with college degrees are a bit less happy than high-school-educated peers.[167] What has not changed is, as Jean Twenge found, it is not education but wealth levels that contribute to more happiness—that wealthier people, on average, are less depressed, less suicidal, less prone to alcoholism and other pathologies than relatively poorer people. That really, she found, had to do more with a certain basic standard of living where most necessities were addressed. Once at that point, wealth no longer played much of a role. This stands to reason that if people were perpetually worried about making a house payment or being able to supply food on the table, it would cause more anxiety.

So expectations once again seem key. Globalists shot their wad at worldwide expectations with the China Virus and all its ramifications, from lockdowns to interrupted supply chains. They followed up by ratcheting up the anxiety dial with the sanctions associated with the Ukraine war. Politically, in the US (as well as Israel and Brazil) elites managed to bombard the public with unending torrents of negative news about President Trump, Prime Minister Netanyahu, and Jair Bosonaro. Their climate doom was unrelenting. Is it any wonder that the disappointed, the malcontents, the disillusioned who took to the streets in 2020 were disproportionately college-educated?[168] "Black Lives Matter" protesters were overwhelmingly white, and pampered. As Noah Smith observed, "frustrated and underemployed elites are uniquely well-positioned to disrupt society. They have the talent, the connection and the *time to organize* radical movements and promulgate radical ideas" (emphasis mine).[169] As he concluded, "a society that generates a large cohort of restless, frustrated, talented, highly educated young people is asking for trouble."

This can be solved either by improving reality or reducing expectations. Fortunately—but slowly—American youth (and/or their parents) have realized that the college degree isn't as important as in previous generations, but that there were well-paying jobs that didn't require a degree.[170] What has changed more than anything is that some, if not many, of these young people seem to now begin to understand that *neither* the college-related job nor the blue-collar/non-college job will fulfill their dreams . . . *because both are work!*

There also appears to be a major turning of the tide when it comes to the awareness of the woke sexual and climate-change propaganda, and a fresh eagerness to confront both. Americans now overwhelmingly back cutting regulations to boost energy production.[171] It could be said we are just one election away from again being the *world's* largest oil and gas producer. Overall, threads and daily active users on Facebook/Meta fell by half as people stopped using the site.[172] The globalist uber-liberal *Washington Post* was set to lose $100 million in 2023, just a decade after Jeff Bezos bought the paper.[173] Even Fox News learned its audiences weren't to be trifled with. After firing the most popular news host on cable, Tucker Carlson, Fox saw its primetime viewership drop by over one third. Small victories similarly reflect the demise of globalist woke, as the Walmart heirs' art center canceled drag shows for kids.[174]

And "Trust the Science?" While as of this writing the major science and medical journals have yet to admit the deadly side effects of the China Virus vax, overall the profession knows it has a problem with truth. A top journal, *Science*, admitted in August 2023 that thousands of its published research papers may have had "exaggerated claims."[175] Just think—three short years ago that would have been labeled "misinformation!" Major voices of one-time liberals, including feminist author Naomi Wolf and Levi's executive Jennifer Sey, were so repulsed by the China Virus vaccine and lockdowns they bolted from the left.[176] And how is that "misinformation" about the 2020 election coming? After all, it was ridiculed by the mainstream media. As of late 2023, nearly *two thirds* of Americans voters thought cheating affected the election. And that doesn't even count the Hunter Biden laptop cover-ups or the social media influencing discussed earlier![177] Internationally there has been a total collapse of trust in the West, mainly because the world perceives America now as possessing a two-tier legal system, a sluggish, amoral crowd of elites who "rig the system behind flimsy legal screens," and celebrity do-gooders who have attached themselves to both the climate and trans movements.[178]

Indeed, a spate of stories late last year, blaming climate change for everything from waking bees up earlier to bumpier airplane flights to the Lahaina fire. Such claims had begun to fall on deaf ears or, worse, be treated with the disdain they deserved. The result was an increasing disregard for anything peddled by the media.

In another triumph, already incited by the film *Sound of Freedom*, activists everywhere stepped up their war on human trafficking. Florida's Attorney General Ashley Moodey called on Facebook (i.e., "Meta") and its CEO Mark Zuckerberg to appear before a statewide council on human trafficking to account for the high use of Facebook to facilitate sex exploitation.[179] In the woke/trans arena, more than sixteen states began legislation to stop the targeting of children for transitioning, while twenty states passed laws to protect female athletes from having to compete with men pretending to be women.[180]

Waves of immigrants (in the US, the majority illegal) racked Sweden, France, and Italy. In France, President Emmanuel Macron had to call out forty thousand officers to put down the Antifa-type rioting by (mostly Muslim) immigrants.[181] Sweden had to employ its army to help police with a surge of immigrant gang killings.[182] Only Poland, which refused to admit migrants, suffered *no* terrorist attacks in the past twenty years.[183]

Under Biden, however, the invasion was stunning and relentless. Millions crossed, so many the Department of Homeland Security could not provide reliable estimates, let alone track the illegals. Wisely, red state governors, such as Ron DeSantis and Greg Abbott, bused the invaders to blue cities, particularly New York, Chicago, and Denver. (DeSantis had an even more clever tactic—flying the illegal criminals to Martha's Vineyard, Massachusetts.)[184]

While it didn't seem to matter that the illegal criminal invasion swamped Texas, Arizona, and southern California, when the hordes reached New York and Chicago, the elites got concerned. With illegals arriving at the rate of six hundred a day in New York City (nearly four thousand in a month), "the mood in City Hall has changed significantly" from a year earlier when the "Sanctuary City" was welcoming illegals. Indeed, not only did Mayor Eric Adams conclude New York was full and that continued influxes were "not sustainable," he also demanded Biden must "control the border" because there is "no more room" in New York City.[185] (It didn't help city finances that the entirety of New York City was crumbling: a plan to renovate aging housing for the poor under the New York Housing Authority saw its initial estimate for repairs nearly double, to $78 billion.)[186] A desperate Adams tried any and all measures to keep the city financially afloat, including fining private businesses $10,000 a month for leaving scaffolding up over ninety days, but those measures were drops in the ocean compared to the crushing demands of the illegal criminal armies.

At one point, New York attempted to re-bus the migrants to upper New York counties, but those counties quickly shut off that option. That, in turn, prompted Democrat governor Kathy Hochul to support revoking the city's right to shelter law, saying "we are truly out of space."[187] Hochul went on to—in a first—blame the Biden administration for the disaster at the border. Meanwhile, Staten Island citizens blasted Adams for lying about the conversion of a former school into a migrant villa. Denver begged Texas border towns, which had suffered for years under the illegal migration, to divert illegals from Denver.[188] Mostly Hispanic residents of a Chicago neighborhood protested the opening of an illegal immigrant shelter there.[189] In Massachusetts, the government called on residents to take illegal criminals into their homes.[190]

Biden was forced to reverse one of his dearest campaign pledges *not* to finish Trump's Wall and ordered the Department of Homeland Security to do so—all the while insisting it wouldn't work and claiming that he was required to spend the money. He waived twenty-six laws to finish building the Wall.[191]

To conclude: We began our discussion of the end of globalism with court cases, so it is fitting we examine more actions from the judiciary. In President Trump's absence, the courts held the line. The Supreme Court, one-third of which was appointed by Trump, struck down Affirmative Action in June 2023; ruled 9–0 in favor of a postal employee's religious freedom; issued an order allowing work to resume on the West Virginia Gas Pipeline, which Biden halted; twice vacated judgments against Oregon bakers who refused to make a same-sex wedding cake; ruled in favor of a Christian graphic artist who was being forced to design homosexual friendly websites; ordered an injunction against the Biden administration saying it "likely" violated free speech by working with Big Tech to censor content; resurrected two whistleblower cases against Medicare and Medicaid for fraud; *unanimously* rejected ethics complaints against Justice Clarence Thomas; and invalidated Biden's student loan forgiveness program.[192] Lower level courts as well have been rolling back woke, global agenda items, including gun bans.[193]

Most important, the Supreme Court in its Trump-era configuration was widely viewed as preparing to overturn the Chevron Doctrine, on which much of the Deep State was built. A four-decades-old decision, the decision in the *Chevron USA v. Natural Resources Defense Council* was the litmus test for Trump's selection of his three Supreme Court nominees. In *Jarkesy v. SEC*, the Fifth Circuit began the process in 2022 by constraining powers of the Securities and Exchange Commission to regulate companies unless explicitly stated.[194] (That case has now headed on appeal to the US Supreme Court.) Trump's judges came to bat with *West Virginia v. EPA*, which ruled that the Environmental Protection Agency couldn't establish emission standards for existing coal plants based on shifts to cleaner forms of energy.[195] Then in *Sackett v. EPA* the court gutted the EPA's absurd regulation of all wetlands as within federal authority.[196]

Obviously, the gigantic ruling in the *Dobbs* case, sending abortion back to the states to be decided by state legislatures, was a blow to the Deep State, as was the *Braun* case which, once again, upheld individual ownership of firearms and reaffirmed the Second Amendment. With a new test of the Chevron doctrine coming before the Court, a serious blow could be struck against the powers of an administrative behemoth. And there were other cases pending with monumental repercussions waiting in the wings, most notably the Brook Jackson whistleblower lawsuit against Pfizer.[197] Jackson observed extensive failures and noncompliance by the drug maker in the Covid vaccine, with extreme implications for *all* the vaccine makers. If fraud was involved in any of the vaccine cases, it could remove the liability protections provided by the federal government and open them all to damages for side effects.

Globalism was not only in retreat: in many instances it was reaching the proportions of a rout. Writing for the *City Journal*, Martin Gurri described the "Elite Panic of 2022," declaring:

> The elites are convinced that their control over American society
> is slipping away. They have conquered the presidency, both houses
> of Congress, and the entirety of our culture; yet their mood is one
> of panic and resentment.[198]

Or, as he put it, "progressive elites sense that they have the power but lack authority. They live in a dread of a reversal in the tide of history . . ."[199] Even at that, sometimes we still mince words. It took Russia's Vladimir Putin to state the obvious, that the New World Order has failed and the elites' "days are numbered."[200] A German MP, Christine Anderson, echoed Putin, promising "We will bring you down" to the World Health Organization, calling the WHO "globalitarian misanthropists."[201]

I like that. "Globalitarian misanthropists." Whatever term one wishes to use, populists across the world have scored major, lasting victories against the spirit of globalism since 2016. As a historian, I always like putting things in terms of a military example. We likely have fought our "Battle of Trenton" or our "Midway." Neither of those won their respective wars. Long, arduous, bloody fighting remained—for years in each case. But each denied the enemy the knockout blow that would have sealed the patriots' doom. Each constituted a shift in time, of attitude, as in the movies, when the hero, having taken the enemy's best, dirtiest punch, gets up, wipes the blood off his lip, and with steel in his eyes marches forward to annihilate his foe. To put it in spiritual terms, it was the moment when the demons realized their god had feet of clay—or, perhaps in this case, lithium.

We have crossed the Delaware. We have landed at Normandy. No one can say as of this moment if Donald Trump can be like Grover Cleveland and recover from a loss, however questionable the circumstances. If he does, however, it could be glorious. He needs to pray that the Lord arms him with fifty mighty men, a dozen flamethrowers, and a giant Terminix van.

Cleaning out the Swamp won't be easy, especially the second time around. Now, my friends, hit the beach!

Acknowledgments

Even monographs are the work of many hands. Special thanks to my editors, Elaine Lafferty and Stephan Zguta; to Tony Lyons for taking a chance with this topic; to Steve Bannon for supporting it the whole way; and to my many readers who have remained loyal over, now, forty years. And a special note of gratitude for President Donald Trump for again giving the United States hope that redemption still might be possible.

Endnotes

INTRODUCTION

1   Roland Robertson, *Globalization* (London: Sage, 1992), 8.
2   Anthony Giddens, *The Consequences of Modernity* (Cambridge, England: Polity, 1990), 64.
3   David Harvey, *The Condition of Postmodernity* (Oxford: Blackwell, 1989), 240.
4   David Peet, *Unholy Trinity: The IMF, World Bank, and WTO*, 2nd ed. (London: Zed, 1988), 2.
5   Email from Robert Barnes to author, July 26, 2023.
6   Email from Charles Calomiris to author, July 26, 2023.
7   Peter Zeihan, *The End of the World Is Just the Beginning: Mapping the Collapse of Globalization* (New York: Harper, 2022), 3.

CHAPTER ONE

1   Louis-Pierre-Edouard, *Les Cabinets et les Peuples* (Miami, HardPress: 2017), 3–5.
2   Adam Zamoyski, *Rites of Peace: The Fall of Napoleon and the Congress of Vienna* (New York: Harper Perennial, 2008), xvii.
3   Paul Johnson, *Napoleon: A Life* (New York: Penguin, 2006), 4.
4   David Chandler, *The Campaigns of Napoleon: The Mind and Method of History's Greatest Soldier* (New York: Macmillan, 1966).

5   Victor Davis Hanson, *Carnage and Culture: Landmark Battles in the Rise of Western Civilization* (New York: Anchor Books, 2001), 62.

6   Vincent Cronin, *Napoleon* (New York: HarperCollins, 1994), 315.

7   Johnson, *Napoleon*, 54.

8   Chandler, *Campaigns of Napoleon*, xxvii.

9   Johnson, *Napoleon*, 89.

10   Martin van Creveld, *Command in War* (Boston: Harvard University Press, 1987), 64.

11   One exception to the English antagonism toward Bonaparte was that of Henry Richard Vassall Fox, the 3rd Baron Holland, who greatly admired many of Napoleon's changes. For example, he noted "the great things he accomplished, and the savings he made, without even the imputation of avarice or meanness, with the sum comparatively inconsiderate of 15 million of France a year, are marvelous, and expose his successors, and indeed all European Princes, to the reproach of negligence or incapacity." (Henry Richard Holland and Henry Edward Holland, *Foreign Reminiscences* [Victoria, Australia: Leopold Classic Library, 2015 (1855)], 139). Holland did not mention the vast amount of plunder Napoleon's troops shipped back to Paris or lifted for themselves.

12   Johnson, *Napoleon*, 6.

13   Thomas Carlyle, *The Works of Thomas Carlyle, Volume 4: The French Revolution* (London: Chapman and Hall, 1896), 320. Legend has it that after dispersing the attackers, Napoleon went into the National Convention halls through a rose hedge and scratched himself to the point he was bleeding. He announced to the delegates that he had "shed his blood" for them.

14   Harold Nicolson, *The Congress of Vienna: A Study in Allied Unity: 1812–1822* (New York: Viking, 1946), 44.

15   Napoleon quoted in the PBS program "Napoleon: Napoleon at War," https://www.pbs.org/empires/napoleon/n_war/campaign/page _6.html.

16   Alan Schom, *Napoleon Bonaparte* (New York: HarperCollins, 1997), 414.

17   Hanson, *Carnage and Culture*, 66.

18   Johnson, *Napoleon*, 97.

19   Chandler, *Campaigns of Napoleon*, 753.

20   Ibid.

21   Zamoyski, *Rites of Peace*, 157; Paul Johnson, *Birth of the Modern: World Society, 1815–1830* (London: Weidenfeld and Nicolson, 1991), 92.

22   Nicolson, *Congress of Vienna*, 96.

23   Zamoyski, *Rites of Peace*, 133.

24   Johnson, *Birth of the Modern*, 72.

25   Zamoyski, *Rites of Peace*, 561.

26   Ibid., 106.

27   Ibid., 122.

28   Johnson, *Birth of the Modern*, 99.

29   Zamoyski, *Rites of Peace*, 142.

30   Ibid., 148. There was a brief interlude when the leading delegates retired to London, which itself became a scandal. The Czar's sister preceded the diplomats in her arrival. Historian Paul Johnson described her as a "small, ugly, squat-nosed widow, full of mischief and malice," and she managed to alienate or insult almost everyone within days of her arrival (Johnson, *Birth of the Modern*, 96).

31   Ibid., 37.

32   David King, *Vienna 1814* (New York: Three Rivers Press, 2008), 194.

33   Johnson, *Birth of the Modern*, 112.

34   Ibid.

35   Zamoyski, *Rites of Peace*, 274.

36   Hilde Spiel, *The Congress of Vienna: An Eyewitness Account*, edited and with an introduction, Trans. Richard Weber (Philadelphia: Chilton Book Company, 1968), xv.

37   Spiel, *Congress of Vienna*, xv.

38   Ibid., xvi.

39   King, *Vienna 1814*, 44.

40   Richard Bright, *Travels From Vienna Through Lower Hungary: With Some Remarks on the State of Vienna During the Congress, in the Year 1814* (Miami: Hardpress, 2019), 13.

41   Ibid.

42   Zamoyski, *Rites of Peace*, 287.

43   Ibid., 309.

44   King, *Vienna 1814*, 69.

45   Zamoyski, *Rites of Peace*, 322.

46   Ibid., 219.

47   Henry Kissinger, *A World Restored: Metternich, Castlereagh and the Problems of Peace, 1812–22* (Brattleboro, VT: Echo Point Books, 2013), 16.

48   King, *Vienna 1814*, 92–93.

49   Ibid.

50   Zamoyski, *Rites of Peace*, 16.

51   Ibid., 550.

52   Ibid., 550.

53   King, *Vienna 1814*, 267.

54   Harriet Martineau, *A History of the Thirty Years' Peace*, 4 vols (London: np, 1877), 1:11.

55   Zamoyski, *Rites of Peace*, 553.

56   Ibid., 559.

57   Ibid., 568.

CHAPTER TWO

1   Orlando Figes, *The Crimean War: A History* (Hampshire, England: Picador Books, 2012); Trevor Royle, *Crimea: The Great Crimean War, 1854–1856* (New York: St. Martin's, 2014).

2   Paul Johnson, *The Birth of the Modern: World Society, 1815–1830* (London: Weidenfeld and Nicolson, 1991), 202.

3   H. L. Wesseling, *The European Colonial Empires, 1815–1919* (Harlow, UK: Pearson, 2004), 85.

4   Peter Zeihan, *The Accidental Superpower* (New York: Twelve Publishers, 2014), 47.

5   Daniel Headrick, "The Tools of Imperialism: Technology and the Expansion of European Colonial Empires in the Nineteenth Century," *The Journal of Modern History*, June 1979, 231–263.

6   Johnson, *Birth of the Modern*, 789.

7   Headrick, "Tools of Imperialism," 244.

8   Ibid., 246.

9   Jerry Keenan, *The Wagon Box Fight* (Boulder, CO: Lightning Tree Press, 1990); Mike Snook, *Like Wolves on the Fold: The Defense of Rorke's Drift* (London: Greenhill Books, 2006).

10   Victor Davis Hanson, *Carnage and Culture: Landmark Battles in the Rise to Western Power* (New York: Anchor Books, 2002).

11   Headrick, "Tools of Imperialism," 252.

12   Richard Fox, *Archaeology, History, and Custer's Last Battle: the Little Big Horn Reexamined* (Norman, OK: University of Oklahoma Press, 1993).

13   David Hackett Fischer, *Washington's Crossing* (New York: Oxford, 2004), 21.

14   Larry Schweikart, *America's Victories: Why the U.S. Wins Wars and Will Win the War on Terror* (New York: Sentinel, 2006), 63–97; David Lee Bergeron, "Fighting for Survival," *U.S. Naval Institute Proceedings*, December 2019, https://www.usni.org/magazines/naval-history-magazine/2019/december/fighting-survival.

15   Headrick, "Tools of Imperialism," 88.

16   David Baker, "Colonial Beginnings and the Indian Response: The Revolt of 1857–58 in Madhya Pradesh," *Modern Asian Studies*, 25, 511–543; Barbara English, "The Kanpur Massacres in India in the Revolt of 1857," *Past & Present*, February 1994, 169–17; and Clare Anderson, *Indian Uprising of 1857–58: Prisons, Prisoners and Rebellion* (New York: Anthem, 2007).

17   Wesseling, *European Colonial Empires*, 54–55.

18   Ibid., 61.

19   Johnson, *Birth of the Modern*, 259–68.

[20] Deauville Walker, *William Carey: Missionary Pioneer and Statesman* (Chicago: Moody, 1951); M.M. Thomas, *Significance of William Carey for India Today* (Makkada, India: Marthoma Dioscean Centre, 1993); Sunil Chatterjee, *William Carey and Serampore* (Calcutta, India: Ghosh Publishing, 1984); and Daniels Potts, *British Baptist Missionaries in India, 1793–1837: The History of Serampore and its Missions* (Cambridge: University Press, 1967).

[21] Jeffrey Cox, *The British Missionary Enterprise since 1700* (New York: Routledge, 2008), 80.

[22] Cox, *British Missionary Enterprise*, 93.

[23] Dorothy Carey was literally raving in her room as Carey baptized his first convert. See James Beck, *Dorothy Carey: The Tragic and Untold Story of Mrs. William Carey* (Grand Rapids, MI: Baker Book House, 1992).

[24] See David Hempton, *The Religion of the People: Methodism and Popular Religion, c. 1750–1900* (London: Routledge, 1996), 110.

[25] Cox, *British Missionary Enterprise*, 92.

[26] Wesseling, *European Colonial Empires*, 57; Wesseling, *Divide and Rule: The Partition of Africa, 1880–1914* (Westport, CT: Prager, 1996).

[27] Sidney Smith, "Indian Missions," *Edinburgh Review*, April 1808.

[28] Cox, *British Missionary Enterprise*, 7.

[29] Ainslie Embree, "Christianity and the State in Victorian India: Confrontation and Collaboration," in R.W. Davis and R.J. Helmstadter, eds., *Religion and Irreligion in Victorian Society: Essays in Honor of R. K. Webb* (London: Routledge, 1992), 151.

[30] Cox, *British Missionary Enterprise*, 16.

[31] Sydney Smith, "Indian Missions," *Edinburgh Review*, April 1808.

[32] R. G. Tiedemann, *Reference Guide to Christian Missionary Societies in China: From the Sixteenth to the Twentieth Century: From the Sixteenth to the Twentieth Century*, 1st ed. (London: Routledge, 2009).

[33] Larry Schweikart and Michael Allen, *A Patriot's History of the United States, from Columbus's Great Discovery to the Age of Entitlement*, 10th Anniversary Edition (New York: Sentinel, 2014), 178–80.

34 Ian Toll, *Six Frigates* (New York: Norton, 2006), 188–253; Donal Barr Chidsey, *The Wars in Barbary: Arab Piracy and the Birth of the United States Navy* (New York: Crown, 1971); Richard Scott, *Jefferson and the Barbary Pirates: America's First Encounter with Radical Islam* (Salem, MA: Winter Island Press, 2019).

35 Johnson, *Birth of the Modern*, 344–49 (quotation on 348).

36 Ibid., 349.

37 Ibid., 349. Also see Maurice Collis, *Raffles* (London: John Day, 1968).

38 Ibid., 351.

39 Charles Tench, *Charley Gordon: An Eminent Victorian Reassessed* (London: Alan Lane, 1978); Brad Faught, *Gordon: Victorian Hero* (Washington, D.C.: Dulles Potomac, 2008); Alice Harell, "Slave trade in the Sudan in the Nineteenth Century and its Suppression in the Years 1877–80," *Middle Eastern Studies,* 1998, 34:113–128.

40 Myles Osborne and Susan Kent, *Africans and Britons in the Age of Empires, 1660–1980* (New York: Routledge, 2015), 41–43; Jessie Page, *The Black Bishop: Samuel Adijai Crowther* (Westport, CT: Greenwood Press, 1979).

41 Osborne and Kent, *Africans and Britons*, 256–58.

42 Johnson, *Birth of the Modern*, 778.

43 Ibid., 781.

44 Wesseling, *European Colonial Empires*, 42

45 Robert A. Huttenback and Lance E. Davis, *Mammon and the Pursuit of Empire: The Political Economy of British Imperialism, 1860–1912* (Cambridge: Cambridge University Press, 1987), 12.

46 Ibid., 38.

47 Ibid., 42.

48 Ibid., 110.

49 Ibid., 301.

50 William Macmillan, *Bantu, Boer and Briton: The Making of the South African Native Problem* (Oxford: Clarendon Press, 1963).

51 David Gilmour, *The Ruling Caste: Imperial Lives in the Victorian Raj* (New York: Farrar, Straus, Giroux, 2005), 27.

[52] Wesseling, *European Colonia Empires*, 43.

[53] Ibid., 47.

[54] Ibid., 48.

[55] Gilmour, *Ruling Caste*, 107–08.

[56] Jan Morris, *Heaven's Command: An Imperial Progress* (London: Faber and Faber, 1973), 382.

[57] Rudyard Kipling, "The White Man's Burden," https://www.kiplingsociety.co.uk/poem/poems_burden.htm.

[58] F. A. Cox, *History of the Baptist Missionary Society, From 1792 to 1842* (London: T. Ward, 1842), v–vi.

[59] Bernard Porter, *The Lion's Share: A Short History of British Imperialism, 1830–1983*, 2nd ed. (London: Longman, 1984), 130; Richard Soloway, *Demography and Degeneration: Eugenics and the Declining Birthrate in Twentieth-Century Britain* (Chapel Hill, NC: University of North Carolina Press, 1990); 39.

[60] Porter, *Lion's Share*, 129.

[61] J. Gallagher and R. Robinson, "Imperialism and Free Trade," *Economic History Review*, second series, VI, 1953, 1–15.

[62] See, for example, Joseph Schumpeter, ed., *Imperialism, Social Classes: Two Essays* (New York: Meridian Books, 1955), 72; David Landes, "Some Thoughts on the Nature of Economic Imperialism," *Journal of Economic History*, December 1961, 513; John Hobson, *Imperialism: A Study* (New York: Cosimo, 2005); V. I. Lenin, *Imperialism: The Highest Stage of Capitalism* (Moscow: Progress Publishers, 1963).

[63] Huttenback and Davis, *Mammon and the Pursuit of Empire*, 5.

[64] Ibid., 6.

[65] Adam Burns, "Retentionist in Chief William Howard Taft and the Question of Philippine Independence, 1912–1916," *Philippine Studies: Historical & Ethnographic Viewpoints*, June 2013, 163–192.

[66] Harry Willis, *Our Philippine Problem: A Study of American Colonial Policy* (New York: Henry Holt, 1905), 186. See also Ralph Minger, *William Howard Taft and United States Foreign Policy: The*

Apprenticeship Years, 1900–1906 (Urbana, IL: University of Illinois Press, 1975).

67 Paul Johnson, *Modern Times: A History of the World from the Twenties to the Nineties*, 2nd ed. (New York: HarperCollins, 1991), 508.

68 Johnson, *Modern Times*, 509.

69 Larry Schweikart and Dave Dougherty, *A Patriot's History of the Modern World, vol. 1: From America's Exceptional Ascent to the Atomic Bomb: 1898–1945* (New York: Sentinel, 2912), 158.

CHAPTER THREE

1 Sara Friedrichsmeyer, et. al., *The Imperialist Imagination: German Colonialism and Its Legacy* (Ann Arbor, MI: University of Michigan Press, 1998); Heinrich Schnee, *German Colonization, Past and Future—the Truth About the German Colonies* (London: George Allen & Unwin, 1926); L. H. Gann, et al., *Colonialism in Africa, 1870–1960: The Economics of Colonialism* (Cambridge: Cambridge University Press, 1969); H. R. Rudin, *Germans in the Cameroons* (New Haven, CT: Yale University Press, 1938); Woodruff Smith, *The German Colonial Empire* (Chapel Hill, NC: University of North Carolina Books, 2012).

2 Oron Hale, *The Great Illusion, 1900–1914* (New York: Harper, 1971), 242.

3 Larry Schweikart and Dave Dougherty, *A Patriot's History of the Modern World, vol. 1, From America's Exceptional Ascent to the Atomic Bomb, 1898–1945* (New York: Sentinel, 2012), 70.

4 Quoted in Barbara Tuchman, *The Guns of August* (New York: Bantam, 1979), 25.

5 Richard Van Alstyne, "Woodrow Wilson and the Idea of the Nation State," *International Affairs*, July 1961, 293–308 (306).

6 Andrew Roberts, *Churchill: Walking with Destiny* (New York: Viking 2019), 82.

7 Roberts, *Churchill*, 82.

8   Jeffrey Sachs and Joseph Stanislaw, "The Commanding Heights," PBS Series, Chapter 2, "The Old Order Falls," transcript, https ://www.pbs.org/wgbh/commandingheights/shared/minitext/tr _show01.html#2

9   Thomas Friedman, *The World Is Flat 3.0: A Brief History of the Twenty-first Century* (London: Picador, 2007).

10   Carroll Quigley, *Tragedy & Hope: A History of the World in Our Time* (New York: Macmillan, 1966), 61.

11   Quigley, *Tragedy & Hope*, 135.

12   Modris Eksteins, *Rites of Spring: The Great War and the Birth of the Modern Age* (Boston, Houghton-Mifflin, 1989), 44, 48, 91.

13   Ibid., 91–92.

14   Tuchman, *Guns of August*, 21.

15   Niall Ferguson, *The War of the World: Twentieth-Century Conflict and the Descent of the West* (New York: Penguin, 2006), 102.

16   Emile Ludwig, "Der moralische Gewinn" ("The Moral Victory"), *Berliner Tabegblatt*, August 5, 2014, 392.

17   Eksteins, *Rites of Spring*, 93.

18   Schweikart and Dougherty, *Patriot's History of the Modern World*, I; 80–81.

19   Johnson, *Modern Times*, 19; Robert Wohl, *The Generation of 1914* (Cambridge, MA: Harvard University Press, 1979).

20   Johnson, *Modern Times*, 19

21   Eksteins, *Rites of Spring*, 93.

22   Johnson, *Modern Times*, 12.

23   Ibid.

24   Johnson, *Modern Times*, 19; Schweikart and Dougherty, *Patriot's History of the Modern World*, I:138.

25   G. D. Sheffield, "Oh! What a Futile War: Representations on the Western Front in Modern British Media and Popular Culture," in Ian Stewart and Susan Carruthers, eds., *War, Culture and the Media* (Trowbridge: Wilts, 1996), 54–74.

26   H. G. Wells, *The War That Will End War* (London: H. G. Wells Library, 2016 [1914]).

[27] Johnson, *Modern Times*, 13.

[28] Ibid., 14.

[29] David Andelman, *A Shattered Peace: Versailles 1919 and the Price We Pay Today* (New York: John Wiley, 2008), 9.

[30] Ibid., 8.

[31] Merle Curti, "Bryan and World Peace," *Smith College Studies in History, xvi*, 1931, 135; Richard Van Alstyne, "Woodrow Wilson and the Idea of the Nation State," *International Affairs*, July 1961, 293–308.

[32] Herbert Croly, *The Promise* (New York: Macmillan, 1912), 160, and his *The Great Society* (New York: Macmillan, 1923).

[33] Croly, *The Promise*, 160.

[34] Van Alstyne, "Woodrow Wilson and the Idea of the Nation State," 296.

[35] Woodrow Wilson, *Congressional Government: A Study in American Politics*, 15th ed. (Boston: Houghton Mifflin, 1925), 4–5.

[36] Ibid., 203.

[37] Van Alstyne, "Woodrow Wilson and the Idea of the Nation State," 298.

[38] Ibid., 300.

[39] Andleman, *Shattered Peace*, 37.

[40] Ibid., 24.

[41] Ibid., 32.

[42] Ibid., 33.

[43] Ibid., 41.

[44] Schweikart and Dougherty, *Patriot's History of the Modern World*, 1:138.

[45] Andleman, *Shattered Peace*, 29.

[46] Johnson, *Modern Times* 30–31.

[47] "H. L.", "The U.S.S.R. and the League of Nations," *Bulletin of International News*, September 1934, 215–224.

[48] "H.L.", "U.S.S.R. and the League of Nations," 217.

[49] Johnson, *Modern Times*, 20.

[50] Ibid., 24.

51 Ibid., 25.
52 John Lewis, *Nothing Less than Victory: Decisive Wars and the Lessons of History* (Princeton, N.J.: Princeton University Press, 2010), 191.
53 Ibid., 192.
54 Walter Mead, *God and Gold: Britain, America, and the Making of the Modern World* (New York: Alfred A. Knopf, 2007), 66.
55 Johnson, *Modern Times,* 26.
56 Schweikart and Dougherty, *Patriot's History of the Modern World,* 1: 161.
57 Johnson, *Modern Times,* 27.
58 Ibid.
59 Ibid., 29.
60 See the Treaty of Versailles, Articles 232–35, https://en.wikisource.org/wiki/Treaty_of_Versailles/Part_VIII#Article_232.
61 Sally Marks, "The Myths of Reparations," *Central European History,* 11, 1978, 231–55 and her "1918 and After: The Postwar Era," in G. Martel, ed., *The Origins of the Second World War Reconsidered: A. J. P. Taylor and the Historians,* 2nd ed. (New York: Routledge, 1999), 13–37.
62 Adam Tooze, *The Wages of Destruction: The Making and Breaking of the Nazi Economy* (New York: Penguin, 2006), 6.
63 Schweikart and Dougherty, *Patriot's History of the Modern World,* 1:215.
64 Ibid.
65 Ibid., 1:216.
66 Tooze, *Wages of Destruction,* 6–7.
67 Schweikart and Dougherty, *Patriot's History of the Modern World,* 1: 163.
68 Mark Mazower, *Dark Continent: Europe's Twentieth Century* (New York: Vintage, 1998), 19.
69 Emily Goldman, *Sunken Treaties: Naval Arms Control Between the Wars* (College Park, PA: Pennsylvania State University Press, 1994), 165; Erik Goldstein and John Maurer, eds., *The Washington Conference, 1921–22: Naal Rivalry, East Asian Stability and the Road to Pearl Harbor* (London: Routledge, 1994).
70 Johnson, *Modern Times,* 14.

CHAPTER FOUR

1   Paul Boyer, *By the Bomb's Early Light* (New York: Pantheon, 1985).
2   See the introduction in Larry Schweikart and Michael Allen, *A Patriot's History of the United States, Fifteenth Anniversary Edition* (New York: Sentinel, 2019), xvii–xxii.
3   Harry Truman, *Memoirs, 1945: Year of Decisions* (New York: Konecky & Konecky, 1955), 417–19.
4   Ibid., 289.
5   Ibid., 14.
6   Ibid., 15; "Last Judgment," *Washington Post*, August 26, 1945.
7   Arthur Compton, "Now That We've Burst the Atom," *Rotarian*, October 1945, 53; "The Bomb and Its Future," *New Republic*, August 20, 1945.
8   Robert Redfield, "Consequence of Atomic Energy," *Phi Delta Kappa*, April 1946, 221; "The Bomb and Man," *Time*, December 31, 1945, 15–16.
9   See Leonard Cottrell, Jr., and Sylvia Eberhart, *American Opinion on World Affairs in the Atomic Age* (Princeton, NJ: Princeton University Press, 1948), 19, 28, 104; George Gallup, ed., *The Gallup Poll: Public Opinion, 1935–1971*, 3 vols. (New York: Random House, 1972).
10   Boyer, *By the Bomb's Early Light*, 22.
11   "The Ultimate Weapon," *Commonweal*, November 23, 1945, 131.
12   Harold Urey, "The Atom and Humanity, October 21, 1945," *Science*, November 2, 1945, 439.
13   Leo Szilard, *Saturday Evening Post*, May 1947, quoted in Boyer, *Bomb's Early Light*, 36.
14   Leo Szilard, "The Physicist Invades Politics," *Saturday Review of Literature*, May 3, 1947, 8, 31–34.
15   Ibid., 33–34.
16   Richard Rhodes, *The Making of the Atomic Bomb* (New York: Simon & Schuster, 2012), 21.
17   Spencer Weart and Gertrude Szilard, eds., *Leo Szilard: His Version of the Facts* (Cambridge, MA: MIT Press, 1978), 22; Rhodes, *Making of the Atomic Bomb*, 21–22.

[18] Weart and Szilard, *Leo Szilard*, 25, 28n.

[19] Ibid., 28n.

[20] Rhodes, *Making of the Atomic Bomb*, 22.

[21] Quoted in Ibid., 25.

[22] Walter Lippmann, "International Control of Atomic Energy," in David Masters and Katharine Way, eds., *One World or None: A Report to the Public on the Full Meaning of the Atomic Bomb* (New York: McGraw-Hill, 1946), 150.

[23] Stephen King-Hall, "World Government or World Destruction?" *Reader's Digest*, November 1945, 14–16.

[24] Frank Tyrrell, "Is the Use of the Atomic Bomb Justified?" *Vital Speeches of the Day*, October 1, 1945, 768.

[25] Boyer, *By the Bomb's Early Light*, 37.

[26] Ibid., 37.

[27] Robert Hutchins, *The Atom Bomb and Education* quoted in Boyer, *Bomb's Early Light*, 38–9.

[28] Norman Cousins, *Modern Man Is Obsolete* (New York: Viking, 1945).

[29] See Reinhold Niebuhr, "The Illusion of World Government," *Foreign Affairs*, April 1949, 379–88; Niebuhr, "The Atomic Issue," *Christianity and Crisis*, October 1, 1945, 5–7.

[30] Harry S. Truman, *Memoirs: 1945: Year of Decision* (New York: Konecky and Konecky,1955), 78–82.

[31] Ibid., 82.

[32] Paul Johnson, *Modern Times: A History of the World from the Twenties to the Nineties*, rev. ed. (New York: HarperCollins, 1991), 437.

[33] Ibid.

[34] James Franck, "The Social Task of the Scientist," *Bulletin of Atomic Scientists*, March 1947, 70.

[35] Sydnor Walker, ed., *The First One Hundred Days of the Atomic Age* (Washington, DC: Woodrow Wilson Foundation, 1946), 44.

[36] *Report on the International Control of Atomic Energy* (Washington, DC: Department of State, March 16, 1946).

37 Radio script for *Exploring the Unknown*, broadcast June 30, 1946, in the Papers of the Atomic Scientists of Chicago, Regenstein Library, University of Chicago, box 12, folder 2, cited in Boyer, *By the Bomb's Early Light*, 65.

38 Harold Urey, "How Does It All Add Up?" in Alice Smith, *A Peril or a Hope: The Scientists' Movement in America, 1945–47*, rev. ed. (Cambridge, MA: MIT Press, 1971), 283.

39 Boyer, *By the Bomb's Early Light*, 67.

40 Harold Urey as told to Michael Amtine, "I'm a Frightened Man," *Collier's*, January 5, 1946.

41 Boyer, *By the Bomb's Early Light*, 69.

42 "Mortals and the Bomb," *Commonweal*, October 28, 1949.

43 Albert Berger, "The Triumph of Prophecy: Science Fiction and nuclear Power in the Post-Hiroshima Period," *Science Fiction Studies*, July 1976, 145.

44 Boyer, *By the Bomb's Early Light*, 146.

45 Ibid.

46 Joseph and Stewart Alsop, "Your Flesh Should Creep," *Saturday Evening Post*, July 13, 1946, 9, 49–50.

47 John Perkins, "Where Is the Social Sciences' Atomic Bomb?" *School and Society*, November 17, 1945, 316–17.

48 A. M. Meerloo, "We need a New Kind of Leader," *New York Times Magazine*, May 26, 1946, 42.

49 Bruce Melvin, "Science and Man's Dilemma," *Science*, March 1, 1946, 241–44.

50 William Ogburn, "Sociology and the Atom," *American Journal of Sociology*, January 1946, 267–68, 272–74.

51 Louis Wirth, "Responsibility of Social Science," *Annals of the American Academy of Political and Social Science*, January 1947, 143–51.

52 Boyer, *By the Bomb's Early Light*, 57.

53 Leonard Cottrell, Jr. and Sylvia Eberhart, *American Opinion on World Affairs* (Princeton, NJ: Princeton University Press, 1948), 33–35, 56–59.

[54] Janet Besse and Harold Lasswell, "Our Columnists on the A-bomb," *World Politics*, October 1950, 74–76.

[55] Boyer, *By the Bomb's Early Light*, 269.

[56] Ibid., 84.

[57] David Bradley, *No Place to Hide* (Boston: Little, Brown and Company, 1948).

[58] Eugene Rabinowitch, "Five Years After," *Bulletin of the Atomic Scientists*, January 1951, 3–5, 12.

[59] Boyer, *By the Bomb's Early Light*, 95–96.

[60] Lewis Mumford, "Kindling for a Global Gehenna," *Saturday Review of Literature*, June 26, 1948; David Lilienthal, "Democracy and the Atom," *NEA Journal*, February 1948, 80.

[61] Edward Long, Jr., *The Christian Response to the Atomic Crisis* (Philadelphia: Westminster Press, 1950), 14–16, 38, 97.

[62] Gallup, *Gallup Poll*, 1: 767.

[63] Herbert Marks, "The Atomic Energy Act: Public Administration Without Public Debate," *University of Chicago Law Review*, Summer 1948, 840–54.

[64] Brian McMahon, "Atomic Energy Publicity," *Vital Speeches of the Day*, February 15, 1949.

[65] Robert Sherwood, "Please Don't Frighten Us," *Atlantic Monthly*, February 1949, 77–78.

[66] Leslie Groves, *Town Meeting of the Air* radio broadcast, February 15, 1949, transcript in William S. Parsons to E.R. Trapnell, February 11, 1949, Parsons Papers, Library of Congress, box 1.

[67] Andrew Roberts, *Churchill: Walking with Destiny* (New York: Viking, 2018), 705.

[68] "The Atlantic Conference & Charter, 1941," Office of the Historian, U.S. State Department, https://history.state.gov/milestones/1937–1945/atlantic-conf.

[69] Stephen Schlesinger, *Act of Creation: The Founding of the United Nations* (New York: Basic Books, 2003), 87.

[70] Ibid., 174.

71 "Proposals for the Establishment of a General International Organization," Pamphlet Number 4, "Pillars for Peace," https ://www.ibiblio.org/pha/policy/1944/441007a.html.

72 Charles Bohlen, *Witness to History, 1929–1969* (New York: W. W. Norton, 1973), 159.

73 Stanley Meisler, *United Nations: A History*. rev. ed. (New York: Grove Press, 2011), 15.

74 Truman, *Memoirs*, 2.

75 Ibid., 23.

76 Winston Churchill, "Sinews of Peace," March 5, 1946, https ://www.nationalchurchillmuseum.org/sinews-of-peace-iron -curtain-speech.html.

77 Meisler, *United Nations*, 26.

78 Ibid., 25.

79 Churchill, "Sinews of Peace."

80 Johnson, *Modern Times*, 440.

81 Meisler, *United Nations*, 25.

82 "The Role of UN Peacekeeping Missions in the Protection of Civilians," OXFAM POLICY COMPENDIUM NOTE, July 2012, https://oxfamilibrary.openrepository.com/bitstream/handle /10546/114587/hpn-role-un-peacekeeping-missions-protection -civilians-170712-en.pdf; "Peacekeepers in Name Only," *Economist*, October 28, 2017, https://www.economist.com/international /2017/10/28/peacekeepers-in-name-only; "UN Staff Accused of Raping Children in Sudan," *Telegraph*, January 2, 2007, https ://www.telegraph.co.uk/news/worldnews/1538476/UN-staff -accused-of-raping-children-in-Sudan.html; "Victims of Peace: Current Abuse Allegations Against U.N. Peacekeepers and the Role of Law in Preventing them in the Future," https://law.bepress .com/cgi/viewcontent.cgi?article=3113&context=expresso; "UN Troops Face Child Abuse Claims," BBC News, November 30, 2005, http://news.bbc.co.uk/2/hi/americas/6195830.stm; Virginia Fortuna claimed that peacekeeping works in *Does*

Peacekeeping Work? (Princeton, NJ.: Princeton University Press, 2008), but Darya Pushkina et al. found that in thirty-two UN peacekeeping deployments, thirteen were full or partial failures and that "what matters most and consistently across all of these missions is the presence or absence of domestic consent to, and cooperation with, deployed [peacekeeping operations]" ("Mission (im)possible? UN Military Peacekeeping Operations in Civil Wars," *European Journal of International Relations*, September 21, 2021). At best, the UN succeeded in half its operations, but at worst, the UN troops' criminal behavior was as bad as the civil wars they sought to stop.

83 Again, this is the conclusion of Pushkina, "Mission (Im)possible."

84 Meisler, *United Nations*, 74.

CHAPTER FIVE

1   Paul Johnson, *Modern Times: A History of the World from the Twenties to the Nineties*, 2nd ed. (New York: HarperCollins, 1991), 659.

2   Peter Zeihan, *The Accidental Superpower* (New York: Twelve, 2014), 1.

3   Ibid., 2.

4   Johnson, *Modern Times*, 659.

5   Richard Peet, *Unholy Trinity: The IMF, World Bank, and WTO*, second ed. (London: Zed Books, 2010), 71.

6   Zeihan, *Accidental Superpower*, 5.

7   Ibid., 6

8   Harold Evans, with Gail Buckland and David Lefer, *They Made America: From the Steam Engine to the Search Engine, Two Centuries of Innovators* (New York: Little Brown, 2004).

9   Zeihan, *Accidental Superpower*, 7.

10 Ibid., 660. See Larry Schweikart and Lynne Pierson Doti, *American Entrepreneur* (New York: AMACOM, 2009), 311–45.

11 Quoted in Adam Tooze, *The Wages of Destruction: The Making and Breaking of the Nazi Economy* (New York: Penguin, 2006), 10.

12   Ibid.

13   Evans, *They Made America*, 388–93.

14   Ibid., 392

15   Ibid., 298.

16   Schweikart and Doti, *American Entrepreneur*, 335–36.

17   Ray Kroc, *Grinding It Out: The Making of McDonald's* (New York: St. Martin's, 2016), passim.

18   Neal Gabler, *Walt Disney: The Triumph of the American Imagination* (New York: Vintage, 2007).

19   Barry J. Eichengreen, *Golden Fetters: The Gold Standard and the Great Depression, 1919–1939* (New York: Oxford University Press, 1995), 205 and passim.

20   Larry Schweikart, *Reagan: The American President* (Nashville, TN: Post Hill Press, 2018).

21   Zeihan, *Accidental Superpower*, 49.

22   See the map on p. 53 of Zeihan, *Accidental Superpower.*

23   Peter Zeihan, *The Absent Superpower: The Shale Revolution and a World Without America* (Austin, TX: Zeihan on Geopolitics, 2016), 138.

24   John Reader, *Africa: Biography of a Continent* (New York: Vintage, 1999), 663.

25   Reader, *Africa*, 673.

26   Larry Schweikart and Dave Dougherty, *A Patriot's History of the Modern World, vol. II: From the Cold War to the Age of Entitlement, 1945–2012* (New York: Sentinel, 2013), 100.

27   Thomas Dichter, *Despite Good Intentions* (Amherst: University of Massachusetts Press, 2003.

28   William Easterly, *White Man's Burden: Why the West's Efforts to Aid the Rest Have Done So Much Ill and So Little Good* (New York: Penguin, 2006), 4.

29   Dichter, *Despite Good Intentions*, ix.

30   Easterly, *White Man's Burden*, 48. Also see his "Can Aid Buy Growth?" *Journal of Economic Perspectives*, Summer 2003, 23–48; William Easterly et. al., "New Data, New Doubts: Comment on 'Aid, Policies, and Growth,'" *American Economic Review*, June 2004, 774–80.

31 Raghuram Rajan and Arvind Subramanian, "Aid and Growth: What Does the Cross-Country Evidence Really Show?" International Monetary Fund manuscript, cited in Easterly, *White Man's Burden*, 49. See also Willard Thorp, *The Reality of Foreign Aid* (New York: Praeger, 1971).

32 Stephen Smith, *Ending Global Poverty: A Guide to What Works* (New York: Palgrave MacMillan, 2003), 59.

33 Harry Truman, *Years of Trial and Hope*, vol. 3., *Memoirs* (Garden City, NY.: Doubleday, 1956), 232.

34 Dichter, *Despite Good Intentions*, 109.

35 "Poverty, INC," The Acton Institute, 2016, https://shop.acton.org /collections/acton-bookshop-dvds/products/povertyinc-dvd.

36 Dougherty and Schweikart, *Patriot's History of the Modern World*, II:108.

37 Hernando de Soto, *The Mystery of Capital: Why Capitalism Triumphs in the West and Fails Everywhere Else* (New York: Basic Books, 2003), passim.

38 World Bank, *Doing Business in 2005: Removing Obstacles to Growth* (Washington, DC: World Bank, International Finance Corporation and Oxford University Press, 2005), 3.

39 Easterly, *White Man's Burden*, 95.

40 Dougherty and Schweikart, *Patriot's History of the Modern World*, II: 108.

41 James Piereson, *Camelot and the Cultural Revolution: How the Assassination of John F. Kennedy Shattered American Idealism* (New York: Encounter Books, 2007), 209.

42 Julius Amin, *The Peace Corps in Cameroon* (Kent, OH: Kent State University Press, 1992), 4, 15–19, 43; Richard Mahoney, *JFK: Ordeal in Africa* (New York: Oxford, 1983), 35.

43 Gerard Rice, *The Bold Experiment: JFK's Peace Corps* (Notre Dame, IN: University of Notre Dame Press, 1985), 2

44 Dougherty and Schweikart, *Patriot's History of the Modern World*, II:113.

45 Henry Fairlie, *The Kennedy Promise: The Politics of Expectation* (New York: Doubleday, 1973), 180–81.

46 Amin, *Peace Corps in Cameroon*, 121; Milton Viorst, ed., *Making a Difference: The Peace Corps at Twenty-five* (New York: Weidenfeld & Nicholson, 1986), 42–3, 59.

47 Patrick Sharma, *Robert McNamara's Other War: The World Bank and International Development* (Philadelphia: University of Pennsylvania Press, 2017), 8.

48 Sharma, *Robert McNamara's Other War*, 11.

49 Ibid., 41.

50 Ibid., 56.

51 Ibid., 56.

52 David Morse, "The Employment Problem in Developing Countries," speech at the Seventh Cambridge Conference on Development, September 1970, in Ronald Robinson and Peter Johnson, eds., *Prospects for Employment Opportunities in the Nineteen Seventies* (London: Cambridge University Overseas Study Committee, 1971), 5–13.

53 Sharma, *Robert McNamara's Other War*, 61.

54 Ibid., 63.

55 Ibid., 123.

56 Ibid., 126 and chart on 127.

57 Richard Peet, *Unholy Trinity: The IMF, World Bank and WTO*, second edition (London: Zed, 2009) 89.

58 Peet, *Unholy Trinity*, 90.

59 Ibid., 95.

60 Ibid., 96.

61 B. T. Johnson and B. D. Schaefer, *The International Monetary Fund: Outdated, Ineffective, and Unnecessary* (Washington, DC: Heritage Foundation, 1999), 54.

62 The United Nations Conference on Trade and Development, *The Least Developed Countries 2000 Report* (New York: United Nations, 2000), 108–110.

63 Peet, *Unholy Trinity*, 134.

64 World Bank, *Articles of Agreement*, February 16, 1989, www. worldbank.org.

65 B. Milanovic, "Can We Discern the Effect of Globalization on Income Distribution? Evidence from Household Budget Surveys," World Bank Policy research Working Paper, 2876, April 2002.

66 B. Milanovic, "Two Faces of Globalization: Against Globalization as We Know It," unpublished paper, 2002, World Bank, cited in Peet, *Unholy Trinity*, 179–80.

67 Schweikart, *Reagan*, 192–285.

68 Charles Calomiris and Stephen Haber, *Fragile By Design: The Political Origins of Banking Crises and Scarce Credit* (Princeton, NJ; Princeton University Press, 2014), 203–82.

CHAPTER SIX

1   Scott Atlas, *A Plague Upon Our House: My Fight at the Trump White House to Stop COVID from Destroying America* (New York: Liberty Protocol, 2021); C. H. Klotz, ed., *Canary in a COVID World: How Propaganda and Censorship Changed Our (My) World* (Las Vegas: Canary House Publishing, 2023).

2   Atlas, *Plague*, 5.

3   Mollie Hemmingway, *Rigged: How the Media, Big Tech, and the Democrats Seized Our Elections* (Washington, D.C.: Regnery, 2021), 61.

4   "The Lab-Leak Hypothesis," *Intelligencer*, January 4, 2021, https://nymag.com/intelligencer/article/coronavirus-lab-escape -theory.html?ref=quillette.com; Nicholas Wade, "Origin of Covid—Following the Clues," May 2, 2021, Medium, https ://nicholaswade.medium.com/origin-of-covid-following-the-clues -6f03564c038; "How Amateur Sleuths Broke the Wuhan Lab Story and Embarrassed the Media," *Newsweek*, June 23, 2021; "Archived Fact-Check: Tucker Carlson Guest Airs Debunked Conspiracy

Theory that COVID-19 Was Created in a Lab," (retraction), *PolitiFact*, May 17, 2021, https://www.politifact.com/li-meng-yan -fact-check/?ref=quillette.com.

5   United States Congress Press Release, "COVID Origins Hearing Wrap Up: Facts, Science, Evidence Point to a Wuhan Lab Leak," March 8, 2023, https://oversight.house.gov/release/covid-origins -hearing-wrap-up-facts-science-evidence-point-to-a-wuhan -lab-leak; "Fauci Was 'Untruthful' to Congress About Wuhan Lab Research, New Documents Appear To Show," *Intercept*, September 9, 2021, https://www.congress.gov/117/meeting /house/114270/documents/HHRG-117-GO24-20211201 -SD004.pdf; "New Details Emerge About Coronavirus Research at Chinese Lab," *Intercept*, September 6, 2021, https://theintercept .com/2021/09/06/new-details-emerge-about-coronavirus-research -at-chinese-lab/; and "Key Scientist in COVID Origin Controversy Misled Congress on Status of $8.9 Million NIH Grant," *Intercept*, July 21, 2023, https://theintercept.com/2023/07/21/covid-origin -nih-lab-leak/.

6   The ever-unreliable Wikipedia page on Covid repeats the now-discredited theory that the disease was spread by Chinese eating bat meat in "wet markets." Wikipedia, "Covid-19," https://en.wikipedia.org/wiki/Origin_of_COVID-19. Accessed November 10, 2023.

7   In October 2020 *Scientific American* firmly stated that it was an "insidious" "myth" that the virus was created in a Wuhan lab (Tanya Lewis, "Eight Persistent COVID-19 Myths and Why People Believe Them," *Scientific American*, October 12, 2020, https ://www.scientificamerican.com/article/eight-persistent-covid19 -myths-and-why-people-believe-them/.) yet as more news leaks out, increasing numbers of Americans believe that it did: Alice Miranda Ollstein, "POLITICO-Harvard poll: Most Americans believe Covid leaked from lab," *Politico*, July 9, 2021, https://www.politico .com/news/2021/07/09/poll-covid-wuhan -lab-leak-498847.

8   "Fauci Adviser Hid Emails from FOIA Requests by Using Personal Account: Records," *New York Post*, June 29, 2023, https://nypost .com/2023/06/29/fauci-adviser-hid-nih-emails-from-foia -requests-during-covid/.

9   "Scientist Who Tried to Squash Wuhan Lab Leak Theory Gets More Cash to Study Viruses," *New York Post*, October 3, 2022, https://nypost.com/2022/10/03/non-profit-tied-to-wuhan-lab -gets-650k-more-to-study-coronaviruses/.

10   "COVID-19 Pandemic," Wikipedia, https://en.wikipedia.org /wiki/COVID-19_pandemic.

11   "What Really Went on Inside the Wuhan Lab Weeks Before Covid Erupted," *The Times*, June 10, 2023, https://archive .is/2023.06.10-172049/https://www.thetimes.co.uk/article/inside -wuhan-lab-covid-pandemic-china-america-qhjwwwvm0.

12   "What Really Went on Inside the Wuhan Lab."

13   "The U.S. Government and the World Health Organization," Kaiser Family Foundation, May 22, 2023, https://www.kff.org /global-health-policy/fact-sheet/the-u-s-government-and-the -world-health-organization/.

14   "What We Do," World Health Organization, March 17, 2020, https://www.who.int/about/what-we-do.

15   Forest Maready, *The Moth in the Iron Lung: A Biography of Polio* (Las Vegas: CreativeSpace Publishing, 2018).

16   Robert F. Kennedy, Jr., *The Real Anthony Fauci: Bill Gates, Big Pharma, and the Global War on Democracy and Public Health* (New York: Skyhorse, 2021), 369.

17   Edward Hooper, *The River: A Journey to the Source of HIV and AIDS* (Boston: Little, Brown, 1999).

18   Chen Wang Q, et., al., "Early Containment Strategies and Core Measures for Prevention and Control of Most Coronavirus Pneumonia in China," *Zhonghua Yu Fang Yi Xue Za*, 54:20, 1–5, *Zhi*, https://www.ncbi.nlm.nih.gov/pmc/articles/PMC7163529/.

19   "China Confirms Sharp Rise in Cases of SARS-like Virus Across the Country," January 20, 2020, France24, https://www.france24

.com/en/20200120-china-confirms-sharp-rise-in-cases-of-sars
-like-virus-across-the-country.

20   Jared Kushner, *Breaking History: A White House Memoir* (New York: Broadside Books, 2022), 335.

21   "How One Model Simulated 2.2 Million U.S. Deaths From COVID-19," CATO at Liberty Blog, April 21, 2020, https ://www.cato.org/blog/how-one-model-simulated-22-million-us -deaths-covid-19#:~:text=It%20meant%20nobody%20 avoids%20crowded,million%20estimate%20depended%20 on%20it; Neil Ferguson, et. al, "Report 8: Impact of Non -Pharmaceutical Interventions (NPIs) to Reduce COVID-19 Mortality and Healthcare Demand," Imperial College COVID-19 Response Team, March 16,2020, https://www.imperial.ac.uk /media/imperial-college/medicine/sph/ide/gida-fellowships /Imperial-College-COVID19-NPI-modelling-16-03-2020.pdf.

22   Covid Data Tracker, Centers for Disease Control and Prevention, Aug. 5, 2023, https://covid.cdc.gov/covid-data -tracker/#datatracker-home.

23   Phillip Magness, "The Failure of Imperial College Modeling is Far Worse than We Knew," *American Institute for Economic Research*, April 22, 2021, https://www.aier.org/article/the-failure -of-imperial-college-modeling-is-far-worse-than-we-knew/.   It is worth noting that many of the most damning challenges to China Virus *medical* research came from economic journals. Economists, it seemed—with the exception of the economic charlatan Paul Krugman—were somewhat more honest and accurate in their reporting even about medical issues than medical researchers.

24   Sabine van Elsland and Ryan O'Hare, "Coronavirus Pandemic Could Have Caused 40 Million Deaths if Left Unchecked," Imperial College London, March 26, 2020, https://www.imperial.ac.uk /news/196496/coronavirus-pandemic-could-have-caused-40/.

25   Atlas, *Plague*, 10.

26   Ibid., 10

27 "Modeler Neil Ferguson Resigns, Nicknamed the 'Master of Disaster,' KFI, May 6, 2020, https://kfiam640.iheart.com /content/2020-05-07-modeler-neil-ferguson-resigns-nicknamed -the-master-of-disaster. Among the ridiculous and outlandishly wrong predictions by Ferguson, he claimed in 2002 that 50,000 people would die from mad cow disease (177 died), or in 2005 that 150 million people would die from the bird flu (282 died), or in 2009 that the swine flu would kill 65,000 (it killed only 457). Such gross errors could always be excused by saying, "See, they listened to me or it would have been worse!"

28 "Trump Administration Restricts Entry into U.S. from China," *New York Times*, February 10, 2020, https://www.nytimes.com/2020 /01/31/business/china-travel-coronavirus.html.

29 "How Anthony Fauci Became America's Doctor," *New Yorker*, April 10, 2020, https://www.newyorker.com/magazine/2020/04/20 /how-anthony-fauci-became-americas-doctor. Within a year, there would be those calling Fauci an American version of Dr. Mengle ("Outrage as Fox News Commentator Likens Anthony Fauci to Nazi Doctor," *The Guardian*, November 30, 2021, https://www .theguardian.com/us-news/2021/nov/30/anthony-fauci-josef -mengele-fox-news).

30 "Trump Trashes Fauci and Makes Baseless Coronavirus Claims in Campaign Call," CNN Politics, October 20, 2020, https ://www.cnn.com/2020/10/19/politics/donald-trump-anthony -fauci-coronavirus/index.html. Note that many, if not most, of Trump's "baseless" claims turned out to be entirely correct.

31 Atlas, *Plague.*

32 Robin Koener, "How the 'Unvaccinated' Got It Right," Brownstone Institute, January 21, 2023, https://brownstone.org/articles/how -the-unvaccinated-got-it-right.

33 "A Year on from Europe's First Lockdown: Italy Mulls New Restrictions," *Euronews*, March 9, 2021, https://www.euronews .com/2021/03/09/a-year-on-from-europe-s-first-lockdown-italy -mulls-new-restrictions.

34 John Carlson and Anders Tegnell, "Swedish Response to COVID-19," *China CDC Weekly*, October 23, 2023, https://www.ncbi.nlm .nih.gov/pmc/articles/PMC8393133/#:~:text=PUBLIC%20 HEALTH%20RESPONSE%20TO%20COVID%2D19%20 IN%20SWEDEN&text=Sweden's%20main%20public%20 health%20response,years%20of%20age%20(5).

35 Kennedy, *Real Anthony Fauci*, xvii–xviii.

36 Bruce Sacerdote et. al., "Why Is All COVID-19 News Bad News?" National Bureau of Economic Research Working Paper 28110, November 2020.

37 Jim A. Kuypers, ed., *Public Communication in the Time of COVID-19: Perspectives from the Communication Discipline on the Pandemic* (Lanham, MD: Lexington Books, 2022), 23.

38 Kennedy, *Real Anthony Fauci*, 151.

39 Ibid., 151; "HIV & AIDS Fauci's First Fraud," documentary film September 6, 2020, https://www.youtube.com/watch?v=wy3frBacd2k.

40 Atlas, *Plague*, 64. Atlas recalled that in his first confrontation with Birx, she referred to a "hair salon" study of masks/infections, which was a) not a study, and b) she simply didn't know the details correctly.

41 Ibid., 14.

42 Sacerdote, "Why is All COVID-19 News Bad News?"

43 Atlas, *Plague*, 45.

44 Ibid., 84.

45 Jim Kuypers, *Partisan Journalism: A History of Media Bias in the United States* (Lanham, MD: Rowman & Littlefield, 2013).

46 Atlas, *Plague*, 62.

47 Kuypers, *Public Communication*, 28; Peter Kerr and Patricia May, "Newspaper Coverage of Fundamentalist Christians, 1980–2000," *Journalism and Mass Communication Quarterly*, 79:2007, 54–72.

48 Gary Taubes, *Good Calories, Bad Calories: Fats, Carbs, and the Controversial Science of Diet and Health* (New York: Anchor Books, 2008).

49 Walter Lippmann, *Liberty and the News* (London: Forgotten Books, 2020), 41–42.

50 Sara Fujimura, "Purple Death: The Great Flu of 1918," *Perspectives in Health*, 8:2009, cited by the Pan American Health Organization, https://www.paho.org/en/who-we-are/history-paho/purple -death-great-flu-1918#:~:text=The%20microscopic%20killer%20 circled%20the,and%20the%20Vietnam%20War%20combined.

51 The number estimated to have died from the Spanish Flu was 675,000, while in December 2020 the number of American Covid deaths was 350,000. See Centers for Disease Control and Prevention, "2020 Final Death Statistics: COVID-19 as an Underlying Cause of Death vs. Contributing Cause," https://www .cdc.gov/nchs/pressroom/podcasts/2022/20220107/20220107. htm.

52 "CDC Reports Fewer COVID-19 Pediatric Deaths after Data Correction," Reuters, March 18, 2022, https://www.reuters.com /business/healthcare-pharmaceuticals/cdc-reports-fewer-covid-19 -pediatric-deaths-after-data-correction-2022-03-18/.

53 "CDC Coding Error led to Overcount of 72,000 Covid deaths," *UK Guardian*, March 24, 2022, https://www.theguardian.com /world/2022/mar/24/cdc-coding-error-overcount-covid-deaths. See "We are Overcounting Covid Deaths and Hospitalizations. That's a Problem," *Washington Post*, January 13, 2023.

54 "Houston, the CDC Has a Problem (Part 2 of 3)," The Ethical Skeptic, October 24, 2022, https://theethicalskeptic .com/2022/10/24/houston-the-cdc-has-a-problem-part-2-of-3/.

55 "Houston, the CDC Has a Problem."

56 "The Vicious Circle of Covid Boondoggles and Bad Data," *Wall Street Journal*, January 26, 2023, https://www.wsj.com/articles /the-vicious-circle-of-covid-boondoggles-and-bad-data-fema-cdc -states-death-certificates-overcounting-11674735182.

57 John Ioannidis, "A Fiasco in the Making? As the Coronavirus Pandemic Takes Hold, We are Making Decisions Without Reliable Data," *STAT*, March 17, 2020, https://www.statnews .com/2020/03/17/a-fiasco-in-the-making-as-the-coronavirus

-pandemic-takes-hold-we-are-making-decisions-without-reliable
-data/.

58 Wendi Mahoney, "Deborah Birx: The Pandemic's Master of Lockdown," Uncoverdc.com, www.uncoverdc.com, June 6, 2023, https://uncoverdc.com/2023/06/06/deborah-birx-the-pandemics -master-of-the-lockdown.

59 Ibid.

60 Ibid.

61 Ibid.

62 J.C. McGinty, "How Many People Might One Person with Coronavirus Infect?" *Wall Street Journal*, February 14, 2020, https ://www.wsj.com/articles/how-many-people-might-one-person -with-coronavirus-infect-11581676200.

63 John Ioannidis, "Coronavirus Disease 2019: The Harms of Exaggerated Information and Non Evidence Based Measures," *European Journal of Clinical Investigation*, April 2020, https://www .ncbi.nlm.nih.gov/pmc/articles/PMC7163529/.

64 Jonathan Rothwell and Sonal Desai, "How Misinformation is Distorting COVID Policies and Behaviors," Brookings Institute, December 22, 2020, https://www.brookings.edu/articles/how -misinformation-is-distorting-covid-policies-and-behaviors/.

65 "False-Positive Results in Rapid Antigen Tests for SARS-DoV-2," *Journal of the American Medical Association*, 5:2022, 485-6; "How Children Are Spoofing Covid-19 Tests With Soft Drinks," BBC, July 5, 2022, https://www.bbc.com/future/article/20210705 -how-children-are-spoofing-covid-19-tests-with-soft-drinks; Daniel Geisler, et. al., "Unexpected False-Positive Rates in Pediatric SARS-CoV-2 Serology Using the EUROIMMUN Anti–SARS -CoV-2 ELISA IgG Assay," *American Journal of Clinical Pathology*, 155:2021;155,773–775; Paget J, Spreeuwenberg, et al., "Global Mortality Associated with Seasonal Influenza Epidemics: New Burden Estimates and Predictors from the GLaMOR Project," *Journal of Global Health*, 9: 2019.

66 "Is it Time for a Reality Check on Rapid COVID Tests?" NPR, January 19, 2023, https://www.npr.org/sections/health-shots/2023/01/19/1149672577/is-it-time-for-a-reality-check-on-rapid-covid-tests#:~:text=%22Rapid%20antigen%20tests%20are%20considerably,home%20tests%20were%20equally%20accurate.

67 Atlas, *Plague*, 23.

68 Carol Graham and Emily Dobson, "Despair Underlies Our Misinformation Crisis: Introducing an Interactive Tool," Brookings Institution, July 13, 2023, https://www.brookings.edu/articles/despair-underlies-our-misinformation-crisis-introducing-an-interactive-tool/. The authors, however, did not make the connection between *what* was the information causing the despair, in this case, hyper-exaggeration of the risk of Covid.

69 Atlas, *Plague*, 35.

70 Ibid., 36.

71 Maja Graso, et. al., "Blaming the Unvaccinated During the COVID-19 Pandemic: The Roles of Political Ideology and Risk Perceptions in the USA," *Journal of Medical Ethics,* June 9, 2023, https://jme.bmj.com/content/early/2023/06/09/jme-2022-108825.

72 Graso, "Blaming the Unvaccinated."

73 "Biden Blames the Unvaccinated for US's COVID-19 Slog," *The Hill,* September 9, 2021, https://thehill.com/policy/healthcare/571593-biden-blames-unvaccinated-for-covid-19s-slog/.

74 "How COVID-19 Threatens Independent Journalism," Open Society Foundations, July 2020, https://www.opensocietyfoundations.org/explainers/how-covid-19-threatens-independent-journalism. The article probably should have been entitled, "How GOVERNMENT HYSTERIA related to COVID-19" threatened all information dissemination.

75 Ananish Caudhun, "The Collateral Damages of Lockdown Policies: A Review of *The Great Covid Panic* by Paul Frijters, Gigi Foster and Michael Baker," *Journal of Behavioral & Experimental Economics,*

June 18, 2022, https://www.ncbi.nlm.nih.gov/pmc/articles /PMC8890786/.

76 Thomas Inglesby, et. al., "Disease Mitigation Measures in the Control of Pandemic Influenza," *Biosecur Bioterror*, 2006, 366–75.

77 Caudhun, "Collateral Damages."

78 A. Sebhatu, et. al., "Explaining the Homogeneous Diffusion of Covid-19 Nonpharmaceutical Interventions Across Heterogenous Countries," *Proceeding of the National Academy of Sciences*, 2020:21201–21208.

79 "What Does the Trucker Convoy Hope to Accomplish?" CTV News, January 28, 2022, https://www.ctvnews.ca/politics/what -does-the-trucker-convoy-hope-to-accomplish-1.5758489.

80 Author interview with David Freiheit, August 18, 2023.

81 J. Gibson, "Hard, Not Early: Putting the New Zealand Covid-19 Response in Context." *New Zealand Economic Papers,* September 2020, 1–8; R. Chaudhry, et al., "A Country Level Analysis Measuring the Impact of Government Actions, Country Preparedness and Socioeconomic Factors on COVID-19 Mortality and Related Health Outcomes. *EclinicalMedicine*, August 2020; https://www .ncbi.nlm.nih.gov/pmc/articles/PMC7372278/, and T.A. Meunier, "Full Lockdown Policies in Western Europe Countries Have no Evident Impacts on the COVID-19 Epidemic, " *medRxiv*. 2020.

82 D. Allen, "Covid-19 Lockdown Cost/Benefits: A Critical Assessment of the Literature," 2021, https://www.sfu.ca/~allen /LockdownReport.pdf.

83 Paul Frijters, et. al., *The Great Covid Panic: What Happened, Why, and What to Do Next* (New York: Brownstone Institute, 2021), 91, Table 3.

84 Ioannidis, "Coronavirus Disease 2019."

85 C. Bjørnskov, "Did Lockdown Work? An Economist's Cross-country Comparison. *CESifo Economic Studies.* 67:2021, 318–331.

86 "Unprecedented Chinese Quarantine Could Backfire, Experts Say," *Washington Post*, January 24, 2020, https://www .washingtonpost.com/health/unprecedented-chinese-quarantine

-could-backfire-experts-say/2020/01/24/db073f3c-3ea4-11ea
-8872-5df698785a4e_story.html.

87   Ibid.

88   Ibid.

89   David Koerner, "COVID-19 and the Trolley Problem: You're on
the Tracks and the Government is Controlling the Switch," FEE
Stories, March 24, 2020, https://fee.org/articles/covid-19-and
-the-trolley-problem-you-re-on-the-tracks-and-the-government-is
-controlling-the-switch/.

90   House of Representatives, Committee on the Judiciary and
the Select Subcommittee on the Weaponization of the Federal
Government, "The Weaponization of CISA: How a 'Cybersecurity'
Agency Colluded with Big Tech and 'Disinformation' Partners to
Censor Americans," June 26, 2023, https://judiciary.house.gov
/sites/evo-subsites/republicans-judiciary.house.gov/files/evo
-media-document/cisa-staff-report6-26-23.pdf.

91   "CISA Was Behind the Attempt to Control Your Thoughts, Speech,
and Life," *Epoch Times*, July 4, 2023, https://www.theepochtimes
.com/opinion/cisa-was-behind-the-attempt-to-control-your
-thoughts-speech-and-life-5373875?utm_source=open&utm
_medium=search.

92   Ibid.

93   "*Berenson v. Biden*: The Potential and Significance," Brownstone
Institute, April 19, 2023, https://brownstone.org/articles/berenson
-v-biden-potential-significance/.

94   "'Censorship-Industrial Complex' Uses Gov't Power to Threaten
Democracy," *New York Post*, March 10, 2023, https://nypost
.com/2023/03/10/censorship-industrial-complex-uses-power-to
-threaten-democracy/.

95   "'Censorship-industrial Complex."

96   "The Truth Cops: Leaked Documents Outline DHS's Plans to
Police Disinformation," *The Intercept*, October 31, 2022, https
://theintercept.com/2022/10/31/social-media-disinformation-dhs/.

97 "Judge Limits Biden Administration Contact with Social Media Platforms in Censorship Case," *Louisiana Illuminator*, July 4, 2023, https://lailluminator.com/2023/07/04/judge-limits-biden-administration-contact-with-social-media-platforms-in-censorship-case/.

98 "To Help Biden, FBI Interfered with 2020 Election," *Daily Signal*, August 26, 2022, https://www.dailysignal.com/2022/08/26/to-help-biden-fbi-interfered-with-2020-election/.

99 "Trump Puts Pence in Charge of Coronavirus Response," *Politico*, February 26, 2020, https://www.politico.com/news/2020/02/26/trump-puts-pence-in-charge-of-coronavirus-response-117790.

100 Kushner, *Breaking History: A White House Memoir* (New York: Broadside Books, 2022, 350.

101 Ibid.

102 Alan Olmstead and Paul Rhode, *Arresting Contagion: Science, Policy, and Conflicts Over Animal Disease Control* (Cambridge, MA: Harvard University Press, 2015), 37.

103 Olmstead and Rhode, *Arresting Contagion*, 39.

104 Ibid., 318–19.

105 Spectator TV, "WHO Special Envoy on COVID-Dr David Nabarron on Lockdowns (Oct. 8, 2020), https://www.youtube.com/watch?v=YdSpil_BQWV0.

106 Kennedy, *Real Anthony Fauci*, 2.

107 Ibid.

108 Ibid.

109 Ibid.

110 "Did Fauci and Collins Receive Royalty Payments from Drug Companies?" *National Review*, May 11, 2023, https://www.nationalreview.com/corner/did-fauci-and-collins-receive-royalty-payments-from-drug-companies/.

111 "Disclosures Show Dr. Fauci's Household Made $1.7 Million in 2020, Including Income, Royalties, Travel Perks and Investment Gains," *Forbes*, January 15, 2022, https://www.forbes.com/sites/adamandrzejewski/2022/01/15/disclosures

-released-dr-fauci-household-profits-exceeded-17-million-in
-2020--included-income-royalties-travel-perks-and-investment
-gains/?sh=37f3b7087d5f.

112 "Patents by Inventor Anthony S. Fauci," https://patents.justia
.com/inventor/anthony-s-fauci.

113 "The NIH Claims Joint Ownership of Moderna's Coronavirus
Vaccine," *Axios*, June 25, 2020, https://www.axios.com/2020/06/25
/moderna-nih-coronavirus-vaccine-ownership-agreements;   "After
Long Delay, Moderna Pays N.I.H. for Covid Vaccine Technique,"
New York Times, February 23, 2023, https://www.nytimes
.com/2023/02/23/science/moderna-covid-vaccine-patent-nih.html.

114 "Is There an Insidious 'Iron Triangle' in American Health
Care?" *The Hill*, June 13, 2022, https://thehill.com/opinion
/healthcare/3519281-is-there-an-insidious-iron-triangle-in
-american-health-care/.

115 Pierre Kory, "The Global Disinformation Campaign Against
Ivermectin—the 'Fix' at the WHO," *Canary in a Covid World*, 63.

116 "Remarks by President Trump at the Operation Warp Speed Vaccine
Summit," December 8, 2020, https://trumpwhitehouse.archives
.gov/briefings-statements/remarks-president-trump-operation
-warp-speed-vaccine-summit/.

117 "Supreme Court Gives Partial OK to Navy for Vaccine
Mandate," NPR, March 25, 2022, https://www.npr.org
/2022/03/25/1086789991/supreme-court-gives-partial-ok-to
-navy-for-vaccine-mandate#:~:text=The%20U.S.%20
Supreme%20Court%20late,COVID%2D19%20or%20face%20
reassignment.

118 "Supreme Court Blocks Biden's Vaccine-or-Test Mandate for Large
Private Companies," January 13, 2022.

119 Kennedy, *Real Anthony Fauci*, xvii.

120 "How Much Herd Immunity Is Enough?" *New York Times*,
December 24, 2020, https://www.nytimes.com/2020/12/24
/health/herd-immunity-covid-coronavirus,html?serchResultPositi
on=2.

121 Kennedy, *Real Anthony Fauci*, 4.

122 Ibid., 5; "U.S. Adults' Estimates of COVID-19 Hospitalization Risk," Gallup, September 27, 2021.

123 Kennedy, *Real Anthony Fauci*, 15.

124 Ibid., 16.

125 Harvey Risch, "Early Outpatient Treatment of Symptomatic, High-Risk COVID-19 Patients That Should be Ramped Up Immediately as Key to the Pandemic Crisis," *American Journal of Epidemiology*, November 2, 2020, https:/pubmed.ncbi.nlm.nih .gov/32458969/.

126 "Hydroxychloroquine Reduces COVID-19 Mortality, Study Finds," *Epoch Times*, October 9, 2023, https://www.theepochtimes .com/health/hydroxychloroquine-reduces-covid-19-mortality -study-finds-5506543.

127 Kennedy, *Real Anthony Fauci*, 27.

128 Mandeep Mehra, et. al., "Hydroxychloroquine or Chloroquine With or Without a Macrolide for Treatment of COVID-19: A Multinational Registry Analysis," *The Lancet*, May 22, 2020, https: //www.thelancet.com /journals /lancet /article /PIIS0140 -6736(20)31180 -6 /fulltext.

129 Kennedy, *Real Anthony Fauci*, 29.

130 Michael Horning and Jim Kuypers, "Journalism Framing in (Times of) Crisis: The Inevitability of Poor Reporting During the COVID-19 Pandemic 23," in Kuypers, *Public Communication*, 23–71 (quotation on 30).

131 CBS, "Large Study Finds Drug Touted by Trump is 'not useful and may be harmful' for COVID-19 Patients," CBS News, May 22, 2020, https://www.cbsnews.com/news /hydroxychloroquine -coronavirus-drug-study-not-helpful-harmful-heart-risks-trump/.

132 "Another Large Study Finds No Benefit to Hydroxychloroquine for COVID-19: The Medication May, in fact, Lead to an Increased Risk of Death," NBC News, May 22, 2020, https://www.nbcnews .com/health/health-news/another-large-study-finds-no-benefit -hydroxychloroquine-covid-19-n1212886.

[133] "Chloroquine, Hydroxychloroquine Linked to Higher Death Risk in COVID-19," Breitbart News, May 22, 2020, https://www.breitbart.com/news/chloroquine-hydroxychloroquine-linked-to-higher-death-risk-in-covid-19/.

[134] "Hydroxychloroquine Provides No Covid-19 Help, Increases Risk, Study Finds," *Wall Street Journal*, May 22, 2020, https://www.wsj.com/articles/malaria-drugs-provide-no-covid-19-help-raise-risk-of-harm-study-finds-11590161735.

[135] Michael Horning and Jim Kuypers, "Journalism Framing in (Times of) Crisis: The Inevitability of Poor Reporting During the COVID-19 Pandemic," *Public Communication*, 31.

[136] Kennedy, *Real Anthony Fauci*, 37.

[137] Ibid., 38.

[138] "Cheap Antiparasitic Could Cut Chance of Covid-19 Deaths by up to 75%," *Financial Times*, January 19, 2021, https://www.ft.come/content/e7cb7fc-da98-4a31-9clf-926c68349c84.

[139] Kennedy, *Real Anthony Fauci*, 43.

[140] Ibid.

[141] Ibid., 59.

[142] Ibid., 60.

[143] "One Hospital Denies Oklahoma Doctor's Story of Ivermectin Overdoses Causing ER Delays for Gunshot Victims: The Hospital Says It Hasn't Experienced Any Care Backlog Due to Patients Overdosing on a Drug that's Been Falsely Peddled as a Covid Cure," *Rolling Stone*, September 5, 2021, https://www.rollingstone.com/politics/politics-new-gunshot-vitims-horse-dewormer-ivermecting-oklahoma-hospitals-covid-1220608/. Merely the headline of the *Rolling Stone* piece's "retraction" is a shockingly poor example of "reporting." The drug had *not* been "falsely peddled." In fact, not peer reviewed studies on ivermectin as a China Virus treatment had been conducted by that point, only related studies and practical experience as in Uttar Pradesh. Second, continuing to refer to ivermectin as a horse dewormer, which is like referring to penicillin as a drug for horse syphilis, is equally silly and dishonest.

144 "Joe Rogan Says He Has COVID-19 And Has Taken the Drug Ivermectin," NPR, September 1, 2021, https://www.npr.org /2021-09/01/1033485152/joe-rogan-covid-ivermecti.

145 "*Rolling Stone* issues 'Update' After Horse Dewormer Hit-Piece Debunked," *Zero Hedge*, September 5, 2021, https://www .zerohedge.com/covid-19/rolling-stone/horse-dewormer-hit-piece -debunked-after-hospital-says-no-ivermectin.

146 "VAERS Data is Crystal Clear: The COVID Vaccines Are Killing an Estimated 1 Person Per 1,000 Doses (676,000 Dead Americans)," Steve Kirsch Newsletter, Substack, August 6, 2023, https ://kirschsubstack.com/p/vaers-data-is-crystal-clear-the-covid?utm _source=post-email-title&publication_id=548354&post _id=135774103&isFreemail=true&utm_medium=email.

147 Steve Kirsch, "Can Anyone Explain the Alarming Rise in Disability in Both the US and UK?" Steve Kirsch's Newsletter, Substack, July 18, 2023, https://kirschsubstack.com/p/can-anyone-explain -the-alarming-rise?utm_source=post-email-title&publication _id=548354&post_id=135232788&isFreemail=true&utm _medium=email'; "BREAKING: VAERS Data Clearly Shows That the COVID Vaccines Are an Unmitigated Disaster for Pregnant Women," July 17, 2022, Steve Kirsch's Newsletter, Substack, https ://kirschsubstack.com/p/breaking-vaers-data-clearly-shows?utm; "COVID Vaccines Have Likely Caused Over 25,000 New Cases of Multiple Sclerosis (MS)," Steve Kirsch's Newsletter, Substack May 28, 2023, https://kirschsubstack.com/p/covid-vaccines-have -likely-caused?utm/; "Apple Valley Village Health Care Center Saw 10x Higher COVID Death Rates After COVID vax Rollout. Isn't it Supposed to Decrease Rates?", Steve Kirsch's Newsletter, Substack August 14, 2023, https://kirschsubstack.com/p/apple -valley-village-health-care?utm.

148 "Peru Declares Health Emergency After Case Explosion of 'Vaccine Side Effect' Linked to Guillain-Barre Syndrome," *Leading Report*, July 10, 2023, https://theleadingreport.com/2023/07/10/peru

-declares-health-emergency-after-case-explosion-of-vaccine-side
-effect-linked-to-guillain-barre-syndrome/.

149 "Kill Shot: Recent Peer-Reviewed Report Finds 1 in 35 People
Who Took Moderna COVID Shot Had Signs of Heart Damage,"
Gateway Pundit, July 27, 2023, https://www.thegatewaypundit
.com/2023/07/killer-doctors-recent-peer-reviewed-report-
finds-1/; "Sex-Specific Differences in Myocardial Injury Incidence
After COVID-19 mRNA-1273 Booster Vaccination," *European
JournalofHeartFailure*,July20,2023,https://onlinelibrary.wiley.com
/doi/full/10.1002/ejhf.2978.

150 "New Emails Show COVID Vaccine Mandates Were Based
on a Lie," *Washington Examiner*, June 20, 2023, https://www
.washingtonexaminer.com/opinion/new-emails-show-covid
-vaccine-mandates-were-based-on-a-lie. A more detailed look at
these sources appears here: Peter McCullough, "E-mails Show
Walensky, Collins, and Fauci Knew mRNA Vaccine was Failing
in January, 2021," Courageous Discourse Substack, June 22,
20223, https://petermcculloughmd.substack.com/p/e-mails-show
-walensky-collins-and?utm.

151 Wendi Mahoney, "Moderna Spikevax Trial Data Show Serious
Adverse Events and Death," UncoverDC.com, July 14, 2023;
"IgG4 Increases with Repeated mRNA Vaccines: Linked to
Disease," UncoverDC.com, May 30, 2022, https://www.uncoverdc
.com/2023/05/30/igg4-increases-with-repeated-mrna-vaccines
-linked-to-disease/.

152 Wendi Mahoney, "Sen. Ron Johonson: Round Two for the
Death Jab," UncoverDC.com, December 8, 2022, https://www
.uncoverdc.com/2022/12/08/sen-ron-johnson-round-two-for-the
-death-jab/.

153 Peter McCullough, "All-Cause Mortality Up After Mass COVID-19
Vaccination," Courageous Discourse, June 20, 2023, https
://petermcculloughmd.substack.com/p/all-cause-mortality-up
-after-mass?utm.

154 Robin Koerner, "How the 'Unvaccinated' Got it Right," Brownstone Institute, January 31, 2023, https://brownstone.org/articles/how-the-unvaccinated-got-it-right/.

155 "Nurse Injured by COVID-19 Vaccine Heading to Trial Against Former Employer," *Epoch Times*, June 7, 2023, https://www.theepochtimes.com/us/nurse-injured-by-covid-19-vaccine-heading-to-trial-against-former-employer-5304112?utm_source=partner&utm_campaign=ZeroHedge&src_src=partner&src_cmp=ZeroHedge.

156 "Covid-19 Researcher Blows the Whistle on Data Integrity Issues in Pfizer's Vaccine Trial," *BMJ*, November 2, 2021, https://www.bmj.com/content/375/bmj.n2635.

157 Steve Kirsch, "Why Covid Litigation Is Our Best Path Forward," newsletter, October 10, 2023, https://kirschsubstack.com/p/why-covid-litigation-is-our-best?utm.

158 "COVID-19 Lockdowns 'Damaged a Generation': Former Chief Medical Officer, *Epoch Times*, June 21, 2023, https://www.theepochtimes.com/world/covid-19-lockdowns-damaged-a-generation-former-chief-medical-officer-5346621.

159 "COVID Crisis Could Push 100 Million People into Extreme Poverty, New World Bank Study Says," FEE Stories, July 1, 2020, https://fee.org/articles/covid-crisis-could-push-100-million-people-into-extreme-poverty-new-world-bank-study-says/.

160 "Zuckerberg: Establishment Asked to Censor COVID-19 Posts That Ended Up Being True," *Epoch Times*, June 10, 2023, https://www.theepochtimes.com/article/zuckerberg-establishment-asked-to-censor-covid-19-posts-that-ended-up-being-true-5325410.

161 "Elon Musk, Matt Taibbi, and a Very Modern Media Maelstrom," *New York Times*, December 4, 2022, https://www.nytimes.com/2022/12/04/business/media/elon-musk-twitter-matt-taibbi.html.

162 "Musk Releases 'Twitter Files' About Platform's Inner Workings," CNN Business, December 3, 2022, https://edition.cnn.com/videos/business/2022/12/03/smr-musk-taibbi-twitter-files.cnn.

163 Ibid.

164 "Latest 'Twitter Files' Alleges Rigged COVID Debate," Newsnation, December 27, 2022, https://edition.cnn.com/videos /business/2022/12/03/smr-musk-taibbi-twitter-files.cnn.

165 Ibid.

166 Koerner, "How the 'Unvaccinated' Got it Right."

167 Ibid.

168 "EXCLUSIVE: Vaccinated Outbreak at CDC Conference Bigger than Reported," *Epoch Times*, August 12, 2023, https://www .theepochtimes.com/mkt_app/health/exclusive-vaccinated -outbreak-at-cdc-conference-bigger-than-reported-5461213?utm.

169 Koerner, "How the 'Unvaccinated' Got it Right."

170 "A Long Term Vision for YouTube's Medical Misinformation Policies," August 15, 2023, https://blog.youtube/inside-youtube/a -long-term-vision-for-medical-misinformation-policies/.

171 Ibid.

172 Loren Graham, *Science in Russia and the Soviet Union* (New York: Cambridge, 1993).

173 David McCullough, *The Path Between the Seas: The Creation of the Panama Canal, 1870–1914* (New York: Simon & Schuster, 1978).

174 Larry Schweikart, *Seven Events that Made America America and Proved the Founding Fathers Were Right All Along* (New York: Sentinel, 2010), 95–116; Gary Taubes, *Good Calories, Bad Calories: Challenging the Conventional Wisdom on Diet, Weight Control, and Disease* (New York: Knopf, 2007).

175 Tracy Beanz, "Could CDC Data Prove COVID-19 Infections in November 2019?" UncoverDC.com, April 5, 2020, https ://www.uncoverdc.com/2020/04/05/could-cdc-data-prove-covid -19-infections-in-november-2019/.

176 Tracy Beanz, "Why Italy?" Uncoverdc.com, March 20, 2020, https://uncoverdc.wpengine.com/2020/03/20/why-italy/.

177 "China Spins Tale That the U.S. Army Started the Coronavirus Epidemic," *New York Times*, March 13, 2020, https://www.nytimes

.com/2020/03/13/world/asia/coronavirus-china-conspiracy
-theory.html.

178   Kennedy, *Real Anthony Fauci*, 423.

179   "Inside the War Between Trump and His Generals," *New Yorker*, August
14, 2022, https://www.newyorker.com/magazine/2022/08/15/inside
-the-war-between-trump-and-his-generals.

180   "Crimson Contagion 2019 Functional Exercise After-Action
Report," Department of Health and Human Services, January
2020, https://int.nyt.com/data/documenthelper/6824-2019-10
-key-findings-and-after/05bd797500ea55be0724/optimized
/full.pdf

181   Kennedy, *Real Anthony Fauci*, 425.

182   Klaus Schwab, "Now Is the Time for a 'Great Reset,'" World
Economic Forum, June 30, 2020), weforum.org/2020/006/now
-is-the-time-for-a-great-reset/.

183   Bill Gates, "Few Countries Will Get 'A Grade' for Coronavirus
Response," BBC, April 2020, bbc.com/news/av/world.52233966.

184   Jeffrey Tucker, "How They Convinced Trump to Lock Down,"
Brownstone Institute, March 23, 2023, https://brownstone.org
/articles/how-they-convinced-trump-to-lock-down/.

185   Tucker, "How They Convinced Trump."

186   David Bell, "What the WHO Is Actually Proposing," Brownstone
Institute, March 3, 2023, https://brownstone.org/articles/what
-the-who-is-actually-proposing/.

187   Ibid.

CHAPTER SEVEN

1   Lindsey Swindall, *Paul Robeson: A Life of Activism and Art* (Lanham,
MD: Rowman & Littlefield, 2015); S. Ross, *Hollywood Left and
Right: How Movie Stars Shaped American Politics* (New York:
Oxford University Press, 2011); R. Schickel, *Intimate Strangers:
The Culture of Celebrity in America* (Oxford: Oxford University

Press, 2011); J. Street, "Celebrity Politicians: Popular Culture and Political Representation," *British Journal of Politics and International Relations*, 6, 435–52.

2   Consider the general consensus today that there are no movie "stars" left. Perhaps Tom Cruise can, on his name, sell a picture. But after the latest *Mission Impossible* movie, even that is not a solid bet. Obvious reasons are that they appear on ads, on cable, or in other "small-budget" films or television, and in general have made themselves "too available." This is all true, but there is another factor: almost all of them have associated themselves with leftist causes, which has led conservatives either consciously or unconsciously to avoid their pictures. Thus, the "star" has alienated half of his or her audience from the start. Cruise, in fact, is no different, in that while he has mostly been apolitical in public, his association with the Church of Scientology and some talk show appearances alienated many mainstream fans.

3   Kenneth Bindas and Craig Houston, "'Takin' Care of Business': Rock Music, Vietnam and the Protest Myth," *The Historian*, November 1989, 1–23.

4   Guy Mitchell, Jr., *Global Warming: The Great Deception* (Savannah, GA: Literary Management Group, 2022), 21–26.

5   Mitchell, *Global Warming*, 46–47.

6   Ibid., 48.

7   Ibid., 56.

8   Ibid., 72.

9   This is nothing new. See "Elmer Gantry," 1950; "Three Billboards Outside of Ebbing, Missouri," 2017; "Doubt," 2008; "The Verdict," 1982.

10 Al Gore, *Earth in the Balance: Ecology and the Human Spirit* (Boston: Houghton-Mifflin, 1992).

11 Paul Johnson, *Modern Times: A History of the World from the Twenties to the Nineties*, rev. ed. (New York: HarperCollins, 1991), 55.

12 Jim Russell, book review of *Earth in the Balance* by Al Gore, Foundation for Economic Education, September 1, 1993.

13 Robert Lowenberg, "The Trivialization of the Holocaust as an Aspect of Modern Idolatry, *St. John's Review*, Winter 1982, 33–43.

14 "Thunberg Says only 'Eight Years Left' to Avert 1.5° Celsius Warming," Climate Home News, January 21, 2020, https://www .climatechangenews.com/2020/01/21/thunberg-says-eight-years -left-avert-1-5c-warming/#:~:text=Thunberg%20said%20there%20 was%20only,wildfires%20and%20rising%20sea%20levels.

15 Leonardo DiCaprio, "We Literally Only Have Eight Years Left," YouTube, https://youtu.be/8LYvIdHGvaI; "Leonardo DiCaprio Puts a Nine-Year 'Ticking Clock' on Climate Crisis— Is He Right?" *The Independent*, January 21, 2022, https://youtu .be/8LYvIdHGvaI/.

16 "Leonardo DiCaprio Uses Oscar Speech to Urge Action on Climate Change," *Scientific American*, February 29, 2016, https ://www.scientificamerican.com/article/leonardo-dicaprio-uses -oscar-speech-to-urge-action-on-climate-change/.

17 "Leonardo DiCaprio: Climate Change Deniers Should Not Hold Public Office," October 4, 2016, https://www.theguardian.com /film/2016/oct/04/leonardo-dicaprio-climate-change-donald -trump-before-the-flood-documentary.

18 "Meryl Streep Is the Last Whale on Earth in Sneak Peek at Climate Change Series 'Extrapolations,'" *Entertainment Weekly*, March 15, 2023, https://ew.com/tv/meryl-streep-last-whale-on-earth -extrapolations-sneak-peek/.

19 "10 Inspirational Quotes from Celebrities on Protecting the Environment," Earth Org, May 28, 2022, https://earth.org /inspirational-quotes-from-celebrities-on-environment/.

20 "Ocasio-Cortez: 'World Will End in 12 Years' If Climate Change Not Addressed," *The Hill*, January 22, 2019, https://thehill.com /policy/energy-environment/426353-ocasio-cortez-the-world-will -end-in-12-years-if-we-dont-address/.

21 "50 Years of Predictions that the Climate Apocalypse is Nigh," *New York Post*, November 12, 2021, https://nypost.com/2021/11/12/50 -years-of-predictions-that-the-climate-apocalypse-is-nigh/.

22 "Bill Gates sees 'A Lot of Climate Exaggeration' Out There: 'The Climate is Not the End of the Planet. So the Planet is Going to be Fine," *Fortune*, September 20, 2023, https://fortune.com/2023/09/20/bill-gates-climate-exaggeration-bloomberg-prince-william-earthshot/?utm.

23 Chris Rojek, *Fame Attack: The Inflation of Celebrity and Its Consequences* (London: Bloomsbury Academic, 2012), ix.

24 "Build Back Better Now: A Letter to the Entertainment Industry," September 2021, https://www.nrdcactionfund.org/build-back-better-entertainment-industry-letter/.

25 "Here's How Celebrities Embraced Climate Discussions at the U.N. General Assembly," KQED, September 27, 2021, https://www.kqed.org/science/1976890/heres-how-celebrities-embraced-climate-discussions-at-the-u-n-general-assembly; C. Rojek, *Celebrity* (London: Reaktion, 2001), and *Fame Attack: the Infatuation of Celebrity and Its Consequences* (London: Bloomsbury, 2012).

26 "Global Citizen Live: Everything You Need to Know," August 26, 2021, https://www.globalcitizen.org/en/content/global-citizen-live-everything-to-know/.

27 Michael Goodman, et. al., "Celebrities and Climate Change," Institute for Interdisciplinary Research into the Anthropocene, June 12, 2022.

28 Rojek, *Fame Attack*, vii.

29 Ibid., 1, 79. Rock singer Bono was involved with twenty-nine mainstream charities, an overexposure of monumental proportions.

30 L. McCutcheon et. al., *Celebrity Worshippers: Inside the Minds of Stargazers* (Baltimore: PublishAmerica, 2004), 166.

31 "Hollywood Should (Mostly) Stay Out of Politics," Morning Consult, October 10, 2018, https://pro.morningconsult.com/articles/hollywood-should-mostly-stay-out-politics.

32 Brian Loader, et. al., "Performing for the Young Networked Citizen? Celebrity Politics, Social Networking, and the Political Engagement of Young People," *Impat5 Factor*, November 20, 2015, 400–19.

33 Anubhay Mishra and Abhinav Mishra, "National v. Local Celebrity Endorsement and Politics," *International Journal of Politics, Culture, and Society*, 27, 2014, 409–25.

34 "Celebrities and Climate Change."

35 Ibid.

36 Mike Goodman, "*Celebritus Politicus*, Neo-liberal Sustainabilities and the Terrains of Care," Gavin Fridell and Martjin Konings, eds, *Contemporary Icons: The Cultural Politics of Neoliberal Capitalism* (Toronto: University of Toronto Press, 2013), 1–15.

37 Goodman, "*Celebritus Politicus*," 3. Goodman criticizes this celebrity activism as all falling within the rubric of "neo-liberal" market structures. In other words, in his view, they are merely puppets.

38 "Celebrities and Climate Change."

39 Ibid.

40 We could call this the "Ross Perot" effect, namely the appeal to a non-politician along basic (to the audience, obvious) principles— seal the border, stop sending US jobs abroad, don't get involved in foreign wars. Problems arise, though, when specifics are needed to back up the general. Ross Perot, in 1992, dropped out of the race temporarily because the demand for specifics of his program had grown too great. Donald Trump met the problem in 2015–16 by developing fleshed-out specific policy proposals, as have Vivek Ramaswamy and Robert F. Kennedy, Jr., in the 2024 presidential race.

41 Rojek, *Fame Attack*, 7.

42 Larry Schweikart, *Reagan: The American President* (Nashville: Post Hill Press, 2018).

43 "Celebrities and Culture Change."

44 J. Repo and R. Yrjola, "The Gender Politics of Celebrity Humanism in Africa," *International Feminist Journal of Politics*, 13, 44–62; D. West, "Angelina, Mia, and Bono: Celebrities and International Development," in L Brainard and D. Chollet, eds., *Global Development 2.0* (Washington, D.C.: Brookings Institute, 2008).

45 A. R. Biccum, "What Might Celebrity Humanitarianism Have to Do with Empire?" *Third World Quarterly*, 37: 2016, 998–1015.

46 Rojek, *Fame Attack* 15.

47 Edward Bernays, *Propaganda* (New York: Horace Liveright, 1928), 48.

48 M. Boykoff, and Mike Goodman, "Cultural Politics of Climate Change: Interactions in Everyday Spaces," in M. Boykoff, ed., *The Politics of Climate Change* (London: Routledge, 2009), 136–154.

49 S. O'Neill, "Image Matters: Climate Change Imagery in U.S., U.K., and Australian Newspapers," *Geoform*, 49:2013, 10–19.

50 S. Moser, "Communicating Climate Change: History, Challenges, Process, and Future Directions," *Wiley Interdisciplinary Reviews: Climate Change*, 1: 2010, 31–53.

51 "Jesus Christ, Streaming Star," *New York Times*, November 26, 2022.

52 "Before the Flood" Film Review, *The Hollywood Reporter*, September 9, 2015, http://www.hollywoodreporter.com/review/before-floodreview-927190.

53 E. G'Sell, "The New 'Inconvenient Truth': Leonardo DiCaprio's New Documentary Wants to Challenge Climate Change Skeptics," *Salon*, October 22, 2016.

54 Dan Brockington, *Celebrity Advocacy and International Development* (London: Routledge, 2014).

55 "Live Aid led to the Patronising 'Save Africa' Industry . . ." *The Guardian*, October 10, 2023, https://www.theguardian.com/global-development/2023/oct/10/live-aid-led-to-the-patronising-save-africa-industry-we-dont-need-a-musical-about-it#:~:text=Live%20Aid%20was%20watched%20by,undoubtedly%20saved%20thousands%20from%20death.

56 "Celebrities and Climate Change."

57 Rojek, *Fame Attack*, 13; L. McCutcheon et al., *Celebrity Worshippers: Inside the Minds of Stargazers* (Baltimore: Publish America, 2002), 18–20.

58 Ibid., 13.

59 M. Borkowski, *The Fame Formula* (London, Routledge, 2008), 371.

60 "Paris Agreement," https://climate.ec.europa.eu/eu-action/international -action-climate-change/climate-negotiations/paris-agreement _en#:~:text=The%20Paris%20Agreement%20sets%20out,support %20them%20in%20their%20efforts.

61 Bjorn Lomborg, *The Skeptical Environmentalist: Measuring the Real State of the World* (Cambridge: Cambridge University Press, 2001), 258.

62 "U.S. Officially Leaving Paris Climate Agreement," NPR, November 3, 2020, https://www.npr.org/2020/11/03/930312701 /u-s-officially-leaving-paris-climate-agreement.

63 Heritage Foundation, "Paris Climate Agreement; Instead of Regulations and Mandates, Embrace Markets," February 25, 2021, https://www.heritage.org/energy-economics/report/paris-climate -agreement-instead-regulations-and-mandates-embrace-markets.

64 International Energy Agency, "Data and Statistics: Total Energy Supply (TES) by Source," https://www.iea.org /data-and-statistics?country=WORLD&fuel=Energy%20 supply&indicator=TPESbySource; "Paris Climate Agreement."

65 U.S. Energy Information Administration, "What Is U.S. Electricity Generation by Energy Source?" February 27, 2020, https://www .eia.gov/tools/faqs/faq.php?id=427&t=3.

66 David Blackmon, reproducing a pdf letter from Prof. Michael Kelly, "Required Reading: The Green Energy Ne-Zero Plan Will Require a Command Economy," Substack, October 13, 2023, https://blackmon.substack.com/p/required-reading-the -green-energy?utm. I completely disagree with Kelly's conclusion. A "command economy" has inefficiencies vastly greater than the free market economy. Russia went broke dedicating only 50 percent of its GDP to the military. This would require the entire GDP, every single year, for twenty-six years.

67 Blackmon, "Required Reading."

68 David Blackmon, "A Reckoning is Coming for Green Energy," https://blackmon.substack.com/p/daily-caller-piece-a-reckoning-is?.

69 Muyu Xu and Shivani Singh, "China's 2020 Coal Output Rises to Highest Since 2015, Undermining Climate Pledges," Nasdaq, January 17, 2021, https://www.nasdaq.com/articles/chinas-2020 -coal-output-rises-to-highest-since-2015-undermining-climate -pledges-2021-01-17.

70 Robert Watson et al., "The Truth Behind the Climate Pledges," Universal Ecological Fund, November 2019, https://pure.iiasa .ac.at/id/eprint/16143/1/The%20Truth%20Behind%20the%20 Climate%20Pledges.pdf.

71 Benjamin Zycher, "Point: Trump Is Absolutely Correct to Withdraw from the Paris Climate Agreement," InsideSources, November 12, 2019, https://www.insidesources.com/trump-is-absolutely-correct -to-withdraw-from-the-paris-climate-agreement/.

72 "Trump: We Are Getting Out of Paris Climate Deal," *The Hill*, June 1, 2017, https://thehill.com/policy/energy-environment/335955 -trump-pulls-us-out-of-paris-climate-deal/.

73 Mitchell, *Global Warming*, 223.

74 "The Government Helped Tesla Conquer Electric Cars. Now It's Helping Detroit, and Elon Musk Isn't Happy," *Washington Post*, September 15, 2021, https://www.washingtonpost.com /technology/2021/09/15/tesla-biden-administration/.

75 "Elon Musk Doubles Down on Ending 'Subsidies' as Competitors Now reap More Benefits," CNN Business, December 7, 2021, https://www .cnn.com/2021/12/07/tech/elon-musk-wsj-government /index.html.

76 "Musk Strikes Again: Tesla's Win on EV Charging Could Split the Industry," Politico, June 16, 2023, https://www.politico.com /news/2023/06/16/tesla-musk-ev-chargers-00101437.

77 "Ford CEO Admits 'Reality Check' When he Took Electric F-150 Truck on Road Trip," *Epoch Times*, August 18, 2023, https://www .theepochtimes.com/article/ford-ceo-admits-reality-check-when -he-took-electric-f-150-truck-on-road-trip.

78 "How Electric Cars Became a Battleground in the Culture Wars," *The Guardian*, August 4, 2023, https://www.theguardian.com /business/2023/aug/04/electric-cars-culture-wars-evs.

79 "Sunday's Energy Absurdity: Idalia and EVs are Not Mixing Well," David Blackmon's Substack, September 3, 2023, https://blackmon .substack.com/p/sundays-energy-absurdity-idalia-and?utm

80 David Blackmon, "Biden's Mad Green Energy and Electric Vehicle Plans Are Falling Apart," *The Telegraph*, September 20, 2023, https://www.telegraph.co.uk/news/2023/09/20/joe-biden-electric -vehicle-uaw-strike-green-energy/.

81 David Blackmon, "Saturday's Energy Absurdity: Ford F-150 Lightning's 'Sales Have Tanked'," Substack, October 14, 2023, https://blackmon.substack.com/p/saturdays-energy-absurdity -ford-f?utm.

82 Hannes Zacher and Cort Rudolph, "Environmental Knowlege is Inversely Associated with Climate Change Anxiety," *Climate Change*, March 23, 2023, https://link.springer.com/article/10.1007 /s10584-023-03518-z.

83 Rojek, *Fame Attack*, 24.

84 Ibid., 72.

85 A. Gilligan, "Africans Don't Rate Bob Geldof, so Why Should We?" *The Telegraph,* July 15, 2010, https://www.telegraph.co.uk/culture /music/7893011/Africans-don't-rate-Bob-Geldof-so-why-should -we.html.

86 Rojek, *Fame Attack*, 39.

87 E. Etzerdorfer, et al., "A Close Response Relationship of Imitational Suicides with Newspaper Distribution," *Archives of Suicide* Research, 27, 2023, 137–45.

88 Guy Mitchell, Jr., *Global Warming: The Great Deception* (Savannah, GA: Literary Management Group, 2022), 15.

89 Mitchell, *Global Warming*, 17. To provide a counter example: From 1988 to 1995 I worked on a then-secret US Air Force aircraft project called the X-30 (National AeroSpace Plane). Its key technology was a scramjet engine capable of reaching Mach 25 thrust. No wind

tunnel on the planet could even get above Mach 8 to test it. So the team used Computational Fluid Dynamics to test models. At regular intervals, they got parts of the plane manufactured to the point they could fire them on the nose cone of missiles and test the higher velocities there. Almost all of the tests *validated* the CFD models.

90 Mitchell, *Global Warming*, 17.

91 John Cook, "Quantifying the Consensus on Anthropogenic Global Warming in the Scientific Literature," *Environmental Research Letters*, 8, May 15, 2013, 1–7.

92 Cook, "Quantifying the Consensus."

93 M. Perry, *Quotations of the Day from Friends of Science* (Washington, DC: Carpe Diem/AEI.org, 2019.

94 *Calgary Herald*, 1999, in ibid.

95 Chris Russill, "Stephen Schneider and the 'Double Ethical Bind' of Climate Change Communication," Bulletin of Science, Technology & Society, 30:1, 2010.

96 "Top Scientist Patrick Brown Says He Deliberately Omitted Key Fact . . ." *UK Daily Mail*, September 5, 2023, https://www.dailymail.co.uk/news/article-12482921/climate-scientist-patrick-brown-wildfires-started-people.html.

97 John Ioannidis, "Why Most Published Research Findings Are False," *PloS Medicine*, August 2005, 696–701, https://www.ncbi.nlm.nih.gov/pmc/articles/PMC1182327/.

98 S. Rasool and Stephen Schneider, "Atmospheric Carbon Dioxide and Aerosols: Effects of Large Increases on Global Climate," *Science*, 173, 138–41; Stephen Schneider, *Global Warming: Are We Entering the Greenhouse Century?* (New York: Vintage 1990).

99 Phillip Magness, "The Failure of Imperial College Modeling is Far Worse than We Knew," *American Institute for Economic Research*, April 22, 2021, https://www.aier.org/article/the-failure-of-imperial-college-modeling-is-far-worse-than-we-knew/.

100 Michael Park, et. al., "Papers and Patents Are Becoming Less Disruptive Over Time," *Nature*, 613, 2023, 138–44, https://www.nature.com/articles/s41586-022-05543-x.

101 Twenge, *Generations*, 446.

102 Ibid., 141.

103 Ibid., 142.

104 Ibid., 171. In the 1950s, only 12 percent of teens agreed with the statement "I am important." By the 1980s, that number ballooned sixfold (173).

105 Ibid., 249.

106 Miles Kimball and Robert Willis, "Utility and Happiness," unpublished paper, October 30, 2006, http://www.econ.yale .edu/~shiller/behmacro/2006-11/kimball-willis.pdf.

107 Twenge, *Generations* 276.

108 Noah Smith, "Will There Be a Millennial Big Chill?" Substack, April 27, 2033, https://noahpinion.substack.com/p/will-there-be -a-millennial-big-chill?utm_source=post-email-title&publication _id=35345&post_id=116649940&isFreemail=true&utm _medium=email.

109 Martha Bailey, et. al., "The COVID-19 Baby Bump: The Unexpected Increase in U.S. Fertility Rates in Response to the Pandemic," National Bureau of Economic Research Working Paper 30569, August 2023, https://www.nber.org/system/files/working _papers/w30569/w30569.pdf.

110 Jean Twenge, *Generations* (New York: Atria Books, 2023); Robert Rudolf and Dirk Bethmann, "The Paradox of Wealthy Nations' Low Adolescent Life Satisfaction," *Journal of Happiness Studies*, 24, 2023, 79–105.

111 Matthew Yglesias, "Why Are Young Liberals so Depressed?" Slow Boring, March 1, 2023, https://www.slowboring.com/p/why-are -young-liberals-so-depressed.

112 "Teen Girls Report Record levels of Sadness, C.D.C. Finds," *New York Times*, February 13, 2023, https://www.nytimes .com/2023/02/13/health/teen-girls-sadness-suicide-violence.html.

113 Jonathan Haidt, "The Dangerous Experiment on Teen Girls," *The Atlantic*, September 21, 2021, https://www.theatlantic.com/ideas /archive/2021/11/facebooks-dangerous-experiment-teen-girls/620767/.

114 Twenge, *Generations*, 317.

115 Karen O'Brien, et. al., "Exploring Youth Activism on Climate Change: Dutiful, Disruptive, and Dangerous Dissent," *Ecology and Society*, October 2018.

116 Thaddeus McCotter, "The WEF and the Climate Cult: Colluding for a World-wide Welfare State," *American Greatness*, September 9, 2023, https://amgreatness.com/2023/09/09/the-wef-and-the -climate-cult/?utm_medium=email&utm_source=act_eng& seyid=87567.

117 Carol Roth, *You Will Own Nothing: Your War with a New Financial World Order and How to Fight Back* (New York: Broadside Books, 2023), xi.

118 Roth, *You Will Own Nothing*, 195.

119 "U.S. Will Need Thousands of Wind Farms: Will Small Towns Go Along?" *New York Times,* December 30, 2022, https://www .nytimes.com/2022/12/30/climate/wind-farm-renewable-energy -fight.html.

120 "Challenges Facing the U.S. Offshore Wind Industry: Inflation, Interest Rates, and Insufficient Subsicies," Reuters, September 6, 2023, https://gcaptain.com/challenges-facing-the-u-s-offshore -wind-industry-inflation-interest-rates-and-insufficient-subsidies/.

121 Ida Auken, "Welcome to 2040: I Own Nothing, Have No Privacy, and Life Has Never Been Better," World Economic Forum, 2016, https://web.archive.org/web/20161125135500/https ://www.weforum.org/agenda/2016/11/shopping-i-can-t-really -remember-what-that-is; video link here: https://www.youtube .com/watch?v=NzpQYLZByQo.

122 Reuters: "Fact Check: The World Economic Forum Does Not have a Stated Goal to have People Own Nothing by 2030," February 25, 2021, https://www.reuters.com/article/uk-factcheck-wef -idUSKBN2AP2T0.

123 McCotter, "WEF and Climate Cult."

124 Twenge, *Generations*, 129.

125 Roth, *You Will Own Nothing*, 9–10. See, for example, the treatment of Ant Group under Jack Ma, who criticized the Chinese Communists' financial programs. He then went missing for several months and it was reported he had given up voting rights. ("Alibaba's Jack Ma Reemerges from Three-Month Absence after Clash with Beijing," *Washington Post*, January 20, 2021, https://www.washingtonpost.com/world/asia _pacific/jack-ma-alibaba-and-china/2021/01/20/eb6b5d32-5adb -11eba849-6f9423a75ffd_story.html.)

126 "China's Social Credit System," Berelsmann Stiftun, https://i.gzn .jp/img/2020/01/08/china-social-credit-system/o1.png.

127 Roth, *You Will Own Nothing*, 14.

128 "Biden Establishes a Ministry of Truth," *Wall Street Journal*, May 1, 2022, https://wsj.com/articles/Biden-establishes-a-ministry-of -truth-disniformation-governance-board-partisan-11651432312.

129 "China Proposes Teaching Masculinity to Boys . . ." NBC News, March 6, 2021, https://www.nbcnews.com/news/world/china -proposes-teaching-masculinity-boys-state-alarmed-changing -gender-roles-n1258939.

130 "The Trans War on the Family," *Spiked*, "January 29, 2023, https ://www.spiked-online.com/2023/01/29/the-trans-war-on-the -family/.

131 Sophie Lewis, *Abolish the Family: A Manifesto for Care and Liberation* (New York: Verso, 2022).

132 "Resolution Adopted by the General Assembly on 25 September 2015, 'Transforming Our World: the 2030 Agenda for Sustainable Development,'" United Nations General Assembly, October 21, 2015, https://sdgs.un.org/2030agenda.

133 "Department of Justice is Using the PATRIOT Act to Investigate Parents," Moms for Liberty, May 12, 2022, https://www .momsforliberty.org/news/do-to-investigat-parents.

134 "The U.S. Birth Rate Hit Another Record Low in 2019," *Business Insider India*, October 9, 2020, https://www.businessinsider.in

/science/health/news/the-us-birth-rate-hit-another-record-low-in
-2019-experts-fear-were-facing-a-demographic-time-bomb-that
-could-be-fast-tracked-by-the-pandemic-/articleshow/78577430.
cms.

135 "California's Baby Bust Has Long Term Consequences," *The Press Democrat*, March 5, 2023, https://www.pressdemocrat.com /article/opinion/pd-editorial-californias-baby-bust-has-long-term -consequences/.

136 Rebecca Traister, "Single Women Are the Most Potent Political Force in America," *The Cut*, February 21, 2016, https://www .thecut.com/2016/02/political-power-single-women-c-v-r.html.

137 "David Shor's Unified Theory of American Politics," *Intelligencer*, July 17, 2020, https://nymag.com/intelligencer/2020/07/david -shor-cancel-culture-2020-election-theory-polls.html.

138 Rod Dreher, "No Families, No Children, No Future," *American Conservative*, October 22, 2020, https://www .theamericanconservative.com/no-families-no-children-no-future -lgbt-30-percent-carle-c-zimmerman/.

139 "Illuminati Opening Ceremony of Gotthard Base Tunnel," Switzerland, 2016, https://www.youtube.com/watch?v=koQZt019P8g.

140 "World's Longest, Deepest Rail Tunnel to Close for Months after Freight Derailment in the Swiss Alps," CNBC, August 17, 2023, https://www.cnbc.com/2023/08/17/gotthard-base-tunnel-worlds -longest-rail-tunnel-to-close-for-months.html.

141 "Elon Musk Says CERN's Large Hadron Collider is 'Demonic Technology,'" https://www.youtube.com/watch?v=dgRCG77ejbs.

142 "'It's Demonic!' Eight-foot gold statue with Twisting Horns . . ." *UK Daily Mail*, January 26, 2023, https://www.dailymail.co.uk /news/article-11680847/Gold-statue-horns-tentacles-paying -homage-Ruth-Bader-Ginsburg-gets-trolled-online.html.

143 "Why is the Strasbourg Parliament Based on the Tower of Babel?" Mattbell.org, June 19, 2016, https://mattbell.org/why-is-the -strasbourg-parliament-based-on-tower-of-babel.

CHAPTER EIGHT

1   Martin Gurri, "The Elite Panic of 2022," *City Journal*, Summer 2022, https://www.city-journal.org/the-elite-panic-of-2022.

2   "'Regulation Has to Be Part of the Answer' to Combating Online Disinformation, Barack Obama Said at Stanford Event," *Stanford News*, April 21, 2023.

3   *NFIB v. OSHA*, 142 S. Ct. 661 (2022).

4   "Elon Musk's Vision of Free Speech Will Be Bad for Twitter," *Washington Post*, April 8, 2022, https://www.washingtonpost.com /outlook/2022/04/08/musk-twitter-equity-discrimination-speech/.

5   Gurri, "Elite Panic."

6   John Davidson, "The Twitter Files Reveal and Existential Threat," *Imprimis*, January 2023. For a large scale infographic on all the suppression and censorship by Twitter, see "INFOGRAPHIC: Key Revelations of the 'Twitter Files'," *Epoch Times*, January 17, 2023, https://www.theepochtimes.com/infographic-key-revelations-of -the-twitter-files_4986669.html?utm.

7   Davidson, "Twitter Files."

8   Ibid.

9   Ibid.

10 "Court Reduces Restrictions on Biden Administration Contact with Social Media Platforms," *Missouri Independent*, September 8, 2023, https://missouriindependent.com/briefs/court-reduces -restrictions-on-biden-administration-contact-with-social-media -platforms/.

11 *State of Missouri et. al. V. Joseph R. Biden et. al.*, No. 23-30445, September 8, 2023, https://storage.courtlistener.com/recap/gov .uscourts.ca5.214640/gov.uscourts.ca5.214640.238.1.pdf; "FIRE Statement on Fifth Circuit's Decision in Missouri v. Biden," September 9, 2023, https://www.thefire.org/news/fire-statement -fifth-circuits-decision-missouri-v-biden.

12 "Analysis of Hunter Biden's Hard Drive Shows He, His Firm took in about $11 million from 2013 to 2018, Spent it Fast," NBC

News, May 18, 2023, https://www.nbcnews.com/politics/national
-security/analysis-hunter-bidens-hard-drive-shows-firm-took-11
-million-2013-2018-rcna29462; "Comer: Mountain of Evidence
Reveals Joe Biden Abused His Public Office for His Family's Financial
Gain," House Oversight Committee, September 28, 2023, https
://oversight.house.gov/release/comer-mountain-of-evidence
-reveals-joe-biden-abused-his-public-office-for-his-familys
-financial-gain%EF%BF%BC/ has the $24 million number.

13   "Ukrainian Prosecutor Gives Proof of Biden Taking Bribes," MSN.
com, August 25, 2023, https://www.msn.com/en-us/news/politics
/ukrainian-prosecutor-gives-proof-of-biden-taking-bribes/ar-AA1g
JKnX?ocid=msedgntp&cvid=e6949c3a61ce4bd4b7b955c6db1cac
a3&ei=8.

14   "Hunter Biden's Chinese Business Partners Sent $250,000 to Joe
Biden's Delaware Home in 2019 . . ." *UK Daily Mail,* September
26,   2023,   https://www.dailymail.co.uk/news/article-12563957
/Hunter-Biden-got-two-payments-China-Joes-Delaware-HOME
-listed-address-Republican-says-obtaining-bank-records.html.

15   Peter Schweizer, *Red-Handed: How American Elites Get Rich Helping
China* (New York: HarperCollins, 2023).

16   "Cooper: One in Six Biden Voters Would Have Changed Their
Minds if they Had Known the Full Story" *Chattanooga Times
Free Press,* November 26, 2020, https://www.timesfreepress.com
/news/2020/nov/26/cooper-biden-voters/.

17   Davidson, "Twitter Files."

18   Joel Pollak and Larry Schweikart, *How Trump Won: The Inside Story
of a Revolution* (Washington, D.C.: Regnery, 2017).

19   Jeff Gerth, "The Press versus the President, Part One," *Columbia
Journalism Review,* January 30, 2023, https://www.cjr.org/special
_report/trumped-up-press-versus-president-part-1.php/. See also
Tyler Durden, "The Dummies Guide to the Russia Collusion
Hoax: Who, What, Where, When, & Why," Zero Hedge, May 26,
2018,   https://www.zerohedge.com/news/2018-05-26/dummies
-guide-russia-collusion-hoax-who-what-where-when-why.

[20] Gerth, "Press versus the President."

[21] C. H. Klotz, et al., eds., *Canary in a Covid World: How Propaganda and Censorship Changed Our (My) World* (New York: Canary House Publishing, 2023).

[22] Tom Jefferson, et. al., "Physical Interventions to Interrupt or Reduce the Spread of Respiratory Viruses," *Cochrane Reviews*, January 30, 2023, https://www.cochranelibrary.com/cdsr /doi/10.1002/14651858.CD006207.pub6/full.

[23] Jennifer Sey, "The Harms of Masking, Part 1," Substack, March 29, 2023, https://jennifersey.substack.com/p/the-harms-of-masking -part-1?utm.

[24] Steve Kirsch, "How I Got Started on My New Career as One of the World's Top 'Misinformation Spreaders,' Substack, January 14, 2023, https://stevekirsch.substack.com/p/the-twitter-dm-thread -that-started?utm.

[25] "SCOTUS Rules Against OSHA COVID-19 Vaccine/Testing Rule . . . So Now What?" Thompson Reuters, January 14, 2023, https://tax.thomsonreuters.com/blog/scotus-ruled-against-the -osha-covid-19-vaccine-testing-ruleso-now-what/.

[26] "High Court Religious Bias Decision Paves Way for EEOC Vax Suits," *Bloomberg Law*, September 26, 2023, https://news .bloomberglaw.com/daily-labor-report/high-court-religious-bias -decision-paves-way-for-eeoc-vax-suits.

[27] "NY Vaccine Mandate for Healthcare Workers 'Null, Void,' Following Judge Ruling," 7 Buffalo, June 16, 2023, https://www .wkbw.com/news/local-news/ny-vaccine-mandate-for-healthcare -workers-null-void-following-judge-ruling.

[28] "UK Now "Hopelessly Divided" Over the Net Zero Program," *Manhattan Contrarian*, September 4, 2023, https://www .manhattancontrarian.com/blog/2023-9-4-uk-now-hopelessly -divided-over-the-net-zero-program.

[29] "UK Now 'Hopelessly Divided.'"

[30] "Britain's Prime Minister Places Himself at the Tip of the Climate Spear," *Daily Caller*, September 23, 2023, https://dailycaller

.com/2023/09/23/britains-prime-minister-places-himself-tip
-climate-spear-david-blackmon/.

31 Eugyppius, "The Administrative Man," Eugyppius: A Plague Chronicle, June 23, 2023, https://www.eugyppius.com/p/the -administrative-man.

32 "Germany Reaches 1 Million Pure Electric Cars, with EVs one-third of new cars in December," *The Driven*, January 11, 2023, https://thedriven.io/2023/01/11/germany-reaches-1-million-pure -electric-cars-with-evs-one-third-of-new-cars-in-december/.

33 "Habeck Wants to Massively Defuse the Heating Law, *Augsburger Allgemeine*, May 26, 2023; "Germany Begins Dismantling Wind Farm for Coal," EuObserver, August 29, 2023, https://euobserver .com/green-economy/157364, https://www.augsburger-allgemeine .de/politik/umstrittener-gesetzentwurf-habeck-will-heizungsgesetz -massiv-entschaerfen-id66624716.html.

34 Robert Bryce, "The Energy Transition Isn't," Substack, July 1, 2023, https://robertbryce.substack.com/p/the-energy-transition-isnt?utm.

35 "Tree Euthanasia? Climate Alarmist Now Warn that Our Forests Will Worsen Global Warming," New American, August 14, 2023, https://thenewamerican.com/us/environment/tree-euthanasia -climate-alarmists-now-warn-that-our-forests-will-worsen-global -warming/.

36 "Scots 'Astonished' as 15.7 Million Trees Felled by SNP to Develop Wind Farms," *Express*, July 22, 2023, https://www.express .co.uk/news/politics/1794037/SNP-cut-down-trees-wind-farms -scotland?s=03.

37 "Biden Forest Service Hands Out Over $100 Million to Advance 'Tree Equity,'" https://dailycaller.com/2023/09/26/biden-forest -service-tree-equity/.

38 "Eugyppius, "German Health Minister Announces New Initiative to Combat Heat Wave Deaths by Calling Old People, Reminding them to Drink Water," Eugyppius: A Plague Chronicle, June 14, 2023, https://www.augsburger-allgemeine.de/politik/umstrittener

-gesetzentwurf-habeck-will-heizungsgesetz-massiv-entschaerfen
-id66624716.html.

39 "What's Next for the Corona-Warn-App?", *Spiegel*, April 2, 2023,
https://www.spiegel.de/netzwelt/apps/wie-geht-es-mit-der-corona
-warn-app-weiter-a-d86d8b9a-adee-42a7-b469-b35a34fa6bda.

40 "White House Cautiously Opens the Door to Study Blocking
Sun's Rays to Show Global Warming," *Politico*, July 1, 2023, https
://www.politico.com/news/2023/07/01/white-house-cautiously
-opens-door-to-study-blocking-suns-rays-to-slow-global-warming
-ee-00104513.

41 "As E-bikes Proliferate, So Do Deadly Fires Blamed on Exploding
Lithium-ion Batteries," AP, July 27, 2023, https://centurylink.net
/news/read/category/news/article/the_associated_press-as_ebikes
_proliferate_so_do_deadly_fires_blamed_on-ap?sc_cid=webmailpo.

42 "Jackson Buys 8 Electric Buses for Transit System, But None of
Them Are Working," *Cowboy State Daily* September 26, 2023,
https://cowboystatedaily.com/2023/09/26/jackson-buys-8
-electric-buses-for-transit-system-but-none-are-working/.

43 "Solar Projects Turn Into Disaster as Groundwater Dries UP,
Leaving Residents Furious: 'Dead Without Water'," *Western
Journal*, June 29, 2023, https://www.westernjournal.com/solar
-projects-turn-disaster-groundwater-dries-leaving-residents
-furious-dead-without-water/; Daryl Orr, "Solar Panels Destroyed
by Large Hail . . ." Twitter, https://twitter.com/WxWyDaryl
/status/1673830414329454592.

44 "Era of 'Unquestioned and Unchallenged' Climate Change Claims is
Over," *Epoch Times*, October 17, 2023, https://www.theepochtimes
.com/article/era-of-unquestioned-and-unchallenged-climate
-change-claims-is-over-5503316.

45 "'Life Is Like It Is': TotalEnergies CEO Defends Strategy Despite
Calls to Cut Fossil Fuel Production," CNBC, July 6, 2023, https
://www.cnbc.com/2023/07/06/totalenergies-ceo-defends-oil-and
-gas-strategy-after-climate-protests.html.

46 "Massive US Oil Caverns Sit Empty in Threat to Energy Security (Biden has Drained 46% of Strategic Petroleum Reserve . . .)", Confounded Interest, July 17, 2023, https://confoundedinterest .net/2023/07/17/massive-us-oil-caverns-sit-empty-in-threat-to -energy-security-biden-has-drained-46-of-strategic-petroleum -reserve-gasoline-prices-up-48-under-bidenomics-us-dollar-down -12-5-since-september-2022/.

47 Noah Smith, "No NEPA Really Is a Problem for Clean Energy," Substack, July 18, 2023, https://www.noahpinion.blog/p/no-nepa -really-is-a-problem-for-clean?utm.

48 "Italy Admits Wildfires Not Caused by Climate Change After Arsonist Caught Red-Handed," *Daily Fetched*, August 1, 2023, https://www.dailyfetched.com/italy-admits-wildfires-not-caused -by-climate-change-after-arsonist-caught-red-handed-watch/; "Greek Officials Arrest 2 for Arson as Multiple Wildfires Continue to Burn," NBC News, August 26, 2023, https://www.nbcnews .com/news/world/greece-wildfires-arrests-deliberate-dry-grass -athens-gale-force-winds-rcna101941; "Vancouver Man Arrested in String of Suspected Arson Fires," *The Columbian*, May 5, 2023, https://www.columbian.com/news/2023/may/05/vancouver-man -arrested-in-december-march-suspected-arson-fires/.

49 "Over 1,600 Scientists and Professionals Sign 'No Climate Emergency' Declaration," *Epoch Times*, August 29, 2023, https ://www.theepochtimes.com/science/over-1600-scientists-sign-no -climate-emergency-declaration-5482554?utm.

50 "800 Spy Cameras Damaged or Stolen as London Revolts Against the Green Agenda," *Breitbart*, October 4, 2023, https://www .breitbart.com/europe/2023/10/04/800-climate-spy-cameras -damaged-or-stolen-as-london-revolts-against-green-agenda/.

51 "Put Brakes on 'Damaging' Drive to Ban Petrol . . ." *UK Daily Mail*, July 20, 2023, https://www.dailymail.co.uk/news /article-12256847/Put-brakes-drive-ban-petrol-diesel-cars-2030 -MPs-industry-leaders-tell-ministers.html.

52   "Number of Transgender Surgeries Performed Each Year has Tripled
     . . ." *UK Daily Mail*, August 23, 2023, https://www.dailymail
     .co.uk/health/article-12437519/Gender-affirming-surgeries-US
     -nearly-tripled-pandemic-dip-study-finds.html.
53   "'Gender Clinics' Shutting Down Due to Red State Bans," *American
     Greatness*, July 27, 2023, https://amgreatness.com/2023/07/27
     /gender-clinics-shutting-down-due-to-red-state-bans/?utm
     _medium=email&utm_source=act_eng&seyid=79630.
54   "REPORT: Distributors Giving UP on Bud Light as They No
     Longer Expect Beer Giant to Recover from Dylan Mulvaney
     Fiasco," *Daily Caller*, July 31, 2023.
55   "Brews & Blues: Anheuser-Busch Restructures with Layoffs,"
     WION, July 27, 2023, https://www.wionews.com/business
     -economy/brews-blues-anheuser-busch-restructures-with
     -layoffs-619813; "Red, White and Brew! Bud Light Resorts to
     Giving Away FREE Beer for Fourth of July," *UK Daily Mail*, June
     29, 2023, https://www.dailymail.co.uk/news/article-12247711
     /Bud-Light-resorts-giving-away-FREE-beer-Fourth-July-struggles
     -reclaim-market.html.
56   A good history of DEI appears in Christopher Rufo, *America's
     Cultural Revolution* (New York: Broadside Books, 2023).
57   "Don't Tread on Me!" Nearly 60% of Americans Want Big
     Business to Stay Out of Politics, New Gallup Poll Reveals," *UK
     Daily Mail*, October 4, 2023, https://www.dailymail.co.uk/news
     /article-12594665/Americans-business-stay-politics-Gallup
     -poll.html. Contrast with "Americans Say 'No Thanks' to 'Woke'
     Corporations: I&I/TIPP Poll, June 19, 2023, https://issuesinsights
     .com/2023/06/19/americans-say-no-thanks-to-woke
     -corporations-ii-tipp-poll/.
58   Alfred Chandler, Jr., *The Visible Hand: The Managerial Revolution
     in American Business* (Cambridge, MA: Belknap, 1977).
59   Larry Schweikart and Lynne Pierson Doti, *American Entrepreneur*
     (New York: Amacom, 2010), 366. Material on the breakthroughs by

non-industry leaders is found in Burton Klein, *Dynamic Economics* (Cambridge, MA: Harvard University Press, 1977).

[60] For these and other business changes see Larry Schweikart, *The Entrepreneurial Adventure: A History of Business in the United States* (Ft. Worth, TX: Harcourt, 2000).

[61] Eugyppius, "The Administrative Man," Pugyppius: A Plague Chronicle, June 23, 2023, https://www.eugyppius.com/p/the -administrative-man.

[62] Eugyppius, "The Meaning of the Rainbow Revolution," Eugypius: A Plague Chronicle, June 11, 2023, https://www.eugyppius.com/p /the-administrative-man.

[63] "Bud Light Distributor Sends Out Public Plea to Bring Back Customers," *Epoch Times*, May 21, 2023, https://www .theepochtimes.com/us/bud-light-distributor-sends-out-public -plea-to-bring-back-customers-5280859?utm.

[64] "Disney Is Crashing and Burning and According to New Data, It's Likely Thanks to Conservatives," RedState, October 6, 2023, https://redstate.com/brandon_morse/2023/10/05/disney-is -crashing-and-burning-and-according-to-new-data-its-likely -thanks-to-conservatives-n2164700.

[65] "Supreme Court Strikes Down Affirmative Action Programs in College Admissions," *SCOTUSBLOG*, June 29, 2023, https://www .scotusblog.com/2023/06/supreme-court-strikes-down -affirmative-action-programs-in-college-admissions /#:~:text=Supreme%20Court%20strikes%20down%20 affirmative%20action%20programs%20in%20college%20 admissions,-By%20Amy%20Howe&text=In%20a%20 historic%20decision%2C%20the,in%20college%20 admissions%20on%20Thursday.

[66] "SUZANNE DOWNING: The 'Woke' Bubble' is About to Burst," *Daily Caller*, June 18, 2023, https://dailycaller.com/2023/06/18 /opinion-the-woke-bubble-is-about-to-burst-suzanne-downing/.

[67] "DEI College Director Fired for Not Being 'Right Kind of Black Person'," *Newsweek*, July 17, 2023, https://www.newsweek

.com/dei-college-director-fired-not-being-right-kind-black
-person-1813481.

68 "DEI Jobs Are Drying Up, But Colleges Keep Pushing Diversity
Studies," *The Federalist*, July 26, 2023, https://thefederalist
.com/2023/07/26/dei-jobs-are-drying-up-but-colleges-keep
-pushing-diversity-studies/.

69 "Ibram Kendi and the Implosion of DEI in Higher
Education," *Washington Examiner*, September 26, 2023, https
://www.washingtonexaminer.com/restoring-america/equality
-not-elitism/kendi-and-implosion-of-dei?utm_source
=deployer&utm_medium=email&utm_content=&utm_campaign
=Beltway+Confidential&utm_term=.

70 Christopher Rufo, "We Have Abolished DEI in Florida,"
Substack, May 15, 2023, https://christopherrufo.com/p
/we-have-abolished-dei-in-florida, and his "Dismantling the
DEI Bureaucracy in Texas," Substack, May 10, 2023, https
://christopherrufo.com/p/dismantling-the-dei-bureaucracy-in
?utm_source=post-email-title&publication_id=1248321&post
_id=124863504&isFreemail=true&utm_medium=email.

71 "Tennessee to Consider Cutting off Federal Government Funding
for Education," *Daily Wire*, September 26, 2023, https://www
.dailywire.com/news/tennessee-to-consider-cutting-off-federal
-government-funding-for-education.

72 "Just 6 Percent of New S&P Jobs Went to White Applicants in the
Wake of George Floyd, Analysis Shows," *Washington Free Beacon*,
September 26, 2023, https://freebeacon.com/latest-news/just-6
-percent-of-new-sp-jobs-went-to-white-applicants-in-the-wake-of
-george-floyd-analysis-shows/.

73 "Braverman: Multiculturalism Has 'Failed' and Threatens
Security," *The Independent*, September 26, 2023, https://www
.independent.co.uk/news/uk/europe-home-secretary-united
-states-multiculturalism-prime-minister-b2418911.html.

74 "'Global Governance Has Failed': PM Modi at G-20 Foreign
Ministers' Meet," NDTV, March 2, 2023, https://www.ndtv.com

/india-news/global-governance-has-failed-shows-experience-of
-last-few-years-pm-narendra-modi-says-at-g20-foreign-ministers
-meet-3826845.

75 Patrick Boyle, "The Death of Globalism," YouTube, https://www
.youtube.com/watch?v=H5ejv-dTAaU.

76 Ibid.

77 "Schroders—Regime Shift: Globalisation Dividend Coming
to an End," *Hubbis*, June 8, 2023, https://www.hubbis.com
/news/schroders-regime-shift-globalisation-dividend-coming-to
-an-end.

78 Ibid.

79 Ibid.

80 "Mexico's Imports from Russia Soar," *Daily Sun*, August 28,
2023, https://www.daily-sun.com/printversion/details/640761
/Mexico%E2%80%99s-imports-from-Russia-soar.

81 Boyle, "Death of Globalism."

82 "CHIPS for America Act & FABS Act," Semiconductor Association,
https://www.infomigrants.net/en/post/19841/in-orbans-hungary
-more-migrants-due-to-labor-shortage.

83 Boyle, "Death of Globalism."

84 "China's Tightening Grip on Foreign Firms Risks Hitting
Investment," *Wall Street Journal*, May 3, 2023, https://www.wsj
.com/articles/chinas-tightening-grip-on-foreign-firms-risks
-hitting-investment-93389517.

85 Noah Smith, "Decoupling Is Just Going to Happen," Substack,
May 21, 2023, https://www.noahpinion.blog/p/decoupling-is
-just-going-to-happen?utm_source=post-email-title&publication
_id=35345&post_id=122906400&isFreemail=true&utm
_medium=email.

86 "China's Tightening Grip."

87 "China's Growing Use of Coal Including the LONGEST Coal
Transporting Railway . . ." *UK Daily Mail*, October 5, 2023,
https://www.dailymail.co.uk/news/article-12599325/Americas
-unionized-strip-club-two-decades-Star-Garden-North

-Hollywood-REOPENS-nine-months-firing-dozen-dancers
-refused-work-without-better-pay-filing-bankruptcy-shutting
-down.html.

88 "China Locks Information on the Country Inside a Black Box,"
Wall Street Journal, April 20, 2023, https://www.wsj.com/world
/china/china-locks-information-on-the-country-inside-a-black
-box-9c039928.

89 "Fasten Your Seatbelts: How to Manage China's Economic
Coercion," MERICS, April 25, 2022, https://www.merics.org
/en/report/fasten-your-seatbelts-how-manage-chinas-economic
-coercion.

90 U.S. Chamber of Commerce, "Statement on Concerns Over PRC
Investment Climate," April 28, 2023, https://www.merics.org
/en/report/fasten-your-seatbelts-how-manage-chinas-economic
-coercion.

91 Adam Lin and Xiaojun Li, "Assessing Public Support for (Non-)
Peaceful Unification with Taiwan: Evidence from a Nationwide
Survey in China," *21st Century China Center Research Paper No.
2023-1*, March 7, 2023, https://papers.ssrn.com/sol3/papers
.cfm?abstract_id=4381723.

92 "Is China's Boom Turning to Bust? Youth Unemployment
Races to a Record High as Economy Suffers Sharp Slowdown,"
This Is Money, July 17, 2023, https://www.thisismoney.co.uk
/money/markets/article-12307787/Is-Chinas-boom-turning
-bust-Youth-unemployment-races-record-high-economy
-suffers-sharp-slowdown.html?ico=mol_desktop_ushome-ne
wtab&molReferrerUrl=https%3A%2F%2Fwww.dailymail
.co.uk%2Fushome%2Findex.html.

93 "How 'Decoupling' from China Became 'De-risking,'" *New York
Times*, May 20, 2023, https://www.nytimes.com/2023/05/20
/world/decoupling-china-de-risking.html.

94 "Interview: Dan Wang, China Specialist," Noah Smith Substack,
May 27, 2023, https://www.noahpinion.blog/p/interview-dan
-wang-china-specialist.

[95] "In Contrast to China, Japan at G-7 Basks in Newfound Appeal to Companies," *Wall Street Journal*, May 21, 2023, https://www.wsj.com/articles/in-contrast-to-china-japan-at-g-7-basks-in-newfound-appeal-to-companies-c3da2ce.

[96] Noah Smith, "How China's 'Debt Traps' Actually Work," substack, October 2, 2023, https://www.noahpinion.blog/p/how-chinas-debt-traps-actually-work?publication_id=35345&post_id=137585987&isFreemail=false&r=dx45b.

[97] "Hundreds in Myanmar Protest Lack of Payment for Land Confiscated for Pipeline Project," *Radio Free Asia*, March 3, 2022, https://www.rfa.org/english/news/myanmar/hundreds-in-myanmar-protest-lack-of-payment-for-land-confiscated-for-pipeline-project-03222018133100.html.

[98] "China Is Investing Billions in Pakistan. Its Workers Are Under Attack," *Wall Street Journal*, November 23, 2022, https://www.wsj.com/articles/china-pakistan-attacks-belt-and-road-11669218179.

[99] "Game of Loans: How China Bought Hambantota," Center for Strategic & International Studies, April 2, 2018, https://www.csis.org/analysis/game-loans-how-china-bought-hambantota

[100] "China's Global Mega-Projects Are Falling Apart," *Wall Street Journal*, January 20, 2023, https://www.wsj.com/articles/china-global-mega-projects-infrastructure-falling-apart-11674166180.

[101] "China's Global Mega-Projects Are Falling Apart."

[102] "China's Huge Asian Investments Fail to Buy it Soft Power," *The Economist*, April 5, 2023.

[103] "China's Loans Pushing the World's Poorest Countries to the Brink of Collapse," AP, May 18, 2023, https://apnews.com/article/china-debt-banking-loans-financial-developing-countries-collapse-8df6f9fac3e1e758d0e6d8d5dfbd3ed6.

[104] Noah Smith, "Four Reasons China Can't Reset the World," Substack, June 20, 2023, https://www.noahpinion.blog/p/four-reasons-china-cant-reset-the

[105] Smith, "Four Reasons."

[106] Ibid.

107 "Brussels Playbook: EU Eyes Chinese Cars—Vestager's Google Break-up Plan—Ukraine Security Vows," *Politico*, June 15, 2023, https://www.politico.eu/newsletter/brussels-playbook/eu-eyes -chinese-cars-vestagers-google-break-up-plan-ukraine-security -vows/.

108 Noah Smith, "Real Estate Is China's Economic Achilles Heel," Substack, June 1, 2023, https://www.noahpinion.blog/p/real -estate-is-chinas-economic-achilles.

109 "China's Recovery Is in Real Peril Now," *Wall Street Journal*, June 13, 2023, https://www.wsj.com/articles/chinas-recovery -is-in-real-peril-now-a985e366; "Fueled by Long Credit Binge, China's Economy Faces Drag from Debt Purge," *Wall Street Journal*, June 22, 2023, https://www.wsj.com/world/fueled-by -long-credit-binge-chinas-economy-faces-drag-from-debt-purge -e4621859?mod=article_inline.

110 "China's Big-City Homeowners Cash Out as Wealth Dream Fades," Caixin Global, June 20, 2023, https://www.caixinglobal.com/2023 -06-20/chinas-big-city-homeowners-cash-out-as-wealth-dream -fades-102067386.html; "China's Property Woes Trigger Shadow Banking Concerns," Reuters, August 17, 2023, https://news.yahoo .com/chinas-property-woes-trigger-shadow-155016153.html.

111 "China Is in Default on a Trillion Dollars in Debt to U.S. Bondholders. Will the U.S. Force Repayment?" *The Hill*, July 4, 2023, https://thehill.com/opinion/international/4075341-china -is-in-default-on-a-trillion-dollars-in-debt-to-us-bondholders-will -the-us-force-repayment/.

112 "China's Premier Holds Meeting with Experts to Save Economy/ Analysts Say Root Cause Systemic with Communism," *Epoch Times*, July 9, 2023, https://www.theepochtimes.com/china/chinas -premier-holds-meeting-with-experts-to-save-economy-analysts -say-root-cause-systemic-with-communism-5383067.

113 Jiayao Liu, et. al., "Sharp Decline in the Number of Foreigners in China Demands Serious Attention," Pekingnology, June 11, 2021,

https://www.pekingnology.com/p/sharp-decline-in-the-number-of-foreigners.

114 See, for example, Japan: "Exclusive: Japan Regulator Sounded Out Top Domestic Banks About China Risks, Sources Say," Reuters, June 19, 2023, https://www.reuters.com/business/finance/japan-regulator-sounded-out-top-domestic-banks-about-china-risks-sources-say-2023-06-19/.

115 "Behind China's Decade of European Deals, State Investors Evade Notice," *Wall Street Journal,* September 30, 2020, https://www.wsj.com/articles/behind-chinas-decade-of-european-deals-state-investors-evade-notice-11601458202.

116 "India's 'Heart' Closer to U.S. than China on Trade, says New Delhi's Commerce Chief at G20 Meeting," *South China Morning Post,* August 26, 2023, https://www.scmp.com/news/china/article/3232385/indias-heart-closer-us-china-trade-says-new-delhis-commerce-chief-g20-meeting.

117 "Indonesia's Mineral Export Bans Face Hot Global Fire," *Asia Times,* July 5, 2023, https://asiatimes.com/2023/07/indonesias-mineral-export-bans-face-hot-global-fire/.

118 "China's Export Restrictions on Germanium and Gallium Shake Up Global Order," *The National Interest,* July 16, 2023, https://nationalinterest.org/blog/techland/china%E2%80%99s-export-restrictions-germanium-and-gallium-shake-global-order-206647.

119 "The End of Hegemony Is Not the End of America," *RealClearWorld,* October 5, 2023, https://www.realclearworld.com/articles/2023/10/05/the_end_of_hegemony_is_not_the_end_of_america_984034.html.

120 Niall Ferguson, "America Still Leads the World, But Its Allies are Uneasy," Bloomberg, June 18, 2023, https://www.bloomberg.com/opinion/articles/2023-06-18/us-can-t-depend-on-ukraine-coalition-to-stop-china-niall-ferguson?srnd=premium.

121 "Do You Avoid the News? You're in Growing Company," *Washington Post,* August 1, 2023, https://www.washingtonpost.com/media/2023/08/01/news-avoid-depressing/?utm.

122 "Trust in Government," Gallup, concluding September 2022, https://news.gallup.com/poll/5392/trust-government.aspx.

123 "Where Are Young People Most Optimistic? In Poorer Nations," *New York Times*, November 11, 2017, https://www.nytimes.com/2021/11/17/upshot/global-survey-optimism.html.

124 "WEF Calls for AI to Rewrite the Bible, Create 'Religions That are Actually Correct," *Slay*, June 10, 2023, https://slaynews.com/news/wef-ai-rewrite-bible-create-religions-actually-correct/.

125 Leo Homan, "Klaus Schwab's Puppet 'Young Global Leaders' Revealed—Trudeau in Canada, Buttigieg in U.S., Macron in France," blog, February 10, 2023, https://leohohmann.com/2022/02/10/klaus-schwabs-puppet-young-global-leaders-revealed-trudeau-in-canada-buttigieg-in-u-s-macron-in-france-and-many-more/#more-8956.

126 Yuval Noah Harari, *Sapiens: A Brief History of Humankind* (New York: Harper, 2015), 389.

127 Harari, *Sapiens*, 391.

128 Yuval Noah Harari, website, https://www.ynharari.com/.

129 "Transhumanism: The Evil Force Behind the New World Order," *Harbinger's Daily*, May 1, 2023, https://harbingersdaily.com/transhumanism-the-evil-force-behind-the-new-world-order/.

130 Ibid.

131 Ibid.

132 Yuval Noah Harari: "We will be beyond the God of the Bible," Reddit, https://www.reddit.com/r/Damnthatsinteresting/comments/xarrhv/yuval_noah_harari_we_will_be_beyond_the_god_of/.

133 "Global Warming? WEF Says Fashion Will Be Abolished by 2030," "The Future of Urban Consumption," World Economic Forum, https://confoundedinterest.net/2023/07/05/global-warming-wef-says-fashion-will-be-abolished-by-2030-humans-will-all-wear-a-uniform-tomorrow-belongs-to/; "The Future of Urban Consumption in 1.5°c World, C-40 Cities Headline Report," https://expose-news.com/wp-content/uploads/2023/06/Arup-C40-The-Future-of-Urban-Consumption-in-a-1-5C-World.pdf.

134 Archbishop Carol Maria Vigano, Twitter, December 17, 2022, https ://twitter.com/ArchbpVigano/status/1604063561093107717.

135 Jim Ferguson, Twitter, "Breaking News: The Hague," https://twitter .com/JimFergusonUK/status/1677405960304746496; "'Paraguay Has Triumphed, Jesus Has Triumphed': Paraguayan Patriots Defeat WEF/CIA Election Coup," National File, May 1, 2023, https ://nationalfile.com/paraguay-has-triumphed-jesus-has-triumphed -paraguayan-patriots-defeat-wef-cia-election-coup/; "Chile: Major Blow to President as Far Right Triumphs in Key Constitution Vote," *The Guardian*, May 8, 2023, https://www.theguardian .com/world/2023/may/08/chile-constitution-committee-vote-jose -antonio-kast-gabriel-boric; "Giorgia Meloni: Italy's Far-Right Wins Election and Vows to Govern for All," BBC News, September 26, 2022.

136 "Could the Dutch Farmer's Party Be the Big Winner from Government Collapse?" July 8, 2023, https://thespectator.com /topic/dutch-farmers-party-government-collapse-netherlands -bbb/?utm.

137 "Slovakia Elections: Populist Fico Grabs Victory," DW, September 30, 2023, https://www.dw.com/en/slovakia-elections-populist -fico-grabs-victory/a-66968108.

138 "New Zealand Elects Its Most Conservative Government in Decades," *New York Times*, October 14, 2023, https://www .nytimes.com/2023/10/14/world/asia/new-zealand-election -national-wins.html; David Blackmon, "The Western Greens Are Collapsing in 2023 Elections, and it is Glorious," substack, October 14, 2023, https://blackmon.substack.com/p/the-western -greens-are-collapsing?utm.

139 Joel Kotkin, "Why Globalism Failed," *Spiked*, July 20, 2023, https ://www.spiked-online.com/2023/07/20/why-globalism-failed/.

140 Iain Davis, "Are We Really at War? Nonsensical Sustainable Development—Part 1," UK Column, February 4, 2023, https ://www.ukcolumn.org/article/are-we-really-at-war-nonsensical -sustainable-development-part-i.

141 "The Russian Economy Is Outperforming Germany's," UnHerd, July 6, 2023, https://unherd.com/thepost/russias-economy-is -outperforming-germanys/.

142 "India Chases Clean Energy, but Economic Goals Put Coal First," December 7, 2022, https://www.ukcolumn.org/article /are-we-really-at-war-nonsensical-sustainable-development-part-I; "India is Right to resist the West's Carbon Imperialism," https ://www.ukcolumn.org/article/are-we-really-at-war-nonsensical -sustainable-development-part-i.

143 "1 Big Thing: Money, People Head for Sun," *Axios*, July 5, 2023, https://www.axios.com/newsletters/axios-deep-dives-612d1fdc -12c6-4865-a39d-a2f2a42c91c7.html; "Gross Domestic Product by State and Personal Income by State, 1st Quarter 2023," BEA, June 20, 2023, https://www.bea.gov/news/2023/gross-domestic -product-state-and-personal-income-state-1st-quarter-2023.

144 "With Much of the U.S. Staying at Home, How Many Jobs can be Done Remotely?" Uchicago News, May 20, 2020, https://news .uchicago.edu/story/much-us-staying-home-how-many-jobs-can -be-done-remotely.

145 Charles Murray, *Coming Apart: The State of White America, 1960– 2010* (New York: Crown, 2012).

146 Derek Thompson, "The Future of the City Is Childless," *The Atlantic*, July 28, 2019, https://www.theatlantic.com/ideas /archive/2019/07/where-have-all-the-children-gone/594133/; Wendell Cox, "America's Dispersing Metros: the 2020 Population Estimates," NewGeography, October 1, 2023, https://www .newgeography.com/content/007037-americas-dispersing-metros -the-2020-population-estimates.

147 John Timpane, "Driving While Suburban," Alan Berger, et. al., eds., *Infinite Suburbia* (Princeton: Princeton Architectural Press, 2017; and Alan Berger, et al., "Interurban: Ground Truthing U.S. Metropolitan Urbanization," in ibid.

148 Joel Kotkin, "Exurbia Rising," *American Affairs*, Spring 2022, https ://americanaffairsjournal.org/2022/02/exurbia-rising/#notes.

149 Gregg Logan and Karl Pischke, "The Top-Selling Master-Planned Communities of Mid-Year 2021, RCLCO, July 2, 2021.

150 "The Shocking Crime Trend Nobody Wants to Talk About," *The Messenger*, September 19, 2023, https://themessenger.com /opinion/the-shocking-crime-trend-nobody-wants-to-talk-about.

151 "Poll: A Third of Seattle Residents Are Considering Leaving, Citing Crime and Costs," *Breitbart*, July 8, 2023, https://www.breitbart .com/politics/2023/07/08/poll-a-third-of-seattle-residents-are -considering-leaving-citing-crime-and-costs/.

152 "'Probably Not Going to Work Out for You': Amazon CEO Plays Bad Cop over Return to Office Mandate," *Breitbart*, August 30, 2023, https://www.breitbart.com/tech/2023/08/30/ probably-not-going-to-work-out-for-you-amazon-ceo-plays -bad-cop-over-return-to-office-mandate/; "Remote Work Is the New Signing Bonus," *Wall Street Journal*, June 26, 2023, https://www.wsj.com/articles/remote-work-is-the-new-signing -bonus-11624680029.

153 "Remote Workers Fleeing Dem-Run Cities, Data Show," *Washington Free Beacon*, June 19, 2023, https://freebeacon.com /latest-news/remote-workers-fleeing-dem-run-cities-data-show/.

154 "New York Loses $1 Trillion in Wall Street Business as Firms Flee the City: Report," *New York Post*, August 21, 2023, https ://nypost.com/2023/08/21/new-york-loses-1-trillion-in-wall -street-business-as-firms-flee-report/.

155 "Upstate NY County Blocks NYC's Bid to Move Homeless North to Ease Migran Shelter Crisis," *New York Post*, October 1, 2023, https://nypost.com/2023/10/01/upstate-county-blocks-nycs-bid -to-shunt-homeless-north-to-ease-migrant-shelter-crisis/.

156 "WEF Confession: Water Crisis Will Succeed in Establishing World Government Where COVID and Climate Change Failed," *Infowars*, September 2023, https: //www.infowars.com/posts/wef-confession-water-crisis-will -succeed-in-establishing-world-government-where-covid-climate -change-failed/.

157 "Poll: More than Half of U.S. Adults Likely to Reject the COVID Vaccine," *American Greatness*, October 2, 2023, https://amgreatness .com/2023/10/02/poll-more-than-half-of-u-s-adults-likely-to -reject-covid-vaccine/?utm_medium=email&utm_source=act _eng&seyid=91963.

158 "'Soros' Open Society Foundations Cuts At least 40 Percent of Staff," *Newsmax*, July 1, 2023, https://www.newsmax.com/newsfront /alexsoros-georgesoros-opensocietyfoundations/2023/07/01 /id/1125656/.

159 "Soros Foundation Worries Trump Will Win in 2024 and 'Imperil' Globalism," *Epoch Times*, September 4, 2023, https://www .theepochtimes.com/us/soros-foundation-worries-trump-win-will -in-2024-and-imperil-globalism-5485994?utm.

160 Noah Smith, "The Elite Overproduction Hypothesis," Substack, August 26, 2022, https://www.noahpinion.blog/p/the-elite -overproduction-hypothesis.

161 "Condé Nast is 'No Longer a Magazine Company,' Its CEO Says," NiemanLab, May 24, 2022, https://www.niemanlab.org/2022/05 /conde-nast-is-no-longer-a-magazine-company-its-ceo-says/.

162 Smith, "Elite Overproduction Hypothesis."

163 Nicholas Barberis et. al., "Extrapolation and Bubbles," *Journal of Financial Economics*, May 4, 2018, 203–227, https://scholar .harvard.edu/files/shleifer/files/extrapolation_bubbles_published _version.pdf.

164 "Inequality and Social Unrest in Latin America: The Tocqueville Paradox Revisited," World Bank Blogs, February 24, 2020, https ://blogs.worldbank.org/developmenttalk/inequality-and-social -unrest-latin-america-tocqueville-paradox-revisited.

165 Miles Kimball and Robert Willis, "Utility and Happiness," Yale University, October 30, 2006, http://www.econ.yale.edu/~shiller /behmacro/2006-11/kimball-willis.pdf.

166 Tim Urban, "Why Generation Y Yuppies are Unhappy," Wait But Why, September 9, 2013, https://waitbutwhy.com/2013/09/why -generation-y-yuppies-are-unhappy.html.

167 "College Grads are More Unhappy at Work than Less Educated . . ." *Medical Daily*, July 19, 2013, https://www.medicaldaily.com /college-grads-are-more-unhappy-work-less-educated-according -new-gallup-poll-understanding-why-key.

168 "Black Lives Matter Marches of 2020 Were Surprisingly White and Educated . . ." Attytood, October 14, 2021, https://www.inquirer .com/columnists/attytood/george-floyd-protest-marches-2020 -white-educated-20211014.html.

169 Smith, "Elite Overproduction Hypothesis."

170 Noah Smith, "Americans Are Falling Out of Love with the Idea of College," Substack, July 27, 2023, https://www.noahpinion .blog/p/americans-are-falling-out-of-love?utm.

171 "EXCLUSIVE: Americans Overwhelmingly Back Cutting Regulations to Boost Energy Production, Poll Shows," *Daily Caller*, August 23, 2023, https://dailycaller.com/2023/08/23/exclusive -americans-support-cutting-regulation-energy-permitting-poll/.

172 "Meta's Threads 'Bombs' as Daily Active Users Halved," Zero Hedge, July 19, 2023, https://www.zerohedge.com/technology /metas-threads-bombs-daily-active-users-halved?utm.

173 "Washington Post Set to lose '$100 million in 2023' One Decade after Jeff Bezos Bought the Paper: Report," Fox News, July 22, 2023, https://www.foxnews.com/media/washington-post-lose-100 -million-2023-one-decade-after-jeff-bezos-bought-paper-report.

174 "Are Walmart Heirs Forsaking the Left? Arts Center They Fund Cancels Drag Shows for Kids," *Daily Signal*, May 26, 2023, https://www .dailysignal.com/2023/05/26/are-walmart-heirs-retreating -left-arts-center-they-fund-cancels-drag-shows-for-kids/.

175 "Top Journal 'Science' Says More than 2,600 of Its Papers May Have 'Exaggerated Claims,'" JustTheNews, August 23, 2023, https://justthenews.com/nation/science/top-government-funded -science-journal-admits-over-2600-its-papers-may-have.

176 John Klar, "Naomi Wolf, Feminist Turncoat," *American Thinker*, June 20, 2023, https://www.americanthinker.com/blog/2023/06 /naomi_wolf_feminist_turncoat.html.

177 War Room, July 26, 2023, https://twitter.com/DC_Draino /status/1684318770112651265; "Half of Americans Agree with the Statement that Joe Biden did not get 81 Million votes."

178 Charles Hugh Smith, "Once Trust Has Been Lost, There's No Going Back," oftwominds.com, May 8, 2023, https://charleshughsmith .blogspot.com/2023/05/once-trust-has-been-lost-theres-no.html.

179 "Moody Calls on Zuckerberg to Respond to 'Stunning' Number of Florida Human Trafficking Cases on Meta Platforms," *The Center Square*, July 10, 2023, https://www.thecentersquare.com/florida /article_a0ffff5c-1f7b-11ee-ae32-0768ce6c6daa.html

180 "States Fight Back Against the Trans Conspiracy to Erase Women," *American Thinker*, May 8, 2022, https://www.americanthinker .com/articles/2023/05/states_fight_back_against_the_trans _conspiracy_to_erase_women.html.

181 "The Worse It Gets in France, the Less American Corporate Media is Covering It And We Know Why," *Liberty Daily*, July 1, 2023, https://thelibertydaily.com/the-worse-it-gets-in-france-the-less -american-corporate-media-is-covering-it-and-we-know-why/; "France Mobilizes 40,000 Officers to Quell Violence as Teen's Death Sparks Outrage," *Epoch Times*, June 29, 2023, https: //www.theepochtimes.com/world/france-mobilizes-40000-officers -to-quell-violence-as-teens-death-sparks-outrage-5364388; "French Police Say 'We're at War With Vermin' as Nationwide Riots Spread Like Cancer," Zero Hedge, July 1, 2023, https: //www.zerohedge.com/markets/french-police-say-were-war -vermin-nationwide-riots-spread-cancer.

182 "Sweden and the Lethal Complacency of the Elites," *Spiked*, October 3, 2023, https://www.spiked-online.com/2023/10/03 /sweden-and-the-lethal-complacency-of-the-elites/.

183 "Wall Street Silver, Terrorist Attacks in Europe in the Past 20 Years," Twitter, July 1, 2021, https://twitter.com/WallStreetSilv /status/1675173815242948608.

184 "Migrants on Martha's Vineyard Flight Say They Were Told They Were Going to Boston," NPR, September 15, 2022, https://www

.npr.org/2022/09/15/1123109768/migrants-sent-to-marthas
-vineyard.

185 "Mayor Eric Adams: Joe Biden Must 'Control the Border' Because 'There Is No More Room' in NYC," *Breitbart*, July 31, 2023, https: //www.breitbart.com/politics/2023/07/31/mayor-eric-adams-joe-biden -must-control-the-border-because-there-is-no-more-room-in-nyc/.

186 "The Bill to Repair NYCHA Projects Doubles—but Pols Won't Fix the System," *New York Post*, July 13, 2023, https://nypost .com/2023/07/13/the-bill-to-repair-nycha-projects-doubles-but -pols-wont-fix-the-system/.

187 "NYC Migrant Arrivals Surge to 600 Per Day Despite Already Out-of-Control Crisis," *New York Post*, October 4, 2023, https ://nypost.com/2023/10/04/nyc-migrant-arrivals-surge-to-600 -per-day-despite-crisis/.

188 "EXCLUSIVE: Sanctuary City Asks Texas Border Towns to Divert MigrantsAwayfromDenver,"*Brietbart*,October4,2023,https://www .breitbart.com/border/2023/10/04/exclusive-sanctuary-city-asks -texas-border-towns-to-divert-migrants-away-from-denver/.

189 "Residents of Hispanic Chicago Neighborhood Protest Opening of Migrant Shelter," *Breitbart*, October 4, 2023, https://www .breitbart.com/immigration/2023/10/04/residents-of-hispanic -chicago-neighborhood-protest-opening-of-migrant-shelter/.

190 "Massachusetts Calls on Residents to Take Border Crossers into their Homes," *Breitbart*, July 17, 2023, https://www.breitbart .com/politics/2023/07/17/report-massachusetts-asking-residents -house-migrants/.

191 "US Agency Waives 26 Laws to Allow Border Wall Construction," *Epoch Times*, October 4, 2023, https://www.theepochtimes.com /us/mayorkas-to-expedite-construction-of-border-wall-in-texas -amid-illegal-immigration-surge-5504330?utm.

192 "Affirmative Action's Fatal Flaw," UnHerd, June 30, 2023, https ://unherd.com/2023/06/affirmative-actions-fatal-flaw/; "Supreme Court Hands Religious Freedom Win to Postal Worker Who Refused to Work on Sunday," Fox News, June 29, 2023, https

://www.foxnews.com/politics/supreme-court-hands-religious-freedom-win-postal-worker-refused-work-Sunday; "Supreme Court Issues Order Allowing Work to Resume on West Virginia Gas Pipeline," *Epoch Times*, July 27, 2023, https://www.theepochtimes.com/us/supreme-court-lets-work-resume-on-manchin-backed-gas-pipe-5427310; "U.S. Supreme Court Again Vacates Judgment Against Oregon Bakers," Center Square, June 30, 2023, https://www.thecentersquare.com/national/article_ac15e6c0-177b-11ee-b4db-971519ad6403.html; *303 Creative LLC v. Elenis*, October 2022, no. 21-476; https://www.supremecourt.gov/opinions/22pdf/21-476_c185.pdf; "Biden Loses 'Ghost Gun' Case, ATF Ban 'Unlawful,'" MSN,; *Biden v. Nebraska*, 143 S. Ct. 2255 (2023), https://www.msn.com/en-us/money/markets/biden-loses-ghost-gun-case-atf-ban-unlawful/ar-AA1dkcfV?ocid=msedgntp&cvid=cba5c7c880a145ada98eab5734cdd9af&ei=8; "Biden Agency 'Likely' Violated Free Speech by Working with Big Tech to Censor Election Content: Court," Fox News, October 5, 2023, https://www.foxnews.com/us/biden-agency-likely-violated-free-speech-by-working-with-big-tech-to-censor-election-content-court; "Supreme Court Unanimously Rejects Ethics Complaints by Democrats Against Justice Clarence Thomas," Blaze Media, April 30, 2023, https://www.theblaze.com/news/supreme-court-ethics-complaints-democrats; *Students for Fair Admissions v. President & Fellows of Harvard College*, 143 S. Ct. 1241 (2022).

193 "Federal Appeals Court Keeps Colorado's Under-21 Gun Ban on Ice," August 29, 2023, https://bearingarms.com/camedwards/2023/08/29/federal-appeals-court-keeps-colorados-under-21-gun-ban-on-ice-n74289.

194 *Jarkesy v. SEC*, 2022, https://www.ca5.uscourts.gov/opinions/pub/20/20-61007-CV0.pdf.

195 *West Virginia V. EPA* 142, S. Ct. 2547 (2022); "Apocalypse Not: What West Virginia v. EPA Really Means," *Pacific Legal Foundation*, July 15, 2022, https://www.edf.org/article/supreme-courts-ruling-climate-change-explained.

196 *Sackett v. EPA*, 143, S. Ct. 1322 (2023).

197 "Brook Jackson Pfizer Whistleblower Lawsuit . . ." YouTube, https://www.youtube.com/watch?v=Qj5egZCcqZo.

198 Gurri, "Elite Panic of 2022."

199 Ibid.

200 Dr. Anastasia Maria Loupis, "World Economic Forum (WEF) Founder Klaus Schwab . . ." Twitter, October 5, 2023, https ://twitter.com/DrLoupis/status/1710171298331037884.

201 "'We Will Bring You Down': German MP Vows to Dismantle WHO's Grip on Governments," Zero Hedge, July 17, 2023, https://www.zerohedge.com/geopolitical/we-will-bring-you -down-german-mp-vows-dismantle-whos-grip-governments.

Index